PIONEER HANDBOOK

PIONEER HANDBOOK

MASTERING FRONTIER LIFE
IN ORLEANS COUNTY, NEW YORK

A. BURRIS

This is a work of fiction depicting life in the 19th century devised to support the content of "Pioneer History of Orleans County, New York" and contains period specific references on a variety of topics. This book should not be considered a modern day survivalist handbook. And though the inclusion of accurate information has been our priority, the Publisher and the author are not experts in any of the fields referenced and make no representations or warranties with respect to the accuracy or completedness of the contents of this work and specifically disclaim all warranties, including without limitation warranties of fitness for a particular purpose. No warranty may be created or extended by sales or promotional materials.

ISBN: 979-8-89416-008-5 (paperback)
ISBN: 979-8-89416-026-9 (hardback)
ISBN: 979-8-89416-002-3 (pdf)
ISBN: 979-8-89416-007-8 (epub)

Copyright © 2024 FOLK STUDIO 451

All rights reserved. Published by FOLK STUDIO 451. No part of this publication may be reproduced,
stored in or introduced into a retrieval system, or transmitted, in any form, or by any means (electrical, mechanical, photocopying, recording or otherwise) without the prior written permission of the publisher.

Other languages available.
Visit *pioneerhistory.us* for more information.

This book is part of a series:
Pioneers of Orleans County, NY
Pioneer History of Orleans County, New York (vol1)
*Pioneer Handbook: Mastering Frontier Life
in Orleans County, New York* (vol2)
Pioneer Cookbook: Wilderness Recipes of Orleans County (vol3)

Visit *folk.studio* for other works.

CONTENTS

PREPARING FOR YOUR JOURNEY 1
PLANNING CAREFULLY; NAVIGATING THE WILDERNESS; NEGOTIATING DIFFICULT TERRAIN; KEY LANDMARKS IN ORLEANS COUNTY; WATERWAYS; MAJOR ROADS; SIGNIFICANT GEOLOGICAL FEATURES

CHOOSING YOUR LAND 31
RECOGNIZING SOIL TYPES; OTHER CONSIDERATIONS

WATER RESOURCES 39
NATURAL WATER SOURCES; GROUNDWATER AND WELLS; CISTERNS AND RAINWATER HARVESTING; WATER FOR IRRIGATION; WATER CONSERVATION PRACTICES; WATER IN DAILY LIFE; SEASONAL CONSIDERATIONS

CLAIMING YOUR LAND 51
THE PROCESS OF CLAIMING LAND; DEFENDING AND MAINTAINING LAND CLAIMS; MAINTAINING THE LAND; THE ROLE OF LOCAL GOVERNMENT AND COMMUNITY; LIFE AS A LAND OWNER

ESTABLISHING A SELF-SUFFICIENT HOMESTEAD 59
WEATHER AND SEASONAL CHANGES; FOOD PRODUCTION AND PRESERVATION; SHELTER BUILDING AND MAINTENANCE; ESSENTIAL CRAFTING; COMMUNITY SUPPORT AND MUTUAL AID; BARN RAISING AND COLLECTIVE LABOR; KNOWLEDGE SHARING AND EDUCATION; INTERACTIONS WITH NATIVE AMERICANS

CLIMATE AND WEATHER PATTERNS 69
CRITICAL SEASONAL ACTIVITIES; STORMS AND NATURAL DISASTERS; WEATHER VARIABILITY AND ADAPTATION; THE ROLE OF COMMUNITY IN DISASTER PREPAREDNESS

SOIL CONDITIONS AND FERTILITY 85
  SOIL MANAGEMENT PRACTICES; CHALLENGES OF SOIL
  MANAGEMENT

FARMING AND AGRICULTURAL PRACTICES 93
  CROP MANAGEMENT; UNDERSTANDING THE LOCAL
  CLIMATE AND SOIL; COMMON CROPS; DIVERSIFICATION
  AND RISK MANAGEMENT; PLANTING TECHNIQUES;
  HARVESTING TECHNIQUES; STORING CROPS; LIVESTOCK
  MANAGEMENT; KEY TYPES OF LIVESTOCK; BREEDING
  PRACTICES; FEEDING AND NUTRITION; BARNS AND
  STABLES; PROTECTION FROM PREDATORS; BASIC
  VETERINARY CARE; ECONOMIC AND CULTURAL VALUE OF
  LIVESTOCK; AGRICULTURAL TOOLS AND TECHNIQUES;
  ESSENTIAL AGRICULTURAL TOOLS

BUILDING AND CONSTRUCTION KNOWLEDGE 121
  SHELTER BUILDING; LOG CABINS; HEATING YOUR HOME;
  BARNS AND OUTBUILDINGS; BUILDING WITH STONE,
  MUD, AND OTHER MATERIALS; SEASONAL CONSTRUCTION
  CONSIDERATIONS; FENCING; TYPES OF FENCES AND THEIR
  USES; BUILDING FENCESTECHNIQUES AND CHALLENGES;
  MAINTAINING FENCES; LAND MANAGEMENT; CLEARING
  THE FOREST; MANAGING FORESTS AND WOODLOTS

NATURAL RESOURCES AND THEIR USE 141
  SUSTAINABLE HUNTING AND TRAPPING; TIMBER AND
  WOOD RESOURCES; TYPES OF WOOD AND THEIR USES;
  TIMBER FOR CONSTRUCTION; TIMBER FOR TOOLS AND
  IMPLEMENTS; THE ENVIRONMENTAL IMPACT OF TIMBER
  USE; TIMBER AS A CASH CROP

IDENTIFICATION OF COMMON PLANTS 157
  COMMON TREES ; BENEFICIAL PLANTS; COMMON
  FORAGED NUTS; EDIBLE MUSHROOMS; SAFE HARVESTING
  PRACTICES; PRESERVATION OF FORAGED FOODS;
  POISONOUS PLANTS

FISHING AND HUNTING 221
FISHING FOR SUSTENANCE; HARVESTING THE BOUNTY OF RIVERS AND LAKES; FISHING TECHNIQUES; FISHING SEASONS; PRESERVING THE CATCH; HUNTING WILD GAME; DEER HUNTING; SMALL GAME HUNTING; WATERFOWL AND GAME BIRDS; PREDATOR CONTROL AND FUR TRAPPING; SEASONAL HUNTING CYCLES; PRESERVATION AND STORAGE

WILDLIFE IDENTIFICATION 231
FISH; BIRDS; REPTILES ; SNAKES; TURTLES; AMPHIBIANS; MAMMALS; ESSENTIAL FOOD SOURCE; VALUED FOR FUR; VALUED FOR MEAT AND HIDES; PREDITORS; PROTECTING LIVESTOCK AND PROPERTY; DEALING WITH PREDATOR ATTACKS; OF BEARS AND BEECH TREES

PEST CONTROL 313
INSECT PESTS AND THEIR IDENTIFICATION; STRATEGIES FOR PEST CONTROL

FIRE MANAGEMENT 333
FIRE BUILDING; TYPES OF FIRES AND THEIR USES; SELECTING AND PREPARING FIREWOOD; FIRE STARTING TECHNIQUES; FIRE SAFETY; PREVENTING HOUSE FIRES; PREVENTING AND CONTROLLING WILDFIRES; EMERGENCY PREPAREDNESS; MANAGING AND MAINTAINING FIRE TOOLS

COMMON AILMENTS AND CAUSES OF DEATH 343
COMMON AILMENTS; COMMON CAUSES OF DEATH

REMEDIES AND PIONEER HEALING PRACTICES 355
FOLK MEDICINE HOME REMEDIES; COLLABORATION WITH NATIVE AMERICANS; COMMON MEDICINAL PLANTS AND THEIR USES; PREPARING AND USING HERBAL REMEDIES; HARVESTING AND DRYING HERBS; UNDERSTANDING THE RISKS AND LIMITATIONS OF HERBAL MEDICINE; POTENTIAL SIDE EFFECTS AND TOXICITY; INTERACTION WITH OTHER TREATMENTS; RECOGNIZING THE LIMITS OF HERBAL MEDICINE

FIRST AID AND EMERGENCY CARE 367
TREATING INJURIES; WOUND CARE; DEALING WITH
BROKEN BONES; TREATING BURNS; MANAGING SHOCK

BUILDING A THRIVING COMMUNITY 373
ESTABLISHING EDUCATIONAL INSTITUTIONS; BUILDING
THE FIRST SCHOOLHOUSE; SCHOOLING PRACTICES;
THE ROLE OF THE SCHOOL IN THE COMMUNITY;
ESTABLISHING RELIGIOUS INSTITUTIONS; ESTABLISHING
LOCAL GOVERNANCE; COOPERATIVES AND MUTUAL
AID SOCIETIES; THE ROLE OF WOMEN IN COMMUNITY
ORGANIZATION

SETTING UP KEY INFRASTRUCTURE 387
POSTAL ROUTES AND POST ROADS; WATER
INFRASTRUCTURE; MILLS AND WATER POWER; STORAGE
INFRASTRUCTURE; COMMUNAL BUILDINGS AND PUBLIC
SPACES; TRANSPORTATION INFRASTRUCTURE

NAVIGATING THE LOCAL ECONOMY 395
CREDIT AND TRADE GOODS; KEY SERVICES VITAL TO
EVERY COMMUNITY; PARTICIPATING IN THE LOCAL
ECONOMY

INTERACTIONS WITH NATIVE AMERICANS 407
NAVIGATING TRADE, COMMUNICATION, AND RESPECT
BUILDING TIES; CONFLICT RESOLUTION

ESSENTIAL CRAFTING FOR HOME AND TRADE 421
PREPARATION OF DAILY NECESSITIES; CLOTHING AND
TEXTILE PRODUCTION; WOOL PRODUCTION; TANNING
HIDES; PREPARING FLAX FOR LINEN; SPINNING WOOL;
WEAVING CLOTH; KNITTING AND CROCHETING; SEWING
AND GARMENT CONSTRUCTION; LEATHERWORKING;
DYEING FABRICS; MENDING AND PATCHING;
SEASONAL PROJECTS; MAKING AND MENDING SHOES;
UNDERGARMENTS AND LINENS

FAMILY RELATIONSHIPS 461
GENDER ROLES; EXTENDED FAMILY AND COMMUNITY
SUPPORT; MARRIAGE AND PARTNERSHIP; FAMILY GROWTH
AND CHALLENGES; CELEBRATIONS AND TRADITIONS

CONCLUSION 467

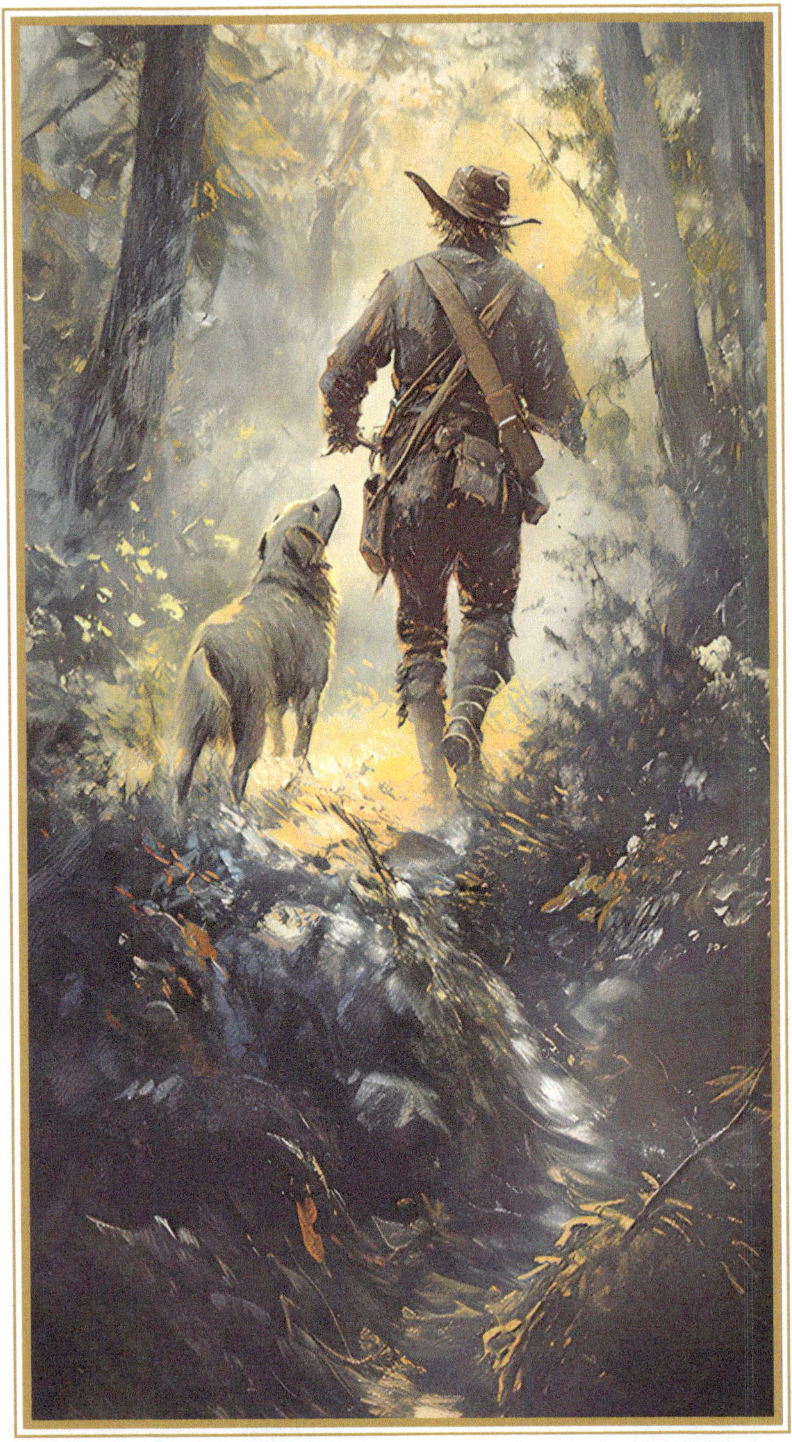

INTRODUCTION

Congratulations, brave traveler, on your decision to break from the comforts of civilization and venture into the untamed wilderness of Orleans County. It is no small feat to leave behind the known and familiar, taking up the mantle of a pioneer in search of land, freedom, and a brighter future for yourself and your family. The path ahead will not be easy, but the rewards are boundless for those with the strength, skill, and perseverance to carve a new life from the wilds. Your courage is commendable, for few possess the fortitude to gamble all they have on the promise of fertile land and the hope of a prosperous homestead.

This book offers practical instructions and time-tested methods to help you navigate the wilderness, acquire and settle your land, and build a life far removed from the comforts of town and city. The lessons in this handbook are designed to guide you through the challenges and triumphs that await.

This is a land of vast promise, difficult trials and significant hardships. In this book you will learn to recognize nature's bounty, the valuable plants and animals, and safeguard yourself against the dangers lurking in the woods and rivers. Whether you are scouting for land, building a cabin, or preparing to weather your first winter, this book shall be your faithful guide, helping you lay the foundation for a life built by your hands upon soil you have claimed and made your own.

The road ahead is long, but with patience and determination, your gamble will indeed pay off. In years to come, you shall look upon the fields you have cleared, the home you have built, and the family you have raised, knowing that the land you stand upon is yours, wrested from the wilderness by your sweat and toil. Let this guide light your way as you embark on this great endeavor—your journey into the wilds of Orleans County and the new life that awaits you.

PREPARING FOR YOUR JOURNEY

Plan carefully for your journey—choose your route, mode of transportation, who to bring with you, and what to pack. Anticipate the challenges of the journey ahead and life in the wilderness once you arrive.

You need to know how to prepare for your long journey, navigate in dense forests, and what key landmarks to look for as your journey progresses.

The trek will be long and arduous, often spanning weeks depending on the weather and road conditions. You must ensure that you are well-supplied and traveling efficiently.

Planning Carefully

Essential Supplies

First and foremost, you must gather the necessities for your new life in Orleans County. Pack enough food to sustain your family for the journey and beyond, as you may not be able to grow crops or hunt immediately upon arrival. Dried meats, grains, flour, salted pork, and hardtack are ideal for the trip.

You'll also need cooking utensils, tools, and seeds to cultivate the land. Don't forget to bring extra clothing, bedding, blankets, and basic medical supplies such as bandages, herbs for common ailments, and remedies for treating injuries or infections. You will build your homestead with tools like axes, saws, hammers, and nails. And you will need supplies for hunting and fishing to sustain yourself once you reach your new land.

Remember that you must also consider the weight of your load—bring what is essential, but be mindful not to overburden your sled or wagon.

Choosing Who Should Make the Journey

When deciding which family members should accompany you, consider each person's strength, health, and endurance. Older family members and very young children may not be suited for such a grueling journey, especially if the terrain is rough and the weather is unforgiving. It may be best to leave some family members with relatives until you have established your homestead. This can allow you to travel more swiftly and with fewer risks.

Those who make the journey should be prepared to help in every possible way. Older children and adults should be capable of handling livestock, managing supplies, and tending to any injuries on the road. Strong and able-bodied individuals are vital to ensuring that the trip is as smooth as possible.

Safety During Travel

Long journeys over rugged terrain require thoughtful planning and pacing. Plan regular stops to rest and regroup rather than attempting to cover too much ground in one day. Travel with others if possible—there is safety in numbers, particularly when crossing wilderness areas where wildlife or dangerous terrain may pose a threat. Set clear goals for each day's travel, but remain flexible to adjust based on road conditions and weather.

Choose campsites with access to fresh water and, if possible, near established trading posts or settlements. These stops can provide an opportunity to replenish supplies or trade for goods that may be needed on the road. Keep a sharp eye on your livestock, which will be essential for hauling your supplies. Fatigue and hunger will affect them as much as it does your family, so rest them frequently and ensure they are well-fed.

With proper planning, determination, and luck, you will reach Orleans County ready to start your new life. Take the time to think through each journey step, and you'll increase the odds of a successful passage into the frontier.

Navigating the Wilderness

As you prepare for your journey into the uncharted wilderness of Orleans County, it will be vital that you understand the natural world around you. In the absence of well-marked roads, nature itself becomes your most reliable guide.

Whether traveling by day or night, recognizing the signs offered by trees, wind patterns, the sun, and stars can help you stay on course. From reading the growth patterns of moss to employing the North Star for direction, the wilderness is filled with subtle clues to keep you oriented.

Blazing trails, following animal tracks, and understanding how to read or create your maps will further ensure your safe passage through the frontier.

Tree Growth Patterns

Trees and vegetation offer subtle yet important clues for orienting oneself in the wilderness, and understanding these natural signs can significantly assist in navigation. In the Northern Hemisphere, moss typically grows more abundantly on the northern side of trees. This occurs because the north side of a tree receives less direct sunlight, creating a cooler, more humid environment ideal for moss growth.

However, it's important to remember that this is not an infallible rule. Moss may grow on other sides of trees in particularly shaded or damp areas, such as near rivers, deep valleys, or dense forests.

In addition to moss growth, consider the tree's overall shape. Trees exposed to steady winds, such as those growing in open fields or on hillsides, often exhibit asymmetrical growth, with branches and foliage leaning slightly toward the prevailing winds. This can help determine local wind patterns and provide another subtle direction indicator.

In more open areas, the southern side of a tree will often display more vigorous growth due to the greater exposure to sunlight. The foliage may be denser, and the bark may appear drier or lighter on the south side.

While these natural signs are helpful, always consider the broader environment. Tree patterns are best used with other navigational techniques, such as observing the sun's position or using natural landmarks, to ensure accurate orientation in the wilderness.

Sun Position and Shadow Sticks

The sun serves as a dependable guide during the day. Observing the sun's position may determine the approximate time of day and ascertain cardinal directions.

To ascertain the cardinal directions using a shadow stick, procure a straight stick or rod and fix it upright in the ground where the sun's rays may cast a shadow.

Mark the extremity of the shadow on the ground with a small stone or other marker. After a quarter to half an hour, mark the shadow's extremity again.

Draw a straight line between these two marks to represent an approximate east-west line, the first mark indicating the west and the second east.

To determine north and south, stand with the west mark on your left and the east mark on your right; north will lie directly before you and south directly behind.

North Star (Polaris)

Polaris, commonly known as the North Star, becomes an invaluable aid for navigation at night. Polaris remains almost fixed in the night sky above the North Pole, making it an excellent reference point for determining true north. This star is easily identified in the northern sky, but first, you must locate it among the stars.

To find Polaris, use the Big Dipper constellation as a guide. The two stars at the edge of the Big Dipper's bowl, known as the "pointer stars," form a straight line that leads directly to Polaris. Once you've located these stars, follow their line upward to find Polaris, the brightest star in that vicinity.

Polaris is not directly overhead unless you are standing at the North Pole, but its height above the horizon corresponds to your latitude. For example, in Orleans County, New York, Polaris will sit roughly 43 degrees above the horizon. This means that, while navigating, you can also estimate your latitude based on Polaris's elevation in the sky.

Polaris's fixed position makes it especially useful for those traveling at night or when other landmarks are obscured. In clear weather, it can guide you without needing a compass, keeping your direction consistent. Remember, Polaris indicates true north, which is slightly different from magnetic north—this subtle distinction can be important when using maps and other tools for long journeys.

Blazing Trails

When forging new paths through dense forests or uncharted territories, it is wise to "blaze" the trail by marking trees or rocks with notches, cuts, or symbols. These marks, which should be clear and easily seen, provide reassurance that the path is correct—whether for those who may follow later or for retracing your steps to return to a previous location.

Blazes are commonly made with an axe or knife, and the marks should be placed at eye level to ensure visibility. The cuts should be deep enough to expose the lighter inner wood of the tree, making it stand out against the dark bark. Care must be taken to angle the marks so that rainwater runs off, preventing the tree from becoming damaged by rot.

In addition to single blazes for straightforward trails, more complex systems can be employed:

DOUBLE BLAZES

Two blazes, one above the other, often indicate a change in direction. The upper blaze should be slightly offset in the direction of the turn.

CROSS MARKS OR ARROWS

Forking or difficult-to-see routes may be marked with arrows or cross marks to clearly show the intended direction.

DISTANCE INDICATORS

For longer journeys, some pioneers mark the miles traveled on the trail to give a sense of progress or proximity to a destination. This can be done with numerical carvings or additional notches.

Blazing is not limited to trees; rocks and other prominent natural features can also be marked with paint, charcoal, or stacked stones (called cairns) when trees are sparse. These additional techniques ensure the trail remains visible in areas where trees are not readily available or where vegetation is too dense for markings to be visible.

It is crucial to blaze consistently and to mark both sides of the trail when necessary to avoid confusion during the return trip. Blazing ensures safe travel through unfamiliar territory and helps prevent travelers from getting lost when familiar landmarks are obscured.

Reading and Creating Maps

Reading and interpreting maps is a considerable advantage when planning your journey into the wilderness. A well-drawn map can save time, prevent wrong turns, and direct you to crucial resources. Any map that indicates the general location of significant landmarks—such as rivers, hills, large rocks, and clearings—is invaluable in a land as wild and untamed as Orleans County. Seek out local or military maps if possible, as they often include terrain, paths, and settlement information.

MAP INTERPRETATION

When reading a map, it is essential to understand how to interpret its symbols and scale. The map's key will reveal how different features—forests, bodies of water, elevation changes—are represented. Contour lines, for instance, can indicate the steepness of hills or mountains, helping you plan your ascent or descent. Make sure you familiarize yourself with the distance scale, as traveling across rugged terrain may take far longer than it appears on paper.

CREATING YOUR MAPS

Without a ready-made map, creating your own as you explore is prudent. Start by marking essential landmarks such as rivers, hills, and unusual rock formations. If you're traveling over several days, mark water sources, safe resting spots, and areas where you have seen wildlife or foraged plants. Note prominent trees or blazed trails that can help you orient yourself if you need to retrace your steps.

While creating your map, it is advisable to use cardinal directions whenever possible. Marking north, south, east, and west will make your map more accessible to follow, especially if you return to the same area later. You may also wish to add symbols for potential dangers, such as areas where predators have been spotted or terrain challenging to cross, to help guide future travelers.

MAINTAINING ACCURACY

It is essential to maintain accuracy in your mapmaking. Use pacing or estimate your travel time between critical landmarks to measure distances, as this can help others who might rely on your map in the future. Consistency in your markings and annotations will ensure that the map remains functional over time.

Maps can be more than just navigation tools—they are discovery records. A well-drawn map guides you and may serve those who follow in your footsteps, preserving knowledge of the land for future generations. Whether purchased or drawn by hand, your map is a lifeline in unfamiliar terrain, giving you a clear picture of the landscape and helping you reach your destination safely.

Compass Navigation

The compass is indispensable for determining direction, regardless of time of day or weather conditions. A simple magnetic compass, relying on the Earth's magnetic field, will invariably point toward the north. With this, you can navigate even in dense forests or unfamiliar territories where prominent landmarks may not be visible.

UNDERSTANDING COMPASS BEARINGS

While a compass will point north, it is essential to understand how to use bearings to navigate effectively. Once determined north, you can set a specific course using the compass's degree markings. For example, if your destination lies to the east, align the compass needle with the north, then turn until the compass dial shows 90 degrees. This will allow you to travel directly east with confidence.

MAINTAINING A STRAIGHT COURSE

It's easy to stray from your intended direction in dense forests or areas with limited visibility. The compass ensures that you stay on course by allowing you to check your bearing at regular intervals. As you travel, pick distant landmarks—such as a tree, hill, or boulder—along the line of your intended direction. Walk to that landmark, recheck your compass, and select a new landmark to maintain a straight path. This method helps avoid the subtle drift that can occur over long distances.

MAGNETIC VARIATIONS AND INTERFERENCE

Though highly reliable, it's essential to be aware that compasses can be affected by magnetic variations and interference. In certain areas, particularly near large deposits of iron ore or other magnetic materials, the compass may not point true north. Be cautious around metal objects or structures, as these can distort the compass needle. Always double-check your readings when encountering such conditions and rely on your surroundings when needed.

USING THE COMPASS WITH A MAP

If you have a map, combining it with your compass can significantly enhance your navigation. Align the map's orientation with true north, then use your compass to establish your location and chart your course. Using both tools together ensures you're navigating with greater precision and clarity, avoiding wrong turns that could delay your journey.

BACKUP NAVIGATION TECHNIQUES

While a compass is a trusted guide, it's wise to learn natural navigation techniques, such as observing the sun, stars, or tree growth patterns, in case your compass is lost or damaged. These methods complement the compass, offering additional ways to find your direction.

Navigating using Natural Landmarks

Mountains, rivers, and valleys are vital reference points for travelers venturing through the wilderness. These natural features help determine direction and can also provide valuable clues about distance and location. Understanding the terrain is crucial for those seeking to navigate effectively in unfamiliar regions, and paying close attention to these features can keep you on course when other markers are absent.

FOLLOWING NATIVE PATHS AND ANIMAL TRAILS

While roads may provide main routes to larger settlements, many areas in this wild country remain accessible only by trails. These narrow paths, often no wider than a footpath or packhorse trail, are vital for reaching remote homesteads, hunting grounds, and new territories. They are essential when you venture deeper into the wilderness, offering routes through dense forests, ridges, and rivers.

Native American paths are precious, as they are well-established, time-honored routes that have connected regions for centuries. Worn smooth by generations of use, these paths often follow the land's natural contours, providing the easiest and most reliable ways through rugged terrain. They avoid steep inclines and treacherous landscapes, preferring gentler slopes, ridgelines, and valleys that facilitate smoother travel. It is wise to learn of these paths from local Native American guides, who possess invaluable knowledge of the region's topography and the safest, most efficient routes.

ANIMAL TRAILS

While not as reliable as human-made paths, animal trails can still be helpful guides when navigating uncharted land. Deer, for example, often creates well-worn trails as they move between feeding areas and water sources. These trails, although narrow, can lead a pioneer to fresh water or open clearings.

Bear, elk, and moose often follow predictable routes between feeding grounds and shelter, leaving broad tracks that can be observed when human trails are absent.

However, it is essential to note that following animal trails requires a degree of caution. While these tracks can provide an efficient route through the wilderness, they can also lead into thick, inaccessible forests or the heart of predator territories. Keep your eyes open for signs of recent animal activity—scat, fur, or tracks—and be aware of potential dangers, especially when predators are more active, such as early morning or dusk.

Finally, human-made trails or animal—made trails often lead to natural resources like fresh water, grazing land, or berry patches. By recognizing these pathways and understanding the behavior of the land and its wildlife, you can gain a greater understanding of the landscape and make your journeys far more efficient and less risky.

MOUNTAINS AND RIDGES

Mountain ranges are among the most reliable landmarks, with their often dramatic and prominent profiles. For instance, a range from north to south offers an excellent natural compass for those moving through the wilderness. If you know the general orientation of a mountain range, you can use it to set your direction or correct your course if you are disoriented. When traveling in valleys or lowlands, look for mountain gaps or passes that might indicate natural routes, often followed by Native American trails or pioneer paths.

RIVERS AND STREAMS

Rivers are among the most consistent guides in the wilderness, as they generally flow toward larger bodies of water, such as lakes or the sea, often leading to settlements, trading posts, or familiar territories. A traveler can usually find a path to a more populated area by following a river downstream. Rivers also serve as natural boundaries, separating regions and providing access to vital resources like fresh water and fish. Be mindful of the river's bends and currents, which can help gauge direction, and note that smaller streams and creeks can be used similarly to lead toward more extensive waterways.

VALLEYS AND LOWLANDS

Valleys, which often run between mountains or hills, tend to form natural corridors that can assist in travel. If you are moving through a valley, note its general direction—this can help orient you about the surrounding terrain. Settlements and farms are often found in valleys due to the fertile soil and access to water, so following a valley can sometimes lead to human habitation.

LAKES AND LARGE BODIES OF WATER

Lakes and larger bodies of water can serve as both a destination and a landmark. Lakes are frequently surrounded by settlements or used as gathering points for traders and hunters. Knowing a lake's location relative to your own can be an excellent anchor point in your navigation.

Moreover, like rivers, lakes are often associated with trade routes or supply stations, making them essential for anyone seeking resources or connections with other travelers.

Be aware of seasonal changes that may affect the visibility or appearance of natural landmarks. In the winter, snow may obscure rivers or flatten the appearance of valleys, while in the summer, dense foliage can obscure distant mountains. Adapting to the changing landscape and understanding how these natural features evolve with the seasons is essential for accurate navigation.

Negotiating Difficult Terrain

Ice Roads

In the heart of winter, when rivers and lakes freeze solid, you may find it easier to create ice roads. These temporary pathways on frozen waterways offer smooth, flat surfaces for sleighs and sleds, cutting down travel time compared to the rugged overland routes. However, caution is essential. Always check the ice thickness regularly to ensure it can bear the weight of your sleds and goods, as thin ice can give way unexpectedly.

Crossing Frozen Rivers

Should you need to cross a frozen river, whether on foot, horseback, or by sled, be aware of the risks. Ice can crack or break without notice, so it is wise to test it ahead of your path. Use a long pole to probe the ice, or better yet, rely on a guide who knows the local conditions and can ensure your safety.

Fords

When traveling during the warmer months, fords offer a natural way to cross shallow rivers. The best fords are found where the water is shallow and the riverbed is firm, often rocky or gravelly, providing solid footing for your animals and good traction for your wagons.

Remember, fords are seasonal by nature, and they may not always be passable. In spring, when rivers swell with snow melt, or after heavy rains, water levels can rise quickly, making the crossing dangerous or impossible. Plan ahead, and be mindful of the seasonal variations of the fords along your journey.

Fords are most useful when the riverbanks slope gently, allowing easy access for wagons and livestock. Steeper banks present a challenge, increasing the risk of accidents or delays. Always scout the ford before crossing to assess the riverbed's depth and firmness. Muddy or sandy beds can trap your wagon wheels, and animals can lose their footing, causing you further delays or harm. Take the time to ensure your path is safe, and you'll avoid many of these potential hazards.

CONSTRUCTED AND IMPROVED FORDS

You may find that early settlers have reinforced or improved fords to make them more reliable. They may have cleared debris from the riverbed, and layed down stones or logs to create a more stable crossing surface, or have built ramps on either side of the river to facilitate access.

These improvements make fords safer and more accessible, especially during periods of high water but they do deteriorate over time. Take care to inspect the construction before attempting to cross.

Key Landmarks in Orleans County

The county's geography is profoundly shaped by several vital waterways, major roads, and significant geological features, which will help you navigate to your new home. They also influence where you settle, cultivate your land, and connect with the broader region as you trade and explore available resources.

As you plan your journey to claim land in Orleans County, it is important to familiarize yourself with its key landmarks, which will aid your navigation and influence your decision on where to settle. The county's landscape is divided into three distinct horizontal bands of terrain.

The northernmost band, stretching from the shores of Lake Ontario to approximately 6-8 miles inland, is a flat to gently rolling plain, with a few ravines cut by streams. Ridge Road runs along a ridge that marks the end of this northern band, rising 8 to 30 feet above the plain.

South of Ridge Road, the terrain begins to undulate more as it leads toward the Niagara Escarpment, a defining geological feature that cuts across the middle of the county. This central band extends about 4-6 miles south from Ridge Road and includes the Erie Canal, which runs east to west, serving as a critical artery for trade and travel through the county.

The southernmost band, south of the escarpment, has flatter terrain extending toward the Orleans/Genesee County line. Understanding these topographical divisions will help guide your choice of land, where you can best farm, settle, and establish vital connections for trade and resources.

WATERWAYS

Orleans County is distinguished by a network of waterways significant for Native Americans and settlers. These rivers, creeks, and lakes provide essential resources for daily sustenance, trade, and transportation, rendering them integral to the history and development of the county.

It is essential to plan your journeys wisely, paying attention to seasons and conditions to avoid natural risks. While the rivers offer a swift means of travel, they are not without danger.

Strong currents, rapids, and waterfalls can make navigation treacherous, forcing travelers to portage their goods. You must be cautious when navigating these waters, as only skilled pilots can safely guide boats through such hazards.

Rivers are subject to the whims of the seasons. In the spring, the rivers swell with melting snow and rain, making them fast and unpredictable, and in summer, dry spells can lower water levels to the point where boats are grounded. So, plan wisely.

Below, you will find a description of each key waterway, how to distinguish it, and what advantage it may give you.

Lake Ontario

As you journey through Orleans County, Lake Ontario is an indispensable landmark. This vast body of water forms the county's northern boundary and is a north-constant reference point.

The lake's clear, cold waters stretch as far as the eye can see, with its shoreline offering a mix of sandy beaches and rocky bluffs.

As you approach, the scent of fresh water will meet you, and the sight of waterfowl—such as ducks and geese—skimming the surface will confirm your proximity. Along the southern edge of Lake Ontario, you will encounter small fishing villages and burgeoning ports where settlers gather to trade goods and fish from the abundant waters.

Oak Orchard River

Flowing through the heart of Orleans County, the Oak Orchard River will guide you through some of the county's most fertile lands. As you follow its meandering course, you'll pass through a diverse range of landscapes—lush wetlands teeming with wildlife, dense woodlands echoing with the calls of birds, and open fields where settlers have begun to cultivate the land.

The river is a lively waterway, with its banks often dotted with the canoes of fishermen and the remnants of early mills built to harness its power. As you draw near its mouth at Point Breeze, you'll notice the river widening, its flow slowing as it meets the vast expanse of Lake Ontario.

Johnson Creek

Though smaller than the Oak Orchard River, Johnson Creek is a vital waterway in the northeastern part of the county. Traveling along its course, you'll notice its gentle flow winding through peaceful, pastoral scenes.

The creek's banks are lined with trees, their roots often exposed where the water has worn away the soil, and you may catch sight of deer or other wildlife coming to drink.

The surrounding farmland, nourished by the creek's waters, stretches out on either side and as you approach its confluence with Lake Ontario, you'll see the landscape open up, with the creek's waters mingling with the enormous lake.

Sandy Creek

Sandy Creek, which flows through the towns of Murray and Kendall, is easily recognized by its sandy bed and floodplain's rich, dark soil. As you follow the creek's winding path, you'll pass through areas where the land rises gently on either side, covered with dense thickets of shrubs and young trees.

The creek's banks are often alive with the sound of frogs and small animals rustling in the underbrush. Near its mouth, where Sandy Creek meets Lake Ontario, the land flattens out, and you'll find marshy areas rich in birdlife and the occasional beaver dam, a testament to the area's natural wealth.

Sandy Creek (South)

Not to be confused with its northern counterpart, South Sandy Creek flows through the southern part of Orleans County.

As you trace its course, you will move through rolling farmlands where the creek's waters are channeled into irrigation ditches, nourishing crops that stretch in orderly rows as far as the eye can see.

The creek is narrower here, often shaded by overhanging branches. As you move downstream, you may come across small, picturesque clearings where the creek's gentle flow provides a soothing backdrop to the surrounding wilderness.

Marsh Creek

Marsh Creek, a tributary of the Oak Orchard River, winds its way through the central parts of Orleans County. As you follow its flow, you'll encounter broad expanses of wetlands where tall reeds sway in the breeze, and the air is filled with waterfowl calls.

The creek's waters, rich in nutrients, support abundant plant and animal life, making this area a haven for hunters and trappers. Further along, where Marsh Creek meets the Oak Orchard River, the land rises slightly, offering a vantage point from which you can see the confluence of these two critical waterways.

Fish Creek

Fish Creek is a small tributary that flows into the Oak Orchard River. It is aptly named for its abundant fish populations, particularly trout, and other freshwater species. Fish Creek will be a valuable fishing resource, supplementing your diet with fresh catch.

As you journey along its banks, you'll notice the creek's crystal-clear waters, where fish dart between the rocks and aquatic plants. The surrounding landscape is of quiet beauty, with rolling hills leading to the flatlands near the Oak Orchard River, where Fish Creek joins the more significant watercourse.

The area is ideal for those seeking tranquility, with the creek's gentle babble providing a constant, soothing presence.

Erie Canal

The Erie Canal, which passes through the southern part of Orleans County, is a marvel of modern engineering and a lifeline for the region. This canal connects the Hudson River in Albany to Lake Erie in Buffalo, cutting across New York State and profoundly impacting the local economy and growth.

The Erie Canal has transformed Orleans County by providing a direct water route for transporting goods and people between the interior of the state and the Great Lakes. It has spurred the growth of towns along its path, including Medina and Albion. The canal facilitates the efficient and profitable transportation of agricultural products, such as grain and apples, contributing significantly to the region's prosperity.

Beardsley Creek

Though lesser known, Beardsley Creek is an important tributary that feeds into the Oak Orchard River. The creek supports local agriculture by providing irrigation water and maintaining soil moisture levels. It also sustains local wildlife populations, offering fish, birds, and small mammals habitats.

Lake Alice and Glenwood Lake

These two long, narrow lakes were formed as hydroelectric resevoirs and were created by damming Oak Orchard Creek. Lake Alice is situated near the village of Waterport, and Glenwood Lake near the Village of Medina. They both support various fish species, are popular spots for fishing, and other outdoor activities.

Both of these waterways were created in the early 20th century and so were not present in the Pioneer's day. They are included here as they may be of interest to 21st century readers.

MAJOR ROADS

The roads in Orleans County are critical for connecting settlements and facilitating trade. Be mindful, however, that road travel is not without its difficulties. Spring rains and melting snow often turn roads into impassable muck, and the heavy snows of winter can block passage entirely. Travel must be planned carefully to avoid the worst of these conditions.

There are a few wagon trails through the area to transport goods and families, though these paths are often rough, with steep hills, rocky ground, and dense forests to navigate. Be prepared to clear obstacles and face wildlife hazards like bears or wolves while traveling through the wilderness.

A yoke of oxen and sled may be your most reliable option for a journey over rough, unpaved roads or through dense forests. Oxen, known for their strength and endurance, is ideal for pulling heavy loads across long distances. A sled, rather than a wheeled wagon, will allow you to traverse rugged terrain, such as muddy trails, rocky paths, and snow-covered roads, without bogging down.

Two major roads have been cut by the Land Company and worked by early settlers to aid land development and make it easier for new pioneers to navigate the landscape.

Ridge Road

Chief among these roads is Ridge Road, an old Indian trail that follows the natural ridge of the ancient shoreline of Glacial Lake Iroquois. This elevated path runs east to west and is one of the most important routes in the county, offering a stable, flood-resistant way across the land.

As you travel along Ridge Road, you will pass through various settlements and farms, with the ridge as a constant guide. The road's high ground affords clear views of the surrounding landscape, allowing you to maintain your course quickly.

Transit Line Road

Running in a north-to-south direction, the Transit Line intersects with Ridge Road, establishing a crucial link between the lakeshore and the southern regions of the county. This route is indispensable for those seeking to reach the interior of Orleans County, where fertile lands await cultivation.

The Transit Line has been hewn through the dense forest, with a swath cleared to a width of 6 rods, permitting the passage of wagons and livestock efficiently. As you journey along this road, you will encounter a variety of terrains—from the orderly ranks of crops in the fertile farmlands to the thick woodlands where the towering trees, once standing shoulder to shoulder, now form a green canopy above.

SIGNIFICANT GEOLOGICAL FEATURES

Orleans County's geological features are more than just exciting landmarks—they're essential for navigation and understanding the land's potential.

Niagara Escarpment
(The Big Ridge)

The Niagara Escarpment, commonly referred to by the locals as the 'Big Ridge,' is a long and steep slope that begins at the south shore of Lake Ontario and runs west through Niagra Falls and beyond, forming a prominent natural divide in the landscape. This ridge is a crucial landmark, serving as a natural barrier and a guide for navigation and settlement.

As you approach the escarpment, the sharp rise in the land will unmistakably signal your location. The fertile lands at its base are highly prized, making them ideal for establishing farms and communities. The sight of the ridge, looming high above the surrounding plains, will orient you and assure you of the rich farming potential of the land below.

Oak Orchard Swamp
(Iroquois National Wildlife Refuge)

The Oak Orchard Swamp, part of which lies within Orleans County, is an expansive wetland known for its challenging terrain and abundant natural resources. As you venture towards the swamp, you will notice a sudden transition from open fields to dense, waterlogged forests—a sure sign you have entered its bounds.

The thick vegetation and treacherous marshes make crossing difficult, but the rewards are plentiful. This area teems with wildlife, providing ample hunting, fishing, and gathering opportunities.

Point Breeze

Point Breeze is a natural convergence point where the Oak Orchard River unites with Lake Ontario's vast expanse, providing a rich environment for commerce and settlement. The area is well-known for its scenic beauty and strategic importance, serving as a critical location for fishing, trade, and travel.

As you draw near, the sight of the river flowing into the mighty lake will tell you that you have arrived at this significant landmark.

Holley Gorge

Holley Gorge was carved by the waters of Sandy Creek near the village of Holley. This deep ravine, with its steep cliffs, wooded slopes, and striking waterfall, presents a dramatic sight and provides numerous hunting, gathering, and fishing opportunities. The sound of rushing water will guide you to the gorge.

Waterfalls of the Oak Orchard River

As you follow the course of the Oak Orchard River through Orleans County, you will encounter several small, picturesque waterfalls and rapids, particularly near Waterport. These natural features have long been valued for the fishing opportunities they provide.

The sound of cascading water will alert you to their presence. Mills built near the falls harness the river's power to provide staples for the community.

Mucklands (Muck Soils)

To the south of Orleans County lie the mucklands, rich, dark, organic soil formed from drained swamps and wetlands. As you draw near these lands, the soil will change beneath your feet, becoming soft and black, indicating that you have reached these fertile grounds.

While these mucklands are yet to be fully utilized, they are well-known to Native Americans and settlers for their remarkable richness. The soil here is ideal for agriculture, promising bountiful harvests for those who cultivate it.

The mucklands were created in the early 20th century. They are included here as the landmark may be of interest to 21st century readers.

The Medina Sandstone Formation

The Medina Sandstone Formation is a significant geological feature underlying much of Orleans County. The sandstone is known for its durability and distinctive reddish-brown color. The stone is used in construction by settlers and has become famous in regional and beyond buildings. Quarrying of Medina sandstone is quite prominent.

Holley Canal Falls

The Holley Canal Falls, situated in the village of Holley, is an artificial waterfall formed during the expansion of the Erie Canal. This notable feature in the local landscape is a testament to human endeavor's transformative power.

As you approach the village, rushing water will guide you to this striking landmark, where the canal's waters cascade down, creating an impressive and dynamic scene.

This feature was created in 1913 during the expansion of the Erie Canal. The falls are included here as the landmark may be of interest to 21st century readers.

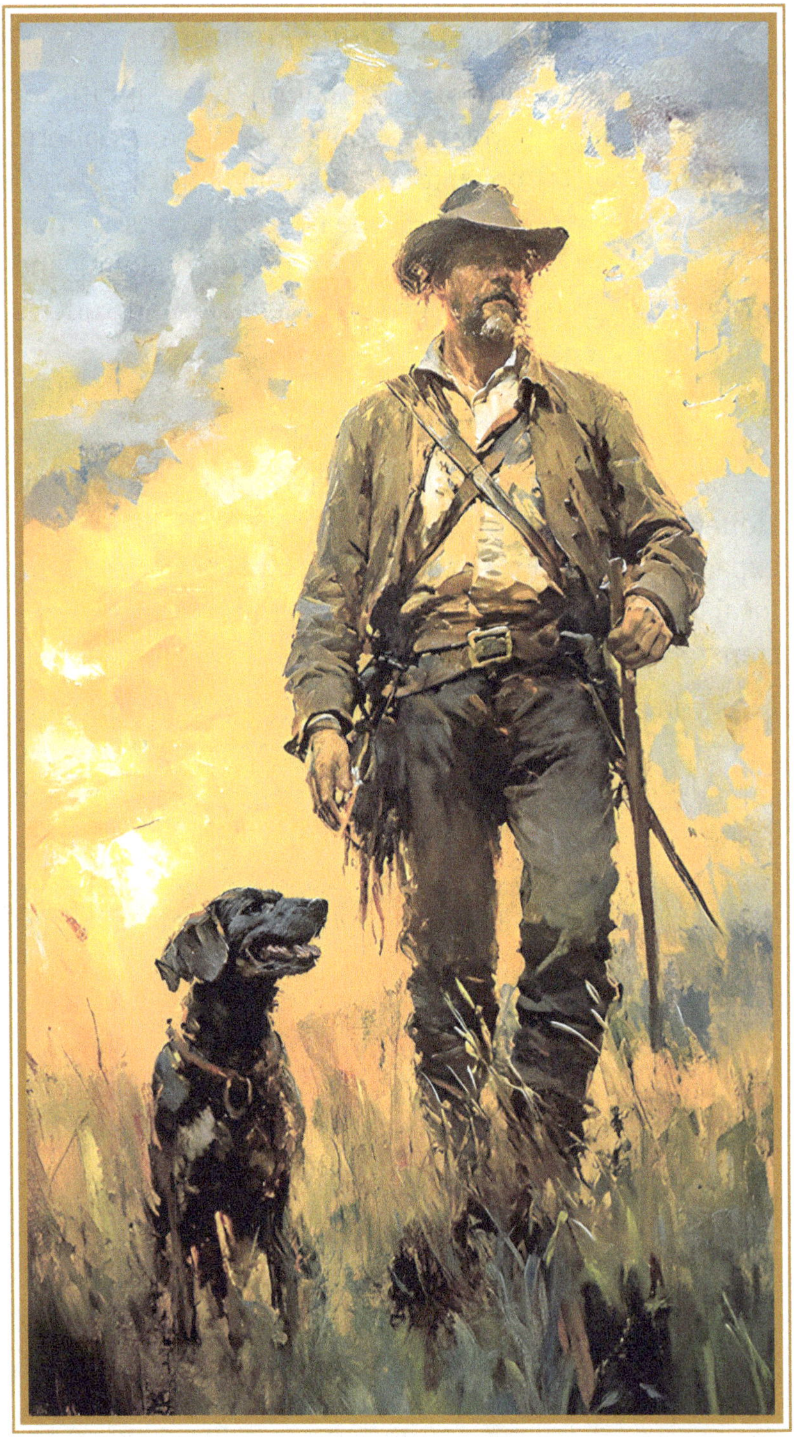

CHOOSING YOUR LAND

Choosing the right land is one of the most critical decisions you will make. The land you settle on will shape your family's future, providing resources for farming, building, and sustaining life. Take the time to choose wisely.

Recognizing Soil Types

Orleans County offers a diversity of soil types, each possessing distinct qualities that greatly influenced the decisions of pioneer farmers. The most common soils include loamy, sandy, clay, and highly fertile muck soils in low-lying areas.

Loamy Soils

THE IDEAL FOR AGRICULTURE

Loamy soil, a balanced blend of sand, silt, and clay, is often regarded as the most desirable soil for farming. It strikes a perfect balance by being well-draining yet capable of retaining moisture, rich in nutrients, and easy to till. This soil type is particularly well-suited for cultivating various crops, making it a prized asset for any settler looking to establish a successful farm.

Settlers fortunate enough to settle on loamy soils enjoy a significant advantage. These fertile soils can support a variety of staple crops, including corn, wheat, oats, and vegetables.

The ease with which loamy soils can be worked makes plowing, planting, and harvesting more efficient, allowing for more extensive and productive farms. Furthermore, loamy soils respond exceptionally well to adding manure or compost, further enriching their fertility and ensuring bountiful harvests year after year.

Sandy Soils

ACCESSIBLE TO WORK, BUT CHALLENGING

Sandy soils, composed chiefly of large, coarse particles, are known for their excellent drainage but are also prone to drying out quickly. These soils often lack nutrients, as both water and nutrients tend to leach away swiftly through the loose structure.

While sandy soils are easy to plow and work, their low nutrient content and poor water retention make them less than ideal for farming. If you settle upon sandy soils, you must adapt your farming practices accordingly. It is wise to plant crops more resistant to drought, such as rye and potatoes, and employ techniques like mulching to help retain soil moisture.

To improve fertility, consider adding organic matter, such as manure or leaf mold, which can aid in retaining both moisture and nutrients. Sandy soils are particularly well-suited for root vegetables and fruits, often thriving in these well-draining conditions.

Clay Soils

FERTILE BUT DIFFICULT TO WORK

Clay soils, made up of beautiful particles, can compact easily, rendering them dense and heavy. While these soils retain water well and are often rich in nutrients, they can be challenging to work, especially when wet, as they become sticky and difficult to till.

You will contend with difficult plowing and planting when dealing with clay soils, particularly wet ones. However, the high fertility of clay soils makes them valuable for growing crops such as corn, beans, and grains, which thrive in rich soil.

To improve the workability of clay soils, consider adding sand or organic matter to break up the density and enhance drainage. It is advisable to avoid working the soil when it is too wet, as this can lead to compaction, which damages the soil structure and may reduce crop yield.

Muck Soils

THE RICH BOUNTY OF DRAINED WETLANDS

Muck soils are found in low-lying areas, mainly where wetlands or swamps have been drained. These soils are dark, rich in organic matter, and highly fertile, making them exceedingly productive for specific crops. However, they are also prone to waterlogging and can be challenging to manage without proper drainage.

Muck soils are a prized resource, especially for growing cash crops like onions, celery, and other vegetables that flourish in nutrient-rich conditions. Managing muck soils, however, requires a thorough understanding of water control, as excessive moisture can lead to crop failure. Settlers who farm on muck lands often invest in drainage ditches or tiles to regulate water levels and prevent waterlogging.

The high fertility of muck soils also allows intensive farming, potentially growing multiple crops per year under the right conditions.

Other Considerations

While soil type in a given area plays a significant role in determining where to establish your farm there are other considerations as well. These considerations are vital for ensuring the land can support your family and future generations.

Lay of Land

VALLEYS AND RIVERBANKS

Areas along rivers and valleys often boast fertile, loamy soils deposited by centuries of flooding. These alluvial soils are rich in nutrients and well-suited for various crops.

Settling in these areas provides the advantage of naturally fertile soil, reducing the need for extensive soil amendments. The proximity to water sources also makes irrigation easier and offers convenient transportation routes for your goods.

UPLANDS AND RIDGES

Uplands and ridges often have well-draining soils, which can be advantageous for growing certain crops and building homes safe from flooding. While they offer better drainage and protection from storms they may also expose you to harsher winds and colder temperatures.

The soils in these areas may be rocky or thin, requiring more effort to clear and cultivate. However, since these locations offer natural protection from floods they provide excellent conditions for fruit orchards, vineyards, and pastures.

WETLANDS AND LOWLANDS

Wetlands and lowlands with muck soils are beautiful for growing specialized crops that thrive in rich, organic soils. With proper drainage, these areas can be transformed into highly productive farmland.

The primary challenge lies in managing water levels to prevent waterlogging, necessitating an investment in drainage systems. Settling in such areas also comes with the risk of flooding during heavy rains or spring thaws.

Proximity to Flood Plains

Flooding is a severe concern near rivers, creeks, and low-lying fields. Spring thaws, heavy rains, and sudden snowmelt can cause rivers like the Oak Orchard River and creeks like Sandy Creek to overflow their banks, resulting in widespread flooding. Floods can wash away crops, erode valuable topsoil, and damage homes and outbuildings.

When choosing the location of your home and farm, it is vital to be aware of flood-prone areas. Settling on higher ground is a common practice to avoid the worst effects of floods. While flood plains are fertile, they are also risky places to plant crops or build permanent structures. As a settler, you must weigh the benefits of rich soil against the dangers of potential flooding.

Proximity to Roads and Waterways

Access to major roads or well-traveled trails is critical for trade, transportation, and communication with nearby settlements. Roads like the Ridge Road or the Genesee Road are commonly used to connect farms to towns and markets. The closer you are to these routes, the easier it will be to transport goods, access services, and trade for necessary supplies.

Waterways are equally important, providing fresh water and a transportation route. Rivers and creeks such as Oak Orchard River or Johnson Creek supply water for daily use and irrigation and serve as natural highways for moving goods. Settling near a water source reduces the labor involved in fetching water and increases access to fertile land often found near riverbanks.

See WATER RESOURCES for more details.

Access to Natural Resources

Consider the availability of timber, stone, and other natural resources needed for building and heating your home, crafting tools, and maintaining a self-sufficient lifestyle. Choosing a site with some natural protection, such as wooded areas, can help insulate your home from the elements. Areas with abundant forests or stone quarries also provide long-term benefits, as they reduce your dependence on outside resources.

Proximity to Towns and Neighbors

While it might be tempting to settle far out for privacy, being isolated can present challenges, particularly in times of need. Proximity to established towns or neighbors offers access to community resources, churches, schools, and mutual aid. Towns are also hubs of economic activity, providing markets for goods and social interaction.

For larger families or those planning to expand, a settlement close to neighboring homesteads can create a support network, such as barn raisings, supplies trading, and educational opportunities for children. On the other hand, smaller families may choose a more remote location if they value solitude or already possess the skills to be entirely self-sufficient.

Family Size and Structure

Access to enough land to grow food and support livestock is critical for larger families. A smaller family might be able to manage on less acreage, but families with many children or extended relatives will need ample room for farming, building outbuildings, and grazing animals. Families planning to grow over time should consider land with potential for expansion.

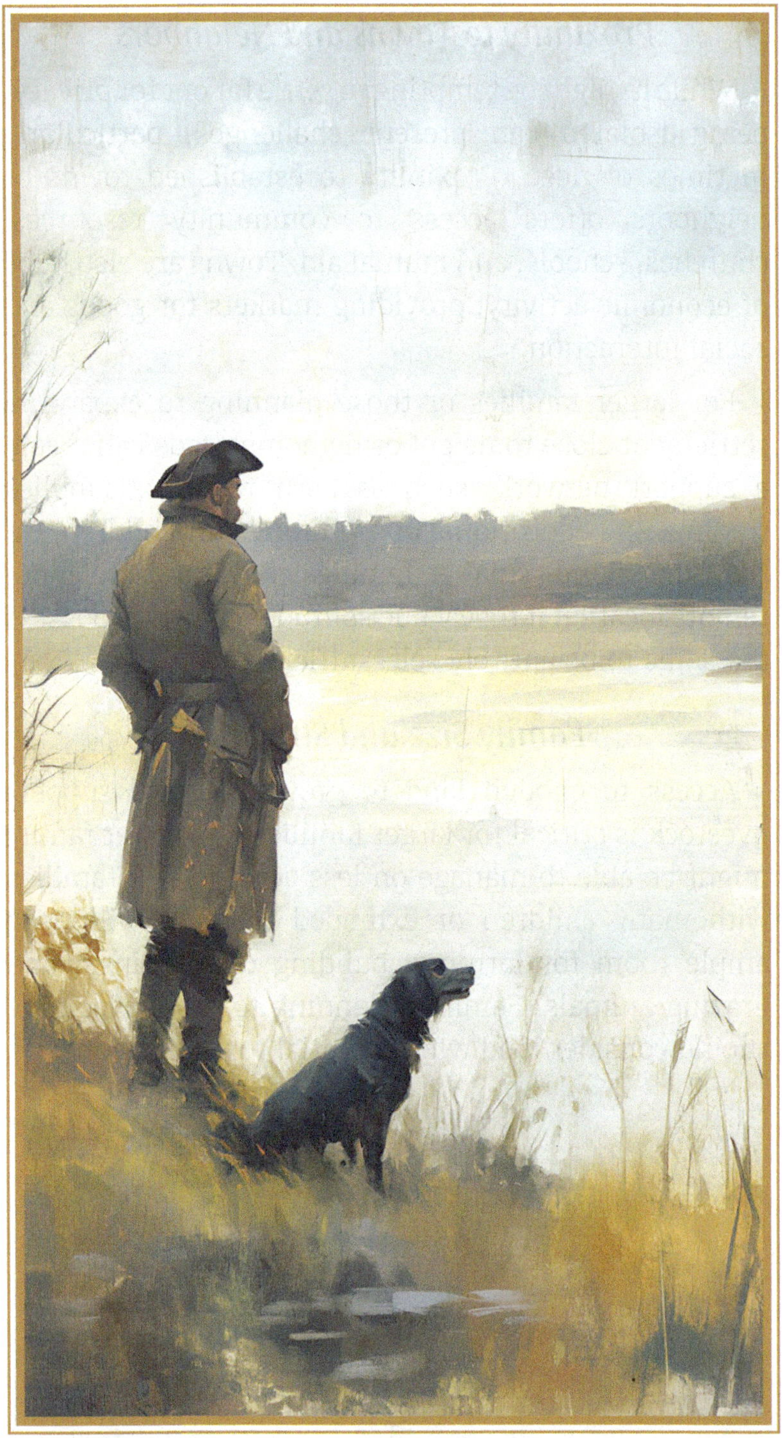

WATER RESOURCES

Before settling on a location for your homestead, you must identify reliable water sources. As an essential resource, water will be a daily concern to ensure you have enough for drinking, cooking, irrigation, livestock, and various household and agricultural tasks.

Natural Water Sources

SPRINGS

Springs are one of the most reliable natural sources of fresh water. These are points where groundwater naturally flows to the surface, often at the base of hills or in low-lying areas. Springs provide a consistent and clean water supply, making them highly prized by pioneers. Settlers usually build their homes near springs to ensure easy access to water.

STREAMS AND RIVERS

Streams and rivers are important water sources for larger homesteads or communities. These flowing bodies of water are used not only for drinking and cooking but also for irrigation, washing, and as a power source for mills. However, you will need to ensure that the water is safe for consumption, as rivers and streams can be contaminated by animal waste, dead vegetation, or upstream activities.

LAKES AND PONDS

Lakes and ponds provide an ample, accessible water supply but require careful management to prevent contamination. These water bodies are used for irrigation, fishing, and watering livestock. However, stagnant water in ponds can become a breeding ground for bacteria and mosquitoes, so it is essential to maintain good hygiene practices around these water sources.

Groundwater and Wells

If you are considering a location for your homestead that does not have an immediate natural water source, you will need to consider the placement of a well or cistern.

DIGGING WELLS

The location of a well is determined by factors such as the water table level, soil composition, and proximity to the homestead. There are a few methods to locate the best spot for a well, including observing the vegetation (certain plants thrive in moist conditions), consulting with experienced well diggers, or even using divining rods, a practice known as dowsing.

The type of well dug depends on the specific needs and resources of your family.

SHALLOW VS. DEEP WELLS

Wells can be shallow or deep, depending on the depth of the water table. Shallow wells, typically less than 30 feet deep, are easier to dig, less expensive, but are more prone to surface runoff contamination.

Deep wells, which can reach over 100 feet, provide cleaner water but require more labor and resources.

WELL CONSTRUCTION

Wells are typically lined with stone, brick, or wooden planks to prevent the walls from collapsing and to keep out debris. The wellhead is often covered with a wooden or stone cap to avoid contamination and accidents. A bucket and windlass system, or later a hand pump, is used to draw water from the well.

Cisterns and Rainwater Harvesting

Cisterns are also used to collect and store rainwater. This method is beneficial in areas where groundwater is inaccessible or during dry seasons when natural water sources are less reliable.

Cistern Construction

UNDERGROUND CISTERNS

Cisterns are typically built underground to keep the water cool and to protect it from evaporation and contamination. These storage tanks are constructed from stone, brick, or concrete and lined with a waterproof material, such as lime plaster or tar, to prevent leaks. Underground cisterns can hold large quantities of water, ensuring a steady supply even during dry periods.

ABOVE-GROUND CISTERNS

In some cases, cisterns are built above ground, often attached to the side of a house or barn. These cisterns are usually smaller and made from wood or metal. They collect rainwater from roofs via gutters and downspouts, storing it for later use. Above-ground cisterns are more susceptible to temperature fluctuations and contamination, requiring regular maintenance and cleaning.

RAINWATER HARVESTING

The most common use of cisterns is for harvesting rainwater. Gutters and downspouts direct rainwater from the roof into the cistern, which is later used. This water is typically used for washing, irrigation, and sometimes drinking and cooking, although it requires filtration and boiling to ensure it is safe for consumption.

Maintenance and Water Quality

KEEPING CISTERNS CLEAN

Cisterns must be cleaned regularly to remove sediment, algae, and other contaminants and maintain water quality. This involves draining the cistern, scrubbing the walls, and sometimes applying a fresh waterproofing material. Keeping the gutters and downspouts clean is also essential to prevent debris from entering the cistern.

WATER TREATMENT

Ensuring the purity of water is a constant concern, as contaminated water can lead to serious health issues, including dysentery, cholera, and other waterborne diseases.

In some cases, settlers add substances like lime or charcoal to the cistern to help purify the water and prevent the growth of algae and bacteria.

In regions where water sources are not clean, it is necessary to boil the water to kill harmful bacteria or used simple filtration methods, such as straining the water through cloth to remove sediment and debris.

Sanitation Practices

PROPER PLACEMENT OF WELLS AND CISTERNS

To protect water sources from contamination, place your well and cisterns a safe distance from potential sources of pollution, such as outhouses, animal pens, and compost heaps. The slope of the land is also essential; wells and cisterns are usually located uphill from these structures to prevent runoff from carrying contaminants into the water supply.

COVERING AND SECURING WATER SOURCES

Cover your well with a lid or cap to prevent debris, animals, or insects from falling in. Cisterns, especially those above ground, should be tightly sealed to keep out dirt, insects, and animals. Regular inspections are necessary to ensure the covers remain secure and the water remains clean.

Managing Waste

Proper waste management is essential for preventing contamination of water sources. Dig outhouses and latrines far from wells and cisterns, and their contents regularly moved to composting pits located away from the homestead. Animal waste should also be carefully composted for use as fertilizer, but always keep it away from water sources.

Filtration and Purification Methods

SAND AND CHARCOAL FILTERS

Simple filtration systems are sometimes used to purify water. These systems often involve passing the water through layers of sand and charcoal, which removed impurities and improved the taste. Charcoal is particularly effective at absorbing odors and organic contaminants, making it a popular choice for water filtration.

BOILING WATER

Boiling is the most reliable method for purifying water, especially for drinking and cooking. By bringing water to a rolling boil for several minutes, settlers can kill bacteria, viruses, and parasites that might be present. Boiling is particularly important for water drawn from rivers, lakes, or rainwater collected in cisterns, as these sources are more likely to be contaminated.

Water for Irrigation

Reliable water sources are essential for agriculture. Choose an efficient irrigation technique and practice water conservation to ensure your crops receive enough water, especially during dry periods.

Irrigation Techniques

SURFACE IRRIGATION

The most common irrigation method used is surface irrigation, where water is directed from a nearby river, stream, or pond into the fields. This can be done by digging channels or ditches that carry the water to the crops. Surface irrigation is relatively simple and inexpensive but requires a reliable water source and careful management to avoid overwatering or flooding the fields.

BUCKET IRRIGATION

In smaller gardens or during drought, you may rely on bucket irrigation, where water is manually drawn from a well or cistern and poured directly onto the plants. This labor-intensive method is used primarily for high-value crops or when other irrigation methods are not feasible.

RAINWATER FOR IRRIGATION

Rainwater collected in cisterns or barrels is often used for irrigation, particularly during dry spells. The rainwater is typically distributed using watering cans or buckets, focusing on crops most sensitive to drought conditions.

Water Conservation Practices

Mulching

Mulch around your crops to conserve water and reduce evaporation. Mulch, made from straw, leaves, or wood chips, helps retain soil moisture and reduces the need for frequent watering. Mulching also suppresses weeds, which compete with crops for water.

Crop Selection and Rotation

Carefully select crops based on their water needs, planting more drought-resistant varieties in areas with less reliable water sources. Practice crop rotation to maintain soil health and moisture levels, reducing the overall water demand on the land.

Timing of Irrigation

Learn to time your irrigation to maximize efficiency. Watering early in the morning or late in the evening, when temperatures are more relaxed and evaporation rates are lower, helps ensure that more water reached the roots of the plants.

Water in Daily Life

Beyond drinking, cooking, and irrigation, water plays a vital role in hygiene, sanitation and domestic tasks.

COOKING AND BREWING

Clean, fresh water is essential for preparing meals and brewing beverages. Contamination can ruin the food or drink and pose a health risk so take great care to follow good sanitation practices.

WASHING AND BATHING

Bathing is often done in a washtub, using water heated on the stove. Water for washing and bathing must be carried in from wells, cisterns, or nearby streams, making it a labor-intensive activity.

You may find that you become more conservative with your water use, reusing water for multiple tasks when possible.

CLEANING AND HOUSEKEEPING

Engage in deep cleaning or "spring cleaning" when water is more abundant in the spring and summer.

LIVESTOCK WATERING

Animals need a consistent supply of water, especially in hot weather or milk production. Build troughs or dig small ponds to collect and store water for your animals. Wells and cisterns also provide water but careful management is necessary to prevent animals from contaminating the water supply.

Seasonal Considerations

Water availability and quality varies with the seasons, and you will need to adapt your water management practices to these changes.

Winter

PREVENTING FREEZING

In the harsh winters of Western New York, preventing water supplies from freezing is a primary concern. Cover or insulate wells and cisterns to retain warmth, and draw water from these sources to store in barrels or pots inside your home to prevent it from freezing. In severe conditions, you will need to break through ice to access water from rivers or ponds.

MELTING SNOW FOR WATER

When other water sources are inaccessible in winter, you may rely on melting snow for water. This temporary solution is labor-intensive and produces relatively small amounts of water, so this should be an emergency measure rather than a primary water source.

Spring Thaw and Flooding

MANAGING RUNOFF

The spring thaw can lead to excessive runoff, sometimes overwhelming wells, flooded fields, and contaminated water supplies. You must be prepared for these conditions by reinforcing well covers, clearing drainage ditches, and monitoring water quality closely during this period.

FLOODED WELLS AND CONTAMINATION

Spring floods can also contaminate wells with silt, bacteria, or chemicals from the surface. In the aftermath of flooding, wells often need to be cleaned, pumped out, and possibly re-dug to ensure the water remains safe.

Summer Droughts

CONSERVING WATER

In the dry summer months, water conservation becomes a top priority. Restrict water use at this time and prioritize essential activities like drinking, cooking, and watering crops. Harvest rainwater during this time to provide a supplementary water source that can be used when wells run low.

PROTECTING WATER QUALITY

High temperatures in summer increase the risk of water contamination from bacteria or algae. You must be vigilant about water quality, boiling drinking water, and using filters to remove impurities. Cisterns and wells must be regularly checked and cleaned to prevent the growth of harmful organisms.

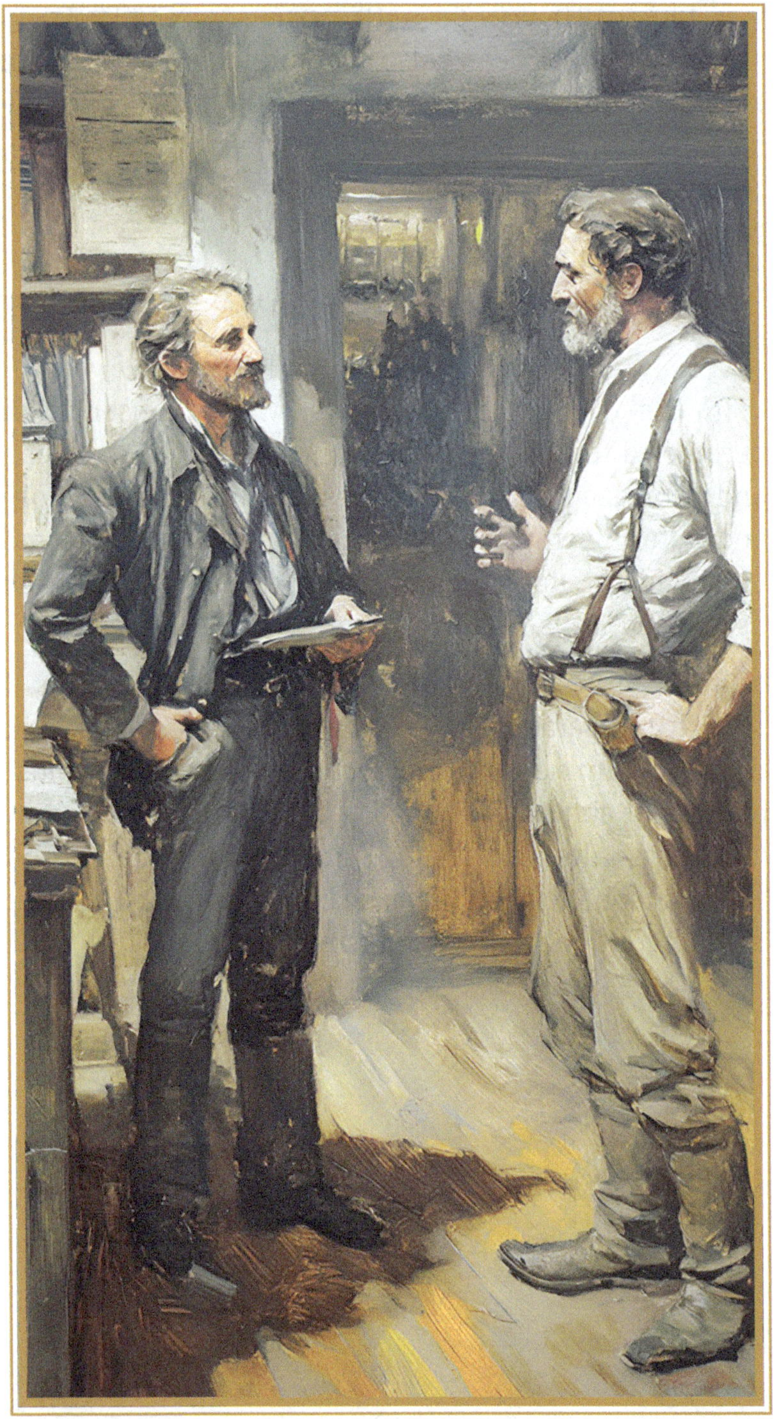

CLAIMING YOUR LAND

Once you have identified which land you wish to take on Article, you must move through the legal processes for claiming, purchasing, and defending the land. This includes knowledge of land grants, homesteading laws, and the role of local government in resolving disputes. The transition from unclaimed wilderness to private property is central to the pioneer experience.

Understanding the processes for claiming and owning land is essential to establishing homesteads legally and securely. Let's start with a bit of history.

COLONIAL AND STATE LAND GRANTS

Before the American Revolution, land in the colonies, including New York, was often granted by the British Crown through colonial charters. These grants were typically given to individuals or groups as rewards for service or to encourage settlement in new areas. After independence, New York continued issuing land grants, focusing on populating and developing frontier areas.

LAND PATENTS

A land patent was an official document issued by the government that granted an individual ownership of a specific parcel of land. These patents were often the result of a land grant and served as the pioneer's legal proof of ownership. Obtaining a patent involved surveying the land, paying fees, and registering the claim with the appropriate government office.

FEDERAL HOMESTEAD ACT OF 1862

While the Homestead Act was not enacted until after the peak of early pioneer settlement in Orleans County, it has significantly encouraged settlement across the American frontier.

The act allows settlers to claim 160 acres of public land, provided they improve the land by building a dwelling and cultivating crops. After five years of continuous residence, the homesteader can apply for a deed to the land.

NEW YORK STATE HOMESTEAD POLICIES

Before the federal Homestead Act, New York State had its own policies to encourage settlement, particularly in the sparsely populated areas of the western part of the state. These policies often involved selling land at low prices or offering it as an incentive for military service or other contributions to the state.

The Process of Claiming Land

Claiming land is now a multistep process requiring knowledge of legal procedures and practical surveying skills. Settlers often work with surveyors, government officials, and neighbors to ensure valid and recognized claims.

SURVEYING THE LAND

Surveying is the first step in claiming land. Professional surveyors, often employed by the government, measure and map the land, dividing it into parcels that can be claimed or purchased. These surveys are critical for establishing clear boundaries and avoiding disputes with neighbors.

MARKING THE LAND

Once a claim is made, settlers often mark boundaries with physical markers, such as stone piles, stakes, or blazed trees (a section of bark removed to reveal the wood beneath). These markers serve as a visible indication of ownership and are essential in areas where formal surveys have not yet been conducted.

LAND OFFICES

You must register land with a government land office to formalize a claim. This involves submitting the survey, paying the required fees, and receiving a certificate or deed as proof of ownership. These documents are essential for defending the claim against challenges and passing the land on to heirs or selling it.

TITLE DEEDS

A title deed is a legal document that transfers land ownership from the government (or a previous owner) to the pioneer. A clear title is crucial for establishing legal ownership and obtaining loans or other financial assistance, as lenders require proof of ownership before offering credit.

DEFENDING AND MAINTAINING LAND CLAIMS

Once you claim and register land, defending that claim against challenges and maintaining the property is an ongoing concern. Legal disputes over land are common, and settlers must be prepared to protect their rights.

BOUNDARY DISPUTES

Disagreements over property boundaries are a common source of conflict among Settlers. These disputes can arise from errors in surveying, misunderstandings about the extent of a claim, or encroachments by neighboring settlers. Resolving such disputes often requires legal intervention, with local courts or arbitration panels reviewing the evidence, such as surveys, deeds, and witness testimony.

SQUATTERS' RIGHTS

In some cases, individuals who have lived on and improved a piece of land for a certain period without formal legal title can claim "squatters' rights." This principle, known as adverse possession, allows settlers who have openly occupied and used the land for several years to gain legal ownership, provided they meet specific legal criteria. However, this often leads to conflicts with those holding formal title deeds.

COURT SYSTEMS

Local courts play a central role in resolving land disputes. These courts are often composed of community members familiar with the regional geography and settlement patterns. Their decisions can affirm, alter, or nullify land claims depending on the evidence presented.

MAINTAINING THE LAND

IMPROVEMENTS AND RESIDENCE

To maintain a claim, settlers must often make "improvements" to the land. This typically means building a dwelling, clearing and cultivating fields, and residing on the property for several years. Failure to meet these requirements can result in the loss of the claim.

TAXATION

Once land is claimed and registered, it becomes subject to property taxes. Paying these taxes is a legal obligation that demonstrates ongoing ownership and residency. Failure to pay taxes can result in fines or even forfeiture of the land.

THE ROLE OF LOCAL GOVERNMENT AND COMMUNITY

Local government and community structures are integral to managing land ownership, resolving disputes, and ensuring that the rules of settlement are followed.

LOCAL AUTHORITY

Township and county governments maintain public land ownership records, such as deeds and surveys. They also manage the allocation of public lands, oversee the construction of roads and public buildings, and administer local land use and property rights laws.

RECORD KEEPING

Land deeds, surveys, and other legal documents are recorded and stored in county courthouses or land offices. These records are essential for verifying ownership, tracing the history of a property, and resolving disputes.

PUBLIC MEETINGS

Town meetings are a forum for settlers to discuss land-related issues, such as road construction, boundary disputes, and communal land management. These meetings are often the first step in resolving conflicts before they escalate to formal legal proceedings.

MUTUAL AID

Settlers often rely on mutual aid within communities to manage land and resolve disputes. Neighbors assist each other with surveying, fence building, and defending land claims. This cooperation is essential in frontier life's often isolated and challenging conditions.

ADJUDICATING DISPUTES

Before formal courts were established, disputes were sometimes resolved through community arbitration, where respected community members would hear both sides and judge. This system relied on local knowledge and the desire to maintain peace and cooperation among settlers.

Life as a Land Owner

Owning land is not just about having a place to live—it is central to a pioneer's identity, economic stability, and legacy.

SELF-SUFFICIENCY

Land ownership provides the basis for self-sufficiency. With owned land, settlers can grow food, raise livestock, and harvest timber, reducing dependence on outside resources. This independence is essential in remote and often isolated frontier life conditions.

INCOME GENERATION

Land also serves as a source of income. Settlers can sell surplus crops, timber, or livestock or lease land to others. Owning land with valuable resources, such as fertile soil or access to water, increases a pioneer's economic opportunities.

SOCIAL STANDING

Owning land elevates a pioneer's social status within the community. Landowners are seen as established and successful members of society, which brings respect and influence to local affairs.

LEGACY AND INHERITANCE

The land is a tangible legacy that settlers can pass on to descendants. Ensuring land ownership is legally recognized and defended is crucial for securing families' future. Many settlers see land as a foundation for building a lasting family legacy, and they work to ensure that it can be passed down through generations.

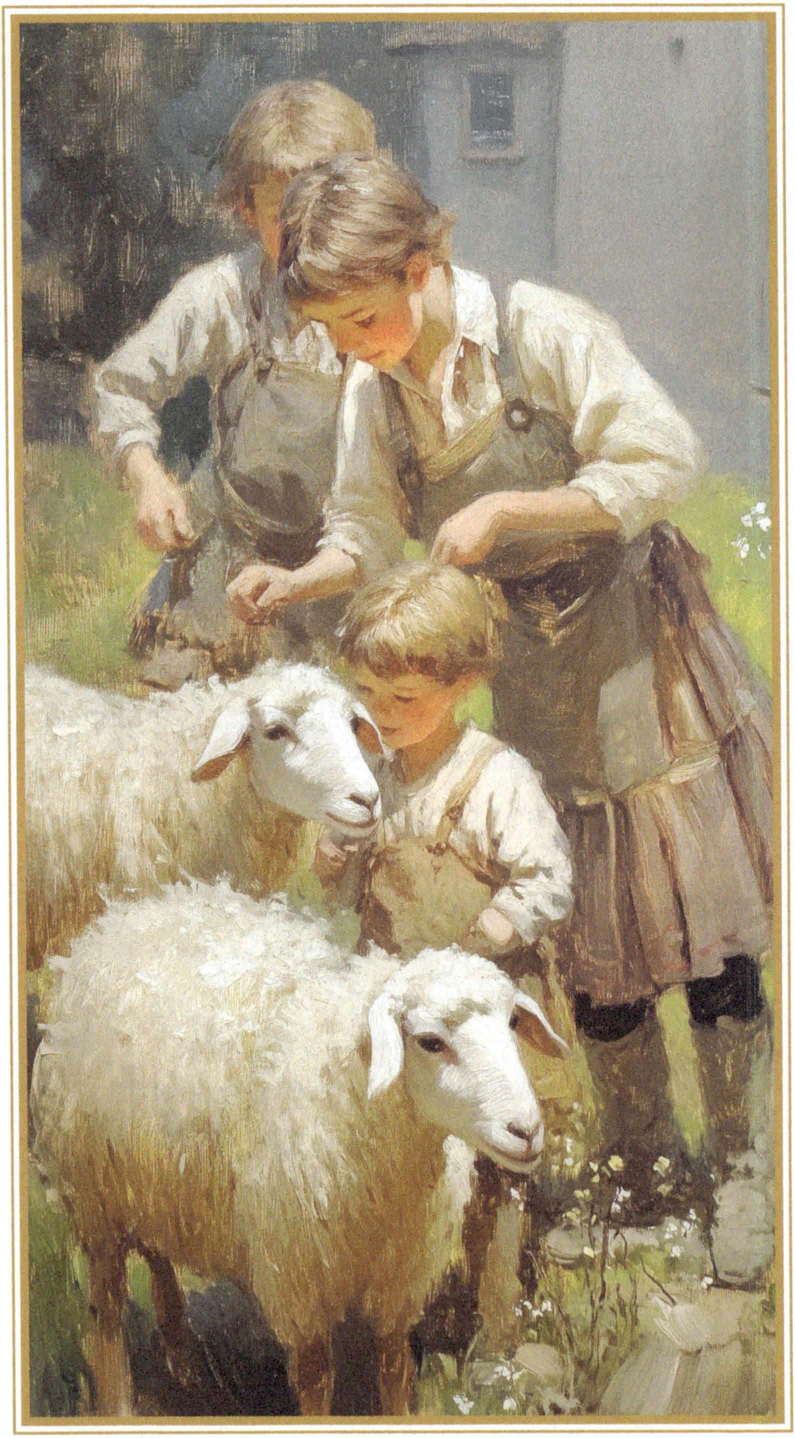

ESTABLISHING A SELF-SUFFICIENT HOMESTEAD

Once you have claimed your land, it's time to begin the business of clearing, building, and living in your new home. The following section is an overview of what you should expect. You will find greater detail later in this volume.

Self-sufficiency is necessary when dwelling in remote regions with limited access to goods and services. You must rely upon your skills and resourcefulness to fulfill basic needs.

You must be ingenious and self-reliant and possess the skills to produce food, build shelters, fashion clothing, and repair tools. Every aspect of your new life will demand a profound understanding of how to make the most of the resources.

WEATHER AND SEASONAL CHANGES

Understanding and adapting to the seasonal changes in Orleans County is crucial for those who settle in the region, as winter weather can be particularly difficult.

Become familiar with local patterns to anticipate and prepare for extreme weather. Use seasonal changes to guide your daily efforts to maximize efficiency.

See CLIMATE AND WEATHER PATTERNS for more details.

FOOD PRODUCTION AND PRESERVATION

FORAGING, FISHING AND HUNTING

To supplement your family's diet, you must hunt wild game and gather edible plants, berries, nuts, and roots. Understanding the local flora and fauna is imperative to avoid poisonous plants and locate the most fruitful hunting grounds. Foraging becomes particularly vital during crop failure or when provisions are scarce. You should also acquire the skills of trapping small game and fishing to secure a steady supply of protein.

See FORAGING, FISHING, or HUNTING section for more details.

GARDENING AND CROP CULTIVATION

A small garden is indispensable for growing vegetables, herbs, and other necessities. A prudent pioneer will practice crop rotation, companion planting, and other husbandry techniques to ensure the most significant yield. Hardy, fast-growing crops such as corn, beans, and squash should be cultivated, as they thrive in the short-growing seasons of frontier lands. Food preservation through drying, smoking, salting, and canning is crucial, particularly in winter when fresh produce is unattainable.

See AGRICULTURAL PRACTICES for more details.

LIVESTOCK MANAGEMENT

Maintaining livestock to supply meat, milk, eggs, and wool is essential. Proper management requires knowledge of breeding, feeding, and protecting the animals from predators and inclement weather. Simple shelters should be erected for the animals, and it is wise to employ rotational grazing to preserve the health of the pastures. In times of scarcity, every part of the animal is utilized—meat, hide, bones, and fat—so that nothing goes to waste.

See LIVESTOCK MANAGEMENT for more details.

SHELTER BUILDING AND MAINTENANCE

LOG CABINS AND SOD HOUSES

Erecting a sturdy shelter should be among the first undertakings upon arrival at your property. Log cabins are customary in wooded areas, as trees may be felled and shaped into logs for construction. To build such a cabin, simple tools such as an axe and saw will be required to cut and fit the logs. Chink the gaps with clay, moss, or mud to guard against the wind and cold.

In regions devoid of trees, sod houses may be constructed from blocks of earth, which offer excellent insulation against both heat and cold.

Often, such shelters are built with the assistance of neighbors in a communal endeavor known as a "house raising" or "bee."

See SHELTER BUILDING for more details.

HEATING AND INSULATION

Maintaining warmth through the harsh winter months is of the utmost concern. A fireplace or wood stove should be employed to heat the cabin. Wood should be gathered throughout the year to ensure a sufficient supply for burning.

Ensure your cabin is well-insulated to retain heat, thus reducing the need for firewood. Utilize animal hides, woven mats, and thick layers of mud or clay to insulate the walls and floors. Hanging heavy blankets or quilts over doors and windows will further block drafts.

See HOME HEATING for more details.

ESSENTIAL CRAFTING

HOMEMADE CLOTHING

As a pioneer family, you must be able to fashion your clothing using available materials. Wool from sheep is spun into yarn, then woven or knitted into garments, while animal hides are tanned and sewn into sturdy leather attire. Simple hand tools such as needles, thread, and looms craft everything from basic shirts and trousers to more intricate garments like coats and dresses. The art of patching and mending should be diligently practiced to prolong the life of clothing.

See MAKING CLOTHING for more details.

TEXTILE PRODUCTION

Beyond making clothing, it may also be necessary to produce textiles for various uses within the home. Wool, flax, and cotton are spun into thread or yarn and woven into fabric upon looms. This fabric is then utilized to create items ranging from bed linens to curtains. Sometimes, one may cultivate flax for linen or rear sheep for wool. Creating textiles is laborious and time-consuming, yet it is an indispensable skill for self-sufficiency.

See TEXTILE PRODUCTION for more details.

SOAP MAKING

Soap is crafted by combining animal fat with lye derived from wood ash. This homemade soap serves to clean clothes, dishes, and the body.

See SOAP MAKING for more details.

LEATHER TANNING

Leather tanning is another essential craft whereby animal hides are processed into durable leather for clothing, footwear, and tools. The tanning process entails soaking hides in water and treating them with tannins from tree bark to preserve and soften the leather.

See LEATHER TANNING for more details.

BLACKSMITHING AND METALWORKING

Blacksmithing is an indispensable skill for both the repair and fabrication of tools. Should you have access to a forge, you may fashion or mend essential items such as axes, plows, and nails. Even without a full forge, basic metalworking skills are invaluable, enabling you to repair broken tools with makeshift materials. As metal is a precious resource, recycling and repurposing as much as possible is prudent.

See REPAIRING METAL TOOLS for more details.

WOODWORKING AND CARPENTRY

Woodworking skills are vital for constructing and maintaining homes, barns, furniture, and tools. One must be well-versed in using hand tools such as saws, chisels, and planes to shape wood for various applications. Carpentry skills are likewise necessary for the making and repairing items such as wagons, fences, and barrels. Working with wood is crucial for the upkeep of a functional homestead and creating items required for daily life.

IMPROVISATION AND INNOVATION

Self-sufficiency frequently requires improvisation when tools break or supplies run short. You must become proficient in discovering alternative uses for everyday objects and crafting tools from available materials. For instance, a broken axe handle might be replaced with a carefully carved branch or a worn-out shoe sole patched with leather from an old saddle. This resourcefulness is essential for survival in an environment where store-bought goods are scarce.

Community Support and Mutual Aid

While individual self-sufficiency is paramount, one will likely rely heavily upon community support and mutual aid to thrive in the wilderness. A prudent pioneer will form alliances with neighbors, sharing resources, labor, and knowledge to foster a strong sense of community, which is essential for survival.

See COMMUNITY STRUCTURES for more details.

BARN RAISING AND COLLECTIVE LABOR

COMMUNITY BUILDING PROJECTS

Significant building endeavors, such as the construction of barns, mills, or churches, are often too laborious for a single family to undertake alone. In such instances, the community unites for a "raising," wherein neighbors labor to complete the project within a day or a weekend. These gatherings serve practical and social purposes, reinforcing community bonds while ensuring all have the requisite infrastructure to support their agricultural and domestic needs.

SHARING TOOLS AND EQUIPMENT

Not every pioneer family can afford or access all the required tools in remote regions. It is customary to share tools and equipment among neighbors. For instance, a family possessing a plow might lend it to their neighbors in exchange for assistance with planting or harvesting. This practice of sharing and bartering ensures that everyone within the community has access to the resources necessary for success.

KNOWLEDGE SHARING AND EDUCATION

PASSING DOWN SKILLS

Skills such as hunting, foraging, farming, and crafting are often transmitted from one generation to the next through hands-on instruction and apprenticeship. Older, more experienced settlers impart their knowledge to the younger or less experienced community members, ensuring that essential survival skills are preserved and passed on. This knowledge exchange is vital for maintaining the community's self-sufficiency as a whole.

INFORMAL SCHOOLS AND LEARNING

Formal education is scarce or nonexistent in many pioneer communities, prompting parents and neighbors to assume the responsibility of instructing the children. Informal schools are frequently established within a community member's home or a shared building, where children are taught essential reading, writing, arithmetic, and practical skills such as farming, cooking, and tool-making. This education is crucial for preparing the next generation to sustain the self-sufficient lifestyle required for survival.

See SCHOOLS for more details.

INTERACTIONS WITH NATIVE AMERICANS

Engagements with Native American tribes form an integral part of daily life. These interactions encompass trade, communication, and navigating complex cultural dynamics. It is essential to maintain peaceful relations for the sake of both survival and mutual prosperity.

Much to be learned from the Native Americans, including using plants for medicine, the best hunting grounds, and navigating the land. A thorough understanding of the intricacies of trade, the significance of effective communication, and the necessity of respecting Native American territories and cultural practices is paramount.

See INTERACTIONS for more details.

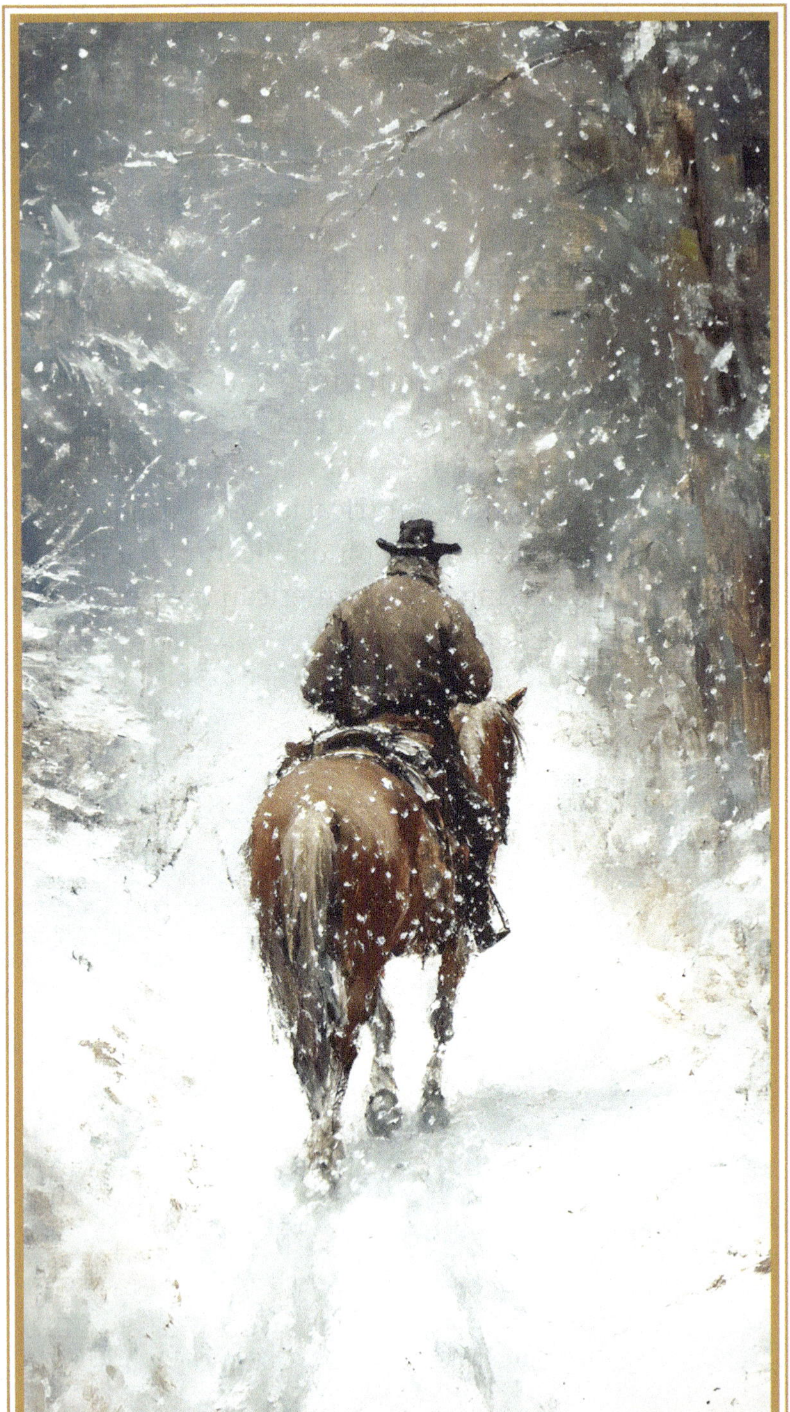

CLIMATE AND WEATHER PATTERNS

As you venture into the Orleans County wilderness to claim your homestead, be prepared for the region's distinctive and often harsh climate. Knowing how the seasons unfold each year will allow you to plan agricultural activities, prepare for the harsh winters, and ensure you have adequate food and fuel supplies for your family to survive.

Winters, beginning in late November and continuing through early March, are long and cold, with temperatures regularly dropping below freezing. You can expect daytime highs to hover between 15°F and 30°F, and snowfall is heavy, often accumulating between 100 and 150 inches over the winter months. The snow will make travel and work difficult, but it will also provide insulation to your crops and wells.

Spring arrives in late March or early April with a thaw that releases the land from winter's grip. Temperatures during this season gradually climb from 40°F to 60°F, making it a vital time for preparing the soil and planting crops.

Summer is mild, with average highs ranging between 70°F and 85°F, perfect for growing crops, though you may encounter periods of heavy rain and humidity.

As summer turns to fall in late September, the cooler temperatures of 50°F to 70°F will signal the harvest season and the need to prepare for the upcoming winter.

Orleans County's weather is unpredictable at times, but its four distinct seasons provide ample opportunity to thrive if you plan wisely and work in rhythm with nature.

Editor's Note: Modern Day Weather (2025). Today, Orleans County experiences similar seasonal patterns, though there have been some changes. Winters are still cold but somewhat milder, with slightly reduced snowfall, typically between 90 and 130 inches. Spring arrives earlier, and the growing season has extended. Summers are warmer, sometimes reaching into the low 90s. These changes have allowed for longer planting periods but also present new challenges with pests and unpredictable weather patterns.

Critical Seasonal Activities

Spring Renewal and Preparation

THAWING AND PLANTING

As the snows of winter recede and the ice begins to melt, the ground will soften, and the earth will thaw, heralding the onset of your planting season. You must be ever mindful of the timing of the last frost, for planting too early may bring ruin should a late frost descend and wither the tender young plants. Observing the blooming of certain flowers or the return of migratory birds are the natural signs that will guide you in choosing the proper moment to commence planting.

MAPLE SUGARING

Early spring is the season to tap sugar maple trees, collecting the sap you will boil down into rich maple syrup and sugar. This task is among the first of the agricultural year, providing a valuable source of sweeteners for your household.

See MAPLE SUGARING for more details.

CLEARING FIELDS

After the long winter, your fields will likely need attention, clearing away the debris—fallen branches and stones—that have accumulated beneath the snow. It is also the time to repair fences and prepare your tools for the busy planting season ahead.

SPRING FORAGING

Spring is the time to gather fresh greens and shoots, such as dandelions, fiddleheads, and wild leeks. These early foods are vital after the long winter, providing fresh nutrients and variety. Spend the early spring days combing the woods and meadows for these young, tender plants, which are both nutritious and flavorful.

Spring is also the season for morel mushrooms, which are eagerly sought after. Morels are often found near dying or recently dead trees, particularly elms, and appearance is eagerly anticipated as one of the first bounties of the season.

See FORAGING for more details.

Summer Growing Season

Summer in Orleans County brings long days filled with sunlight, perfect for cultivating corn, wheat, oats, and vegetables. Yet, with these long days come long hours of labor. You must tend your fields, pulling weeds and ensuring your crops receive sufficient water.

MANAGING LIVESTOCK

Your livestock will demand more excellent care during the summer months as they are turned out to pasture. You must observe them, ensure their health, protect them from predators, and manage the production of milk, eggs, and other animal products.

SUMMER FORAGING

Summer is the peak season for berries and wild fruits. Gather blueberries, raspberries, and blackberries for fresh eating, preserving, and baking. Though smaller than cultivated varieties, wild strawberries are also collected and often used in jams or desserts.

Throughout the summer, foraged for wild greens and herbs, such as lamb quarters and purslane. These are fresh in salads or cooked, and some are dried for winter use. Summer is also the time to gather herbs like mint, sage, and thyme, which are used both for cooking and medicinal purposes.

See FORAGING for more details.

PRESERVING THE HARVEST

As your fruits and vegetables reach their peak, the work of preserving food for the winter begins. You must dry, pickle, or store your produce in root cellars, securing enough to sustain your family through the cold months. Begin cutting and storing hay now to feed your livestock when winter arrives.

Autumn Harvest and Preparation for Winter

HARVESTING CROPS

Autumn is the busiest time of the year, as the crops you have tended all summer must now be gathered. The timing of your harvest is critical—you must bring in your crops before the first frost, which can damage or destroy them. This season demands intense labor, with every hand in the family working from dawn to dusk.

See HARVESTING for more details.

FALL FORAGING

Gather nuts and seeds rich in fats and proteins for the colder months. Beech nuts, walnuts, and hickory nuts are collected, often in large quantities, for winter storage. These nuts are sometimes ground into flour or whole in cooking and baking.

See NUTS for more details.

WILD APPLES AND CRABAPPLES

Gather wild apples and crabapples in the fall for making cider, preserves, and jellies. While smaller and usually more tart than cultivated varieties, these fruits are valued for storing them for long periods without spoiling.

See CRABAPPLES for more details.

PROCESSING AND STORING FOOD

Once the harvest is complete, your focus must shift to processing and storing the bounty. Grains are threshed, ground into flour, or stored in silos or barns. Vegetables and fruits are canned, dried, or preserved in other ways. Meat, such as pork and beef, should be salted, smoked, or cured to ensure it lasts through winter.

See PRESERVING THE HARVEST for more details.

FIREWOOD AND FUEL

Ensuring you have enough firewood to last through the cold months is imperative as winter approaches. This task involves cutting, splitting, and stacking wood—a labor-intensive endeavor. It is often said that wood warms you twice: once when you cut it and once when you burn it.

See FIRE MANAGEMENT for more details.

PREPARING FOR THE COLD

Your home must be well-prepared for the coming chill. Be sure to seal windows and doors to keep out drafts, clean the chimneys, and add extra insulation to your sleeping areas, such as quilts or animal hides. The shelters for your livestock must also be fortified against the cold, and additional feed stored to ensure their survival through the winter.

Winter Survival and Maintenance

LONG, COLD WINTERS

Winter in Orleans County is harsh and unforgiving, with heavy snowfall and freezing temperatures. You must be well-prepared to endure it. During this season, agricultural work essentially ceases, and your focus will shift to staying warm and well-fed.

WINTER FORAGING

Even in winter, some foraging opportunities remained. Gathered pine needles to make a tea rich in vitamin C, a remedy against scurvy and colds. Evergreens like spruce and fir also provide needles for teas and are sometimes used as flavorings in cooking.

ROOT VEGETABLES

Certain root vegetables, such as burdock and Jerusalem artichokes, can be dug up in winter if the ground is frozen. These roots provide a valuable carbohydrate source and can be stored or used fresh in cooking.

FOOD AND FUEL MANAGEMENT

You will rely heavily on the food stores preserved in the fall. Root cellars, larders, and smokehouses are essential for keeping food from spoiling. Firewood must be used conservatively to ensure it lasts the entire winter, as constantly burning the fire is necessary for cooking and heating your home.

See FIRE MANAGEMENT for more details.

REPAIR AND CRAFTING

Winter is also a time for indoor tasks, such as repairing tools, making clothing, and crafting household items. You might spend this time mending farm equipment, spinning wool, weaving cloth, and sewing garments.

Children can be tasked with small chores, such as feeding the animals or gathering eggs, contributing to the household's needs during the long winter months.

See ESSENTIAL CRAFTING for more details.

COMMUNITY AND SOCIALIZING

Though winter often brings isolation, it is also a season for community gatherings. Neighbors may come together for quilting bees, barn raisings, or church services. Such gatherings are vital for maintaining social bonds and providing mutual support in the harsh environment.

Storms and Natural Disasters

In this region of Western New York, storms and natural disasters are frequent, and your ability to foresee and manage these challenges will be vital to the survival and prosperity of your settlement. A thorough understanding of the typical weather events—such as blizzards, floods, and thunderstorms—is essential. This knowledge will guide you in the construction of your shelter, the protection of your crops, and the safeguarding of your livestock. Moreover, an awareness of areas prone to flooding and the dangers of tornadoes should greatly influence the selection of your homestead.

The knowledge of how to face these natural disasters is passed down through the generations, with each family learning from the experiences of those who came before them. This shared wisdom is invaluable, helping you adapt to your surroundings and survive the many challenges of the natural world.

WEATHER VARIABILITY AND ADAPTATION

One of the foremost challenges you will encounter as a settler is the unpredictable nature of the weather from year to year. Some winters may be harsher than others, bringing deeper snow and prolonged cold, while summers might bring drought or heavy rains, severely affecting your crops. You must be adaptable and resilient, drawing upon your knowledge of the land and the seasons to make the most of the conditions each year may present.

These are the typical weather events and natural disasters for which you must be prepared.

Blizzards

Surviving the Winter's Fury

CHARACTERISTICS

Blizzards are among the most feared natural disasters in Western New York. These fierce snowstorms bring heavy snowfall, powerful winds, and bitterly cold temperatures. A blizzard can rage for several days, leaving behind deep snowdrifts that may bury homes and barns, rendering travel impossible and isolating communities from much-needed supplies.

PREPARATION

You must be thoroughly prepared for blizzards, particularly during winter. Your home should be fortified against the cold with extra insulation, such as thick quilts, animal hides, and walls packed with straw. Firewood must be carefully stockpiled, often requiring months of labor to ensure enough to last through the winter. Food supplies, including preserved meats, grains, and root vegetables, should be stored in cellars and pantries to prevent starvation should travel become impossible.

SURVIVAL STRATEGIES

During a blizzard, your family may need to remain indoors for days on end, relying on stored provisions and the warmth of the hearth. Livestock requires special care; barns should be packed with extra hay for insulation and feed. Regular checks on your animals are essential, ensuring they have sufficient food and water and are well-protected from the biting cold.

Floods

Navigating the Rising Waters

CHARACTERISTICS

Flooding is a severe concern near rivers, creeks, and low-lying fields. Spring thaws, heavy rains, and sudden snowmelt can cause rivers like the Oak Orchard River and creeks like Sandy Creek to overflow their banks, resulting in widespread flooding. Floods can wash away crops, erode valuable topsoil, and damage homes and outbuildings.

FLOOD PRONE AREAS

When choosing the location of your home and farm, it is vital to be aware of flood-prone areas. Settling on higher ground is a common practice to avoid the worst effects of floods. While flood plains are fertile, they are also risky places to plant crops or build permanent structures. You must weigh the benefits of rich soil against the dangers of potential flooding.

MITIGATION EFFORTS

Some settlers build levees or dikes to protect their land from rising waters, while others dug drainage ditches to divert water away from their homes and fields. During times of flood, livestock should be moved to higher ground, and valuable tools and supplies should be stored in elevated locations to prevent water damage. After a flood, the focus turns to recovery, with the community often coming together to repair damaged structures and replant the fields.

Thunderstorms and Lightning

Facing Nature's Electrical Fury

CHARACTERISTICS

Thunderstorms are frequent during the warmer months, often bringing heavy rain, strong winds, and lightning. Lightning strikes pose a significant danger, especially to wooden structures, which can easily catch fire. The strong winds may topple trees and damage roofs, while the heavy rains can lead to flash flooding.

BUILDING FOR SAFETY

Construct your home with lightning rods, which help direct lightning strikes safely into the ground, thus reducing the fire risk. Build your house with steep roof to quickly shed rainwater and to better withstand the force of high winds. Barns and other outbuildings should be similarly constructed to protect livestock and stored crops from the storm's fury.

PROTECTING LIVESTOCK

During a thunderstorm, your livestock is particularly vulnerable to lightning strikes, especially if left in open fields. It is prudent to bring animals into barns or other shelters at the first sign of a storm to shield them from the danger of lightning and the risk of being spooked by the loud thunder.

Tornadoes

Preparing for Nature's Most Violent Storms

CHARACTERISTICS

Though less common than blizzards or floods, tornadoes are a deadly threat in Western New York. These violent storms can develop with frightening speed, causing immense destruction with their powerful winds and flying debris. A tornado is capable of tearing apart buildings, uprooting trees, and killing livestock and people caught in its path.

TORNADO RISK AREAS

You must be keenly aware of the signs of an approaching tornado—dark, greenish skies, a low, rumbling roar, and funnel-shaped clouds. While tornado-prone areas are often avoided for settlement, in regions where tornadoes are a risk, it is wise to build storm or root cellars that can double as shelters during a storm.

SURVIVAL TACTICS

When the ominous signs of a tornado are seen or suspected, you must swiftly seek shelter in an underground cellar or the sturdiest part of your dwelling, often a small interior room devoid of windows. Gather your family together, and wait for the storm to pass before emerging once the danger has diminished. After the storm, your attention must immediately turn to rebuilding, tending to injured livestock, and restoring your damaged crops.

Windstorms

Battling the Tempest

CHARACTERISTICS

Windstorms, whether powerful gales or fierce straight-line winds are another peril. These storms can burn trees, scatter crops, and damage buildings. Though not as catastrophic as tornadoes, windstorms are still a significant threat, mainly if your homestead lies in a wooded area.

PROTECTIVE MEASURES

To safeguard against such dangers, you should clear the trees near your home to reduce the risk of falling limbs or entire trees causing harm. Ensure that your roof is securely fastened and that shutters or sturdy wooden boards protect windows. Planting or constructing windbreaks, such as rows of trees or fences, will help shield your crops and buildings from the brunt of the wind.

CROP MANAGEMENT

In drought, focus on saving as much of your harvest as possible by prioritizing water for your most valuable crops. Learn to recognize the signs of an approaching drought, and consider planting early in the season or selecting crops that can endure with minimal water.

THE ROLE OF COMMUNITY IN DISASTER PREPAREDNESS

In these wild lands, the strength of your community is the greatest safeguard against disaster. When storms or calamities strike, neighbors band together to fortify homes, share supplies, and offer shelter to those in need. In the aftermath, the collective effort of rebuilding, replanting, and restoring what was lost is what ensures the survival and prosperity of the settlement.

It is also important to recognize that some in your community may be more vulnerable when disaster strikes. The young, the elderly, those in poor health or living alone, or families struggling with fewer resources may find it harder to recover.

As a pioneer, it is your responsibility to look out for such neighbors. Whether it's helping to reinforce their homes, providing extra food or tools, or simply offering a hand when needed, your care for these individuals strengthens the bonds that hold your community together. In doing so, you create a safer and more resilient settlement, where every member—no matter their circumstances—has the chance to thrive.

SECURING PROPERTY

When a windstorm approaches, secure any loose objects, such as tools, equipment, and stored crops, to prevent them from being blown away or damaged. Bring your livestock into barns or other secure shelters to protect them from the storm's force.

Drought
Managing Water Scarcity

CHARACTERISTICS

Though Western New York is generally blessed with ample water, there are times when droughts occur, particularly in the summer months. These prolonged dry spells can cause wells to run dry, crops to wither, and forage for your livestock to become scarce. A drought threatens your food supply and, if prolonged, could lead to famine.

WATER CONSERVATION

You must learn to conserve water during these dry periods by employing mulching to retain moisture in the soil, planting drought-resistant crops, and rotating your pastures to prevent overgrazing. Wells should be managed with care, and cisterns used to collect and store rainwater when it does fall.

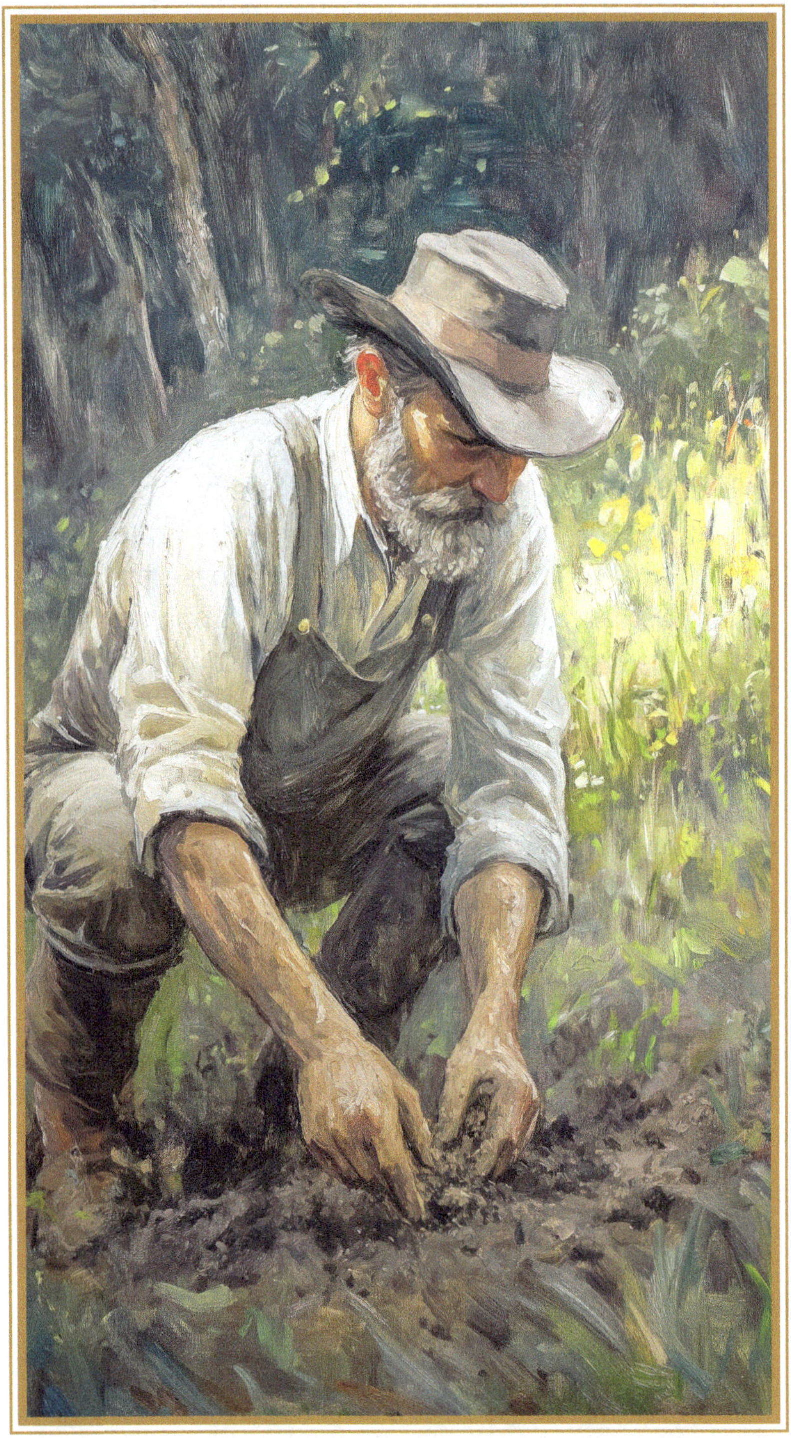

SOIL CONDITIONS AND FERTILITY

Understanding the soil conditions and fertility of the land is of utmost importance as you establish your farm and strive for long-term sustainability. The quality and type of soil will dictate which crops may thrive, how readily the land can be tilled, and your farm's overall productivity. Careful consideration of these factors is essential to ensuring your farm's success and the bountiful harvests you seek.

Soil Management Practices

Once you have settled on your land, various soil management practices must be employed to maintain soil fertility and ensure sustainable farming. These methods are rooted in centuries of agricultural wisdom and are adapted to the specific conditions of Orleans County.

Crop Rotation

Crop rotation involves planting different types of crops in the same field in successive seasons or years. The aim is to prevent the soil from depleting specific nutrients, as other crops have varying nutrient needs and contribute differently to the soil.

You might rotate between cereals like wheat or corn, legumes like beans or peas, and root crops like potatoes or turnips. Legumes are especially valuable in crop rotation, as they can fix nitrogen in the soil through root nodules, replenishing an essential nutrient often depleted by other crops.

Rotating your crops can reduce the risk of soil depletion, manage soil-borne pests and diseases, and ultimately increase crop yields. This practice also helps maintain a balance of organic matter in the soil, improving its structure and water-holding capacity.

Manuring

Recycling Nutrients

Manure from your livestock is a vital source of nourishment for the land. Manuring involves spreading animal waste over fields to enrich the soil with organic matter and essential nutrients such as nitrogen, phosphorus, and potassium.

The manure from cows, horses, pigs, and chickens is collected yearly and often composted to reduce its volume and odor. It is then spread over the fields, typically in the fall after the harvest or early spring before planting begins. In some instances, settlers create manure piles near the fields, allowing the manure to decompose further and become even more prosperous in nutrients before being applied to the soil.

Manure provides essential nutrients to the soil and improves its structure, enhancing its ability to retain moisture and resist erosion. Regular application of manure helps maintain the fertility of your fields, leading to higher crop yields over time.

Fallowing Fields
Restoring Soil Health

Fallowing involves leaving a field unplanted for a season or more, allowing the soil to rest and recover. During this period, natural processes replenish soil nutrients and improve fertility.

As a settler, you may designate a portion of your land to remain fallow each year, allowing weeds and natural vegetation to grow. These plants will eventually be plowed under, returning organic matter to the soil. Sometimes, you may graze livestock on fallow fields, which helps control weeds and adds manure to the soil.

Fallowing helps break cycles of pests and disease by removing the host plants, thereby reducing the strain on the soil. It also allows the soil to rebuild its nutrient levels naturally, making it more fertile when brought back into production. This practice is critical in areas with poorer soils or where continuous cropping has led to significant soil exhaustion.

Green Manuring

Enhancing Soil with Cover Crops

Green manuring involves planting cover crops, such as clover, rye, or buckwheat, which are not harvested but plowed back into the soil to increase their organic matter and nutrient content.

You may plant these cover crops during the offseason, such as in late summer or early fall. These crops proliferate and cover the soil, protecting it from erosion and suppressing weeds. Before the cover crops reach maturity, they are plowed under, adding valuable organic material to the soil and enhancing its fertility for the next planting season.

Green manuring dramatically improves soil structure by increasing nutrient levels and helping to control weeds. The organic matter added from the cover crops enhances the soil's ability to retain water and nutrients, leading to healthier and more vigorous crop growth in the following seasons. This practice is precious in maintaining soil fertility without relying solely on animal manure, offering a sustainable way to keep the land productive year after year.

Composting

Creating Rich Soil Amendments

Composting is breaking down organic materials, such as plant waste, kitchen scraps, and animal manure, into a rich soil amendment that can be added to your fields to enhance soil fertility.

As a settler, you would create compost piles near your home or barn, layering green materials like vegetable scraps and grass clippings with brown materials like straw, leaves, and wood ash. The compost is regularly turned to introduce air, which helps to speed up the decomposition process. After several months, the compost becomes ready to spread over your fields or use in your garden.

Compost enriches the soil with a wide range of nutrients and improves its texture, making it easier to work and more productive. Additionally, composting provides an efficient way to recycle waste materials on the farm, reducing the need for external inputs and supporting sustainable farming practices that will serve you well over the long term.

Challenges of Soil Management

Despite your best efforts, you will encounter several challenges in maintaining soil fertility over the long term.

Soil Exhaustion

Continuous cropping, without proper rotation, manuring, or fallowing, can lead to soil exhaustion, where the soil's nutrients are drawn out faster than they can be replenished. You must rotate your crops and practice fallowing and manuring to avoid this. However, should the land be overworked, the soil may become so depleted that yields are significantly reduced, forcing you to seek new, more fertile ground.

Erosion

Soil erosion, particularly on slopes and in regions with heavy rainfall, can carry away the fertile topsoil, leaving behind poorer, less productive subsoil. This erosion not only diminishes the land's productivity but can also make farming more laborious and less rewarding.

Techniques such as contour plowing, building terraces, and planting cover crops are employed to reduce erosion and protect the soil. It is wise to avoid plowing fields too steep or prone to erosion, leaving them as pastures or woodlots instead.

Pest and Disease Management

Soil-borne pests and diseases can accumulate in the soil significantly when the same crop is grown repeatedly in the same field, leading to reduced yields and crop failures.

Crop rotation is the most effective method for managing these soil-borne pests and diseases. By changing the types of crops you plant each year, you can disrupt the life cycles of pests and lessen the occurrence of soil-borne diseases.

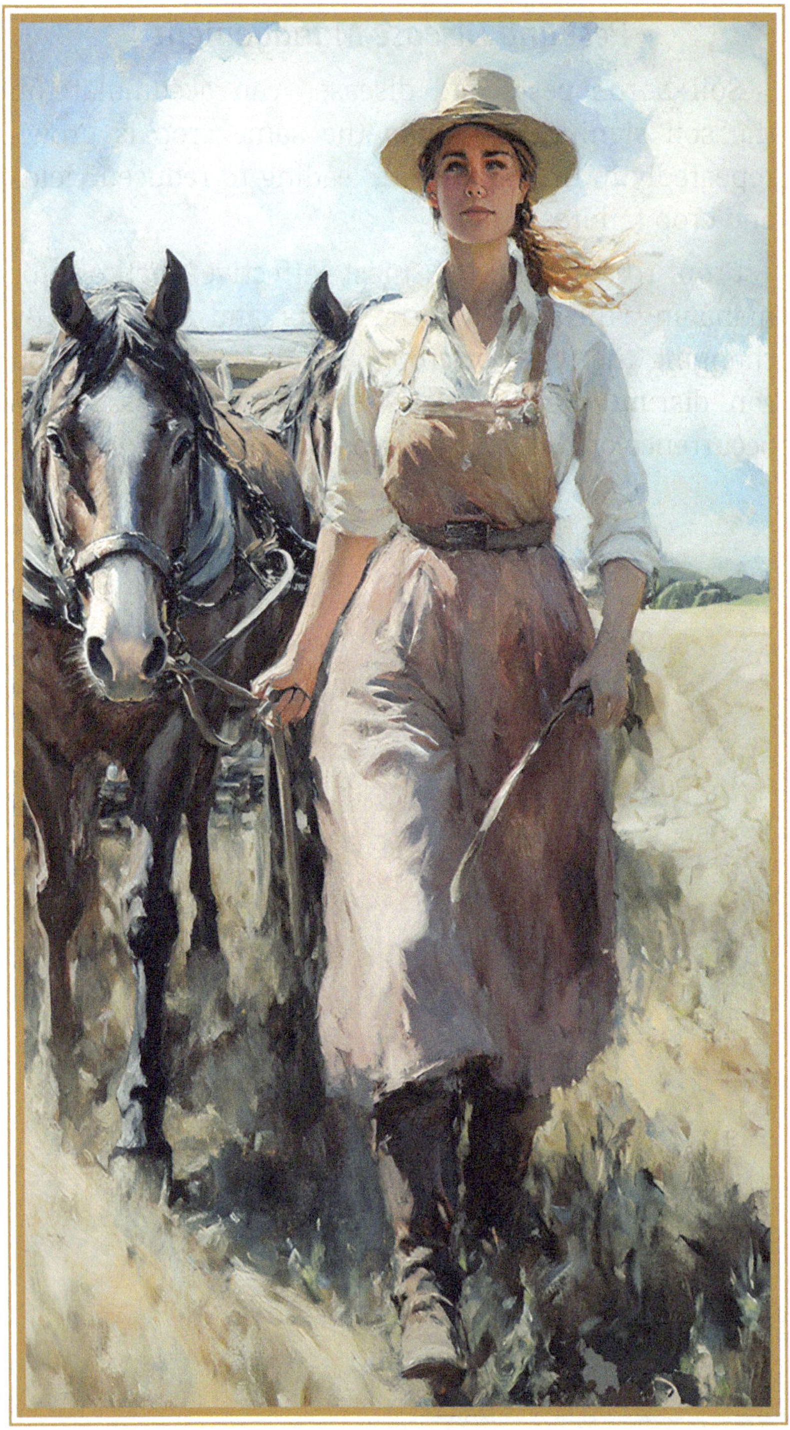

FARMING AND AGRICULTURAL PRACTICES

Crop Management

Choosing suitable crops is crucial and can determine whether you have a bountiful harvest or a year of hardship. The region's climate, soil conditions, and length of the growing season all influence which crops will thrive. Rely on a blend of traditional knowledge, experimentation, and adaptation to select the best crops for your farm. This careful selection ensures that your efforts in the field will yield the sustenance and prosperity you seek.

UNDERSTANDING THE LOCAL CLIMATE AND SOIL

The climate of Orleans County is characterized by cold winters, warm summers, and a growing season that generally extends from late spring to early fall. The soils in this region vary, from the fertile loams found in river valleys to the more challenging clays and sands in upland areas. You must choose crops that can thrive under these conditions, carefully considering factors such as:

Frost Tolerance

Early and late frosts can severely damage or even destroy your crops. Therefore, it is wise to select hardy crops that can withstand frost or mature quickly enough to be harvested before the first frost in the fall.

Soil Requirements

Different crops have different needs. Some require rich, loamy soils with good drainage, while others may do well in poorer, sandier soils. A thorough understanding of soil fertility and structure is essential for determining the most suitable crops to plant.

Water Needs

Crops requiring much water should be planted where irrigation is feasible, or the soil retains moisture well.

COMMON CROPS

Knowing which crops are best suited to the local climate and soil conditions. Commonly grown crops include wheat, corn, oats, potatoes, and beans, staples of the pioneer diet.

The crops you select are essential for providing food for your family but also play a significant role in trade, feeding your animals, and maintaining soil fertility. Choosing wisely will ensure the prosperity and sustainability of your farm.

Wheat
The Staple Grain

Wheat is a staple of the pioneer diet, primarily for making bread, a daily food item. Wheat is also used in porridge, biscuits, and other baked goods.

Wheat varieties that are well suited to the climate of Orleans County are chosen for high yields and ability to mature before the first frost. Wheat can be grown on various soil types, though it thrives best in well-drained loamy soils.

Settlers typically sow wheat in the fall (winter wheat) or early spring (spring wheat). Winter wheat has the advantage of maturing early the following summer, allowing for a second crop or using the field for grazing. Wheat is often rotated with other crops to prevent soil depletion.

Corn (Maize)
Versatile and Vital

Corn is another staple crop, serving as a primary food source for humans and livestock. It is used in various forms, including cornmeal for bread and mush, hominy, and roasted or boiled corn.

Corn is highly adaptable to different soil types and can tolerate the summer heat. It is a significant crop because it can be stored easily and provides a high-calorie yield. Corn can also be used as animal feed, making it doubly valuable.

Corn is typically planted in late spring after the danger of frost has passed. Settlers often use the "Three Sisters" planting method inherited from Native Americans, where corn is planted with beans and squash. The beans fix nitrogen in the soil, benefiting the corn, while the squash provides ground cover to retain moisture and suppress weeds.

Oats

A Dual Purpose Crop

Oats are primarily grown as feed for livestock, particularly horses and cattle, but they also serve as a food source for settlers and are used in oatmeal and baking. Oats are a critical crop for maintaining the health and productivity of farm animals, which are essential for transportation, plowing, and providing milk and meat.

Oats are chosen for their ability to grow in poorer soils and under more excellent conditions. They are hardy and resistant to many diseases, making them a reliable crop in less-than-ideal growing seasons.

Oats are usually planted in early spring and harvested in late summer. They are often grown in rotation with other crops to improve soil health, as oats can help suppress weeds and add organic matter back into the soil after harvest.

Potatoes

The Reliable Root

Potatoes are a dietary staple, providing a significant source of carbohydrates, vitamins, and minerals. They are easy to store and can be prepared in many ways, making them a versatile and essential food.

Potatoes thrive in the excellent, moist soils of Orleans County, especially in the mucklands and loamy soils. Once established, they are less susceptible to frost damage, making them a reliable crop.

Potatoes are typically planted in early spring, with tubers (seed potatoes) placed in furrows and covered with soil. The plants require hilling (adding soil around the base) to protect the tubers from sunlight and pests. Potatoes are harvested in late summer or early fall, stored in excellent, dry conditions, and can last throughout the winter.

Beans

The Nitrogen Fixer

Beans are a vital source of protein in the pioneer diet. They are dried for long-term storage and can be used in soups, stews, and baked dishes. Beans are also crucial in crop rotation and soil health.

Beans are chosen for their ability to grow in various soil types and climates. They are precious because of their nitrogen-fixing ability, which improves soil fertility for future crops.

Beans are often planted alongside corn in the "Three Sisters" method or rows. They require little maintenance and are harvested in late summer. Dried beans can be stored easily and are a crucial winter food.

Rye and Barley
Hardy Grains for Bread and Beer

Rye and barley are essential for making bread, porridge, and beer. Rye is often used to make hearty, dark bread, while barley is necessary for brewing beer and feeding livestock.

Rye and barley are hardy crops that tolerate poor soils and cooler climates. They are often planted in areas where other grains like wheat might struggle, such as in sandy or clay soils.

Rye and barley are typically planted in the fall (winter rye) or early spring (spring barley). These grains are valuable for resilience and are often grown in rotation with other crops to improve soil structure and prevent erosion.

DIVERSIFICATION AND RISK MANAGEMENT

Don't rely solely on a single crop. Instead, diversify crops to mitigate the risks of poor weather, pests, and disease. This approach ensures that if one crop fails, others can still provide food and income. Crop diversity also helps maintain soil fertility and reduces the likelihood of complete crop failure due to disease or pests.

ADAPTING TO THE ENVIRONMENT

Be flexible and adapt crop choices to the specific conditions of the land and the changing environment. For example:

DROUGHT RESISTANT CROPS

In years of low rainfall, plant more drought-resistant crops like beans and potatoes, which can survive with less water.

FLOOD TOLERANT CROPS

In low-lying areas prone to flooding, crops that can withstand wet conditions, like corn or barley, are favored.

PERENNIAL CROPS

Plant perennial crops, such as fruit trees and berry bushes, that require less annual maintenance and can provide food year after year.

PLANTING TECHNIQUES

Once your soil has been prepared with plows and harrows, the time comes to employ the proper planting methods. Settlers use various techniques, each suited to the type of crop and the conditions of the land, to ensure the most excellent chance of a successful harvest.

Row Planting

Row planting calls for the sowing of seeds in straight, evenly-spaced rows. This practice allows for easier weeding, cultivating, and harvesting. Corn, beans, and potatoes are often planted in rows, and when tools such as seed drills or planters are available, they ensure seeds are evenly placed at the correct depth. However, when such tools are scarce, you will rely on simple hand tools, such as hoes or sticks, to create furrows and sow the seeds.

Row planting permits better airflow between plants, helping to reduce the spread of disease and simplifying the application of manure or compost directly to the roots. Tools like hoes make it easier to manage weeds, keeping the soil around your crops free from competition.

Broadcast Sowing

Broadcast sowing involves scattering seeds by hand over a wide area and lightly covering them with soil. This method is commonly used for grains like wheat and oats.

After scattering the seeds, a plow or rake is often used to cover them with a thin layer of soil, ensuring good contact with the earth and protection from birds and other animals.

Broadcast sowing is quick and effective for planting large fields, though it requires skill to ensure even distribution. It is beneficial for crops that do not require precise spacing.

Hill Planting

Hill planting is preferred for larger crops like squash, pumpkins, and melons. In this approach, seeds are sown in small mounds or "hills," spaced far enough apart to allow these spreading plants to flourish. Corn is also commonly planted this way, especially in the traditional "Three Sisters" method, where corn, beans, and squash are grown together.

Using hoes, you will shape the hills and plant the seeds by hand. The raised soil around the young plants aids their growth, offering essential benefits such as improved drainage and warmer soil. In cooler climates, these mounds help the soil warm more quickly in the spring, necessary for successful germination. Hill planting also simplifies managing weeds and watering individual plants, ensuring that each one thrives.

HARVESTING TECHNIQUES

When your crops have ripened, the success of your efforts rests upon efficient harvesting, for it is essential to preserve the quality of the produce and ensure that nothing is lost to waste.

Hand Harvesting

Your crops, particularly vegetables, fruits, and grains, will be gathered by hand. Scythes, sickles, or even your bare hands will be employed to bring in the harvest. For grains, the stalks are cut and bound into sheaves, then left to dry in the field before threshing. Vegetables must be carefully pulled or dug from the earth to avoid damage, and fruits are picked by hand, often with ladders to reach the highest branches.

Harvesting by hand is laborious and requires precise timing, for crops must be collected at the height of ripeness. Inclement weather can swiftly ruin the yield, so it is imperative that you work swiftly and diligently to gather the crops before they are spoiled.

Threshing

Once the grain is harvested, threshing must be done to separate the grain from the stalks and husks. This task is traditionally done by hand, using a flail, or having animals tread the grain. As time passes, mechanical threshers may be employed to ease this labor.

To thresh by hand, the sheaves of grain are spread upon the threshing floor, and the grain is beaten from the stalks with a flail. Afterward, the grain is winnowed and tossed into the air so the wind may carry away the lighter chaff, leaving the heavier grain behind. Threshing is a crucial part of grain production, requiring skill and effort. The care with which you thresh and winnow will significantly affect your grain for food, seed, and future harvests.

STORING CROPS

Proper storage becomes paramount once your harvest is brought in, ensuring that your hard-earned crops last through the long winter and beyond.

Root Cellars

Root cellars are essential for storing root vegetables such as potatoes, carrots, turnips, and other perishable goods like apples. These underground chambers maintain a cool, stable temperature and high humidity, perfect for preserving the freshness of your crops.

A well-built root cellar is dug into the ground and lined with stone or wood, with small vents or doors to allow for proper ventilation, preventing mold and rot growth.

It will be necessary to check your root cellar regularly, removing any spoiled produce before it can affect the rest. To keep your crops fresh, store them in sand, straw, or sawdust layers to maintain moisture and prevent direct contact between the vegetables.

Granaries

Granaries store dried grains such as wheat, oats, and corn. The key to preserving grain is keeping it dry and safe from pests. Granaries are typically raised on stilts or platforms to protect the grain from moisture and rodents.

The structure must be well-ventilated to prevent mold while remaining tightly sealed to keep out vermin. Make a habit of inspecting your stored grain regularly, watching for any signs of pests such as weevils or rodents. Stir or turn the grain periodically to ensure even drying and prevent moisture from accumulating.

Silos and Barns

Silos are tall, cylindrical structures used to store animal feed, such as silage or hay, while barns serve multiple purposes, housing not only tools and equipment but also crops that need shelter from the elements.

Silos preserve the feed by keeping it protected and allowing it to ferment, thus maintaining its nutritional value. In barns, careful organization is necessary to prevent damage to stored crops and make the daily care of livestock more efficient. Always ensure your feed remains dry and free from mold, as spoiled feed can endanger the health of your animals.

Livestock Management

Managing livestock is both a complex and essential part of pioneer life. Choosing the suitable breeds, providing proper nutrition, and ensuring adequate shelter and protection require a settler to be resourceful and well-informed. The success of your farm often hinges upon the health and productivity of your animals, as they are indispensable in providing your family with food, materials, and economic opportunities.

KEY TYPES OF LIVESTOCK

Settlers typically raise various livestock, each serving specific purposes on the homestead. The most common animals include cattle, pigs, chickens, and sheep, though horses, goats, and other animals also play essential roles.

Cattle

MILK PRODUCTION

Dairy cattle are vital for providing milk, which can be consumed fresh or turned into butter, cheese, and other dairy products. A family cow is often one of the first animals acquired because of its ability to provide a steady supply of nourishment. Jersey, Guernsey, and Ayrshire breeds are famous for their high milk yields.

MEAT

Cattle are also raised for beef, providing a substantial source of protein. Beef cattle, such as Hereford or Angus, are slaughtered in the fall when the animals are heaviest. The meat is preserved by salting, smoking, or drying, ensuring a food supply through the winter.

LABOR

Oxen, a type of castrated male cattle, is essential for heavy labor, such as plowing fields, hauling logs, and transporting goods. They are valued for strength and endurance, making them indispensable on pioneer farms.

MANURE

Cattle manure is a valuable byproduct used to fertilize crops and improve soil fertility. Manure is collected and spread over fields in the fall or spring, enriching the soil with essential nutrients.

Pigs

MEAT PRODUCTION

Pigs are an efficient source of meat, producing a large quantity of pork in a relatively short time. They can be fattened on kitchen scraps, acorns, and other foraged foods, making them easy to raise. Pioneer families typically slaughter pigs in the fall, preserving the meat by salting, smoking, or turning it into sausages.

LARD

In addition to meat, pigs provide lard, which is used for cooking, baking, and making soap and candles. Lard is a versatile fat that is essential in the pioneer household.

LOW MAINTENANCE

Pigs require relatively little care compared to other livestock. They are hardy animals that can thrive on diverse diets and in various climates. Settlers often allow pigs to forage in the woods, where they can find acorns, roots, and other natural foods.

Chickens

EGG PRODUCTION

Chickens are raised primarily for eggs, providing reliable protein and other nutrient sources. Eggs are a staple in the pioneer diet and can be used in various dishes, from breakfast to baking.

MEAT

Chickens also provide meat, with older hens or surplus roosters being slaughtered for food. Chicken meat is often eaten fresh but can be preserved by drying or canning.

FEATHER USE

In addition to eggs and meat, chickens provide feathers, which are used for stuffing pillows, mattresses, and quilts. Feather beds are highly valued for warmth and comfort in the winter.

PEST CONTROL

Chickens play a role in controlling pests around the homestead. They forage for insects, grubs, and seeds, helping to reduce pest populations in gardens and fields.

Sheep

WOOL PRODUCTION

Sheep are primarily raised for wool, spun into yarn, and woven into cloth. Wool is essential for making clothing, blankets, and other textiles, providing warmth during the cold winters. Breeds like Merino or Lincoln are popular for high-quality wool.

MEAT

In addition to wool, sheep provide mutton, a staple meat in the pioneer diet. Mutton is often eaten fresh but can be preserved through drying or salting.

LANOLIN

Sheep also produced lanolin, a natural oil found in wool. Lanolin is used in soap making, as well as in balms and ointments to protect and heal skin.

GRAZING MANAGEMENT

Sheep are grazed on pastures, helping to manage the growth of grasses and weeds. They are often rotated between different pastures to prevent overgrazing and to allow the land to recover.

BREEDING PRACTICES

Successful livestock management demands careful attention to breeding practices. To keep your animals healthy and productive over time, selecting the best breeding pairs and managing the risks of inbreeding is essential.

Selective Breeding

Engage in selective breeding to enhance the quality and productivity of your livestock. Choose animals with desirable traits—such as high milk yield in cows, rapid growth in pigs, or thick wool in sheep—for breeding, ensuring these favorable qualities are passed on to the next generation.

Select breeding animals based on their performance and physical characteristics. Keep detailed livestock records, tracking their lineage and performance, to make informed decisions about which animals to breed. This practice will gradually improve the quality of your livestock over the years.

Managing Breeding Seasons

The timing of breeding is crucial to ensure that births occur at the most advantageous times of the year, typically in spring or early summer. This timing allows young animals to grow and strengthen during the warm months, better preparing them for the challenges of the coming winter.

Control breeding by keeping males and females separated until the desired breeding season. This management ensures that offspring are born when conditions are optimal for survival, reducing the risk of loss due to cold or lack of food.

FEEDING AND NUTRITION

Feeding livestock is a year-round concern, and different strategies are employed depending on the season.

Grazing and Foraging

SUMMER FEEDING

During the warmer months, livestock are primarily fed by grazing on pastures. Pastures are managed carefully, rotating animals between fields to prevent overgrazing and to allow grasses to recover. Animals like cattle, sheep, and goats are also driven to graze in open fields, forests, and meadows.

WINTER FEEDING

When pastures are covered with snow in winter, rely on stored hay and grain to feed livestock. Hay is cut and dried during the summer and stored in barns or haystacks to provide feed through the cold months. Grain crops, such as oats and corn, are also grown and stored for winter feeding.

Supplemental Feeding

ROOT VEGETABLES

Root vegetables like turnips, beets, and carrots are grown specifically for livestock feed, especially in the winter. These vegetables are stored in root cellars and fed to animals to supplement hay and grain.

KITCHEN SCRAPS AND BYPRODUCTS

Use every available resource to feed pigs and chickens, including kitchen scraps and byproducts from food processing, such as whey from cheese making or leftover grains from brewing.

SHELTERING AND PROTECTION

Protecting livestock from harsh weather and predators is a constant concern. Build sturdy shelters to keep animals safe and healthy.

BARNS AND STABLES

CONSTRUCTION

Barns and stables are essential structures built to house your livestock during the harsh winter months and to provide shelter during storms. These buildings must be well-ventilated and insulated to protect the animals from extreme cold. Barns are often constructed with thick wooden walls and thatched or shingled roofs to keep out the elements and ensure the safety and comfort of your livestock.

WINTER CARE

In winter, animals are kept in barns with deep bedding made of straw or hay, which provides insulation against the cold. This bedding also absorbs waste, helping to keep the animals clean and warm. Manure is regularly removed and piled outside to decompose into compost, which will be invaluable for use in your fields come spring.

PROTECTION FROM PREDATORS

FENCING

Fences are essential for keeping your livestock contained and protecting them from predators such as wolves, coyotes, and bears. Wooden rails, stone walls, or brush are commonly used to create barriers around your pastures and homesteads, providing a first line of defense against these threats.

GUARD ANIMALS

Keeping guard animals, particularly dogs, is a wise practice to protect your livestock. Dogs can be trained to alert you to the presence of predators and to help keep your animals safe from harm.

NIGHT SHELTERING

To further protect your livestock from nocturnal predators, bringing them into barns or closer to the homestead at night is typical. Chickens should be housed in secure coops to prevent attacks from foxes, raccoons, and other small predators. By taking these precautions, you can ensure the safety of your animals through the night.

BASIC VETERINARY CARE

Maintaining the health of your livestock is of utmost importance, as sick animals can result in the loss of valuable resources.

OBSERVATION

You must rely heavily on careful observation to detect any signs of illness or injury in your animals. Early intervention is essential, so you must become skilled at recognizing symptoms such as lameness, weight loss, or unusual changes in behavior. Keeping a close watch on your livestock will allow you to address issues before they become serious.

HOME REMEDIES

With limited access to professional veterinary care, you often rely on home remedies to treat common ailments. Settlers commonly use herbal medicines and poultices and perform simple surgeries, such as castration or dehorning.

QUARANTINE

Sick animals are often isolated from the rest of the herd to prevent the spread of disease. This practice is critical in avoiding contagious illnesses like foot and mouth disease or cholera in pigs.

DISEASE PREVENTION

Maintaining clean barns and stables is essential for preventing disease. Regular mucking out of stalls, proper ventilation, and clean water supplies helped reduce the risk of infections.

DIET AND NUTRITION

A balanced diet is critical for keeping animals healthy. Ensure that livestock can access clean water, various feeds, and mineral supplements like salt licks which provide essential nutrients.

ECONOMIC AND CULTURAL VALUE OF LIVESTOCK

Livestock is not merely a source of food and raw materials; it also holds great economic and cultural importance.

ECONOMIC VALUE

Livestock often represent one of the most valuable assets a pioneer family can possess. They can be sold, traded, or bartered for goods and services, making them a cornerstone of economic stability. Cattle, in particular, symbolize wealth and prosperity; owning a large herd is a clear mark of success and affluence.

LIVESTOCK MARKETS

Livestock markets serve as vital centers of commerce within pioneer communities, where farmers gather to buy and sell animals. These markets offer the opportunity to acquire new breeding stock, sell surplus animals, or trade for other necessary supplies, thus supporting the economic life of the settlement.

COMMUNITY EVENTS

Livestock are central to many community events and traditions. Fairs, cattle drives, and shearing days are more than just work—they are essential social gatherings where settlers can exchange knowledge, celebrate their achievements, and support one another in the challenges of pioneer life.

Agricultural Tools and Techniques

Possessing the right tools and knowing how to use and maintain them is vital to the success of any farm. These tools enable you to clear land, prepare the soil, plant crops, manage fields, and harvest your produce efficiently. These techniques have been developed and refined over time to maximize productivity and ensure that your hard work yields the best possible results.

ESSENTIAL AGRICULTURAL TOOLS

The tools you will rely on are often simple yet highly effective, crafted to maximize human and animal power. Here are some of the most essential tools in a pioneer's arsenal:

Plows

PREPARING THE GROUND

The plow is one of the most vital tools for breaking up and turning over the soil to prepare it for planting. This process, known as plowing or tilling, is essential for creating a seedbed, controlling weeds, and incorporating organic matter into the soil.

WOODEN PLOW

Early settlers often used wooden plows, which were lightweight and more accessible to handle but less durable and practical in tough soils.

IRON PLOW

As technology advances, iron plows become more common. These are much stronger and can cut through the heavy clay soils prevalent in parts of Orleans County. The "moldboard" plow, which turns the soil more effectively, is especially valued.

HORSE DRAWN PLOW

Larger farms often employ horse-drawn plows, allowing more efficient tilling of expansive fields. Horses are generally preferred over oxen for their speed, though oxen may still be used in rougher terrain.

MAINTENANCE

Keeping your plows sharp and free of rust is essential. Regularly sharpen the plow blades and clean them after each use to ensure they remain effective. A well-maintained plow can serve you for many years, even with heavy use.

Harrows

Refining the Seedbed

After the plowing, the soil often needs further breaking down and leveling. Harrows are employed to smooth out the plowed field, breaking up clods of soil and covering seeds after planting. This process helps create a fine, even seedbed, which is ideal for the successful germination of your crops.

SPIKE TOOTH HARROW

This type has long, straight teeth that drag through the soil, breaking up clumps and leveling the surface. It is commonly used for lighter soils and seed covering.

DISC HARROW

Featuring circular blades that cut into the soil, disc harrows are more effective in heavier soils and can handle more substantial clods and debris. They also help to incorporate organic matter more thoroughly into the soil.

TECHNIQUE

Harrowing is typically done after plowing but before planting and sometimes after sowing seeds to cover them with a thin layer of soil. Proper timing and technique are essential to avoid compacting the soil or damaging young plants.

Scythes

Harvesting by Hand

Scythes are indispensable tools for manually cutting hay, grain crops, and tall weeds, particularly before the advent of mechanized reapers and mowers.

A scythe is a long, curved blade attached to a wooden handle known as a snath. The curvature of the blade allows for a smooth, sweeping motion, enabling you to cut through vegetation with minimal effort.

Using a scythe requires both skill and strength. You will need to learn to swing the scythe in a rhythmic motion, keeping the blade low and parallel to the ground to cut crops close to the roots. Regular sharpening of the blade is essential to maintain its cutting efficiency.

Scythes must be frequently sharpened with a whetstone, and the blade should be kept clean and rust-free. The wooden snath also requires care, often treated with oil to prevent it from drying out and cracking.

With proper maintenance, a scythe can serve you well through many harvests.

Sickles

Precision Cutting

Sickles are more diminutive, handheld tools used for cutting grain, particularly in areas where precision is needed, such as around fences, near the ground, or in smaller fields. They are also commonly employed for harvesting crops like flax and pruning.

A sickle is equipped with a short, curved blade featuring a serrated edge, making it well-suited for gripping and slicing through stalks in a controlled manner.

Harvesting with a sickle is labor-intensive but allows for greater control in tight spaces or when working with delicate crops. The sickle is wielded sweepingly, with the worker grasping a handful of stalks and cutting them close to the ground.

Like the scythe, the sickle's blade requires regular sharpening to maintain effectiveness. The serrated edge should also be kept clean and rust-free to ensure longevity.

Hoes

Versatile Hand Tools

Hoes are multipurpose implements essential for weeding, cultivating the soil, and planting. They are particularly invaluable for the upkeep of vegetable gardens and small-scale farming endeavors.

DRAW HOE

With its flat blade set at a right angle to the handle, the draw hoe is used for chopping and drawing soil towards oneself. It proves ideal for creating furrows, covering seeds, and breaking up the soil.

PUSH HOE

With a slightly angled blade, the push hoe is designed for pushing through the soil, making it well-suited for weeding and cultivating between rows of crops.

TECHNIQUE

Proper home use requires a steady rhythm to prevent fatigue and ensure thorough cultivation. The blade should be kept sharp, enabling it to easily cut through soil and weeds.

MAINTENANCE

Though simple in design, hoes must be kept sharp and clean. The wooden handles should be treated with oil to prevent splintering and to ensure a firm and comfortable grip. With regular care, a hoe will serve you faithfully for many years.

Rakes

CLEARING AND GATHERING

Rakes serve many purposes, from gathering hay and straw to clearing debris from fields and gardens. They are indispensable tools for preparing fields for planting and gathering cut crops after the harvest.

Rakes are made with either wooden or metal tines, with the spacing and length of the tines varying according to their intended use. Hay rakes have longer, more widely spaced tines to gather loose hay, while garden rakes have shorter, more closely set tines for smoothing soil.

TECHNIQUE

Raking requires a gentle, sweeping motion to avoid damaging the soil or crops. The rake is drawn towards the user, gathering debris or crops into piles for accessible collection.

MAINTENANCE

Wooden rakes are prone to wear and breakage, so settlers often repair them by replacing broken tines or reinforcing the handle. While more durable, metal rakes still require maintenance to keep them rust-free. Proper care ensures that your rake remains a reliable tool for many seasons.

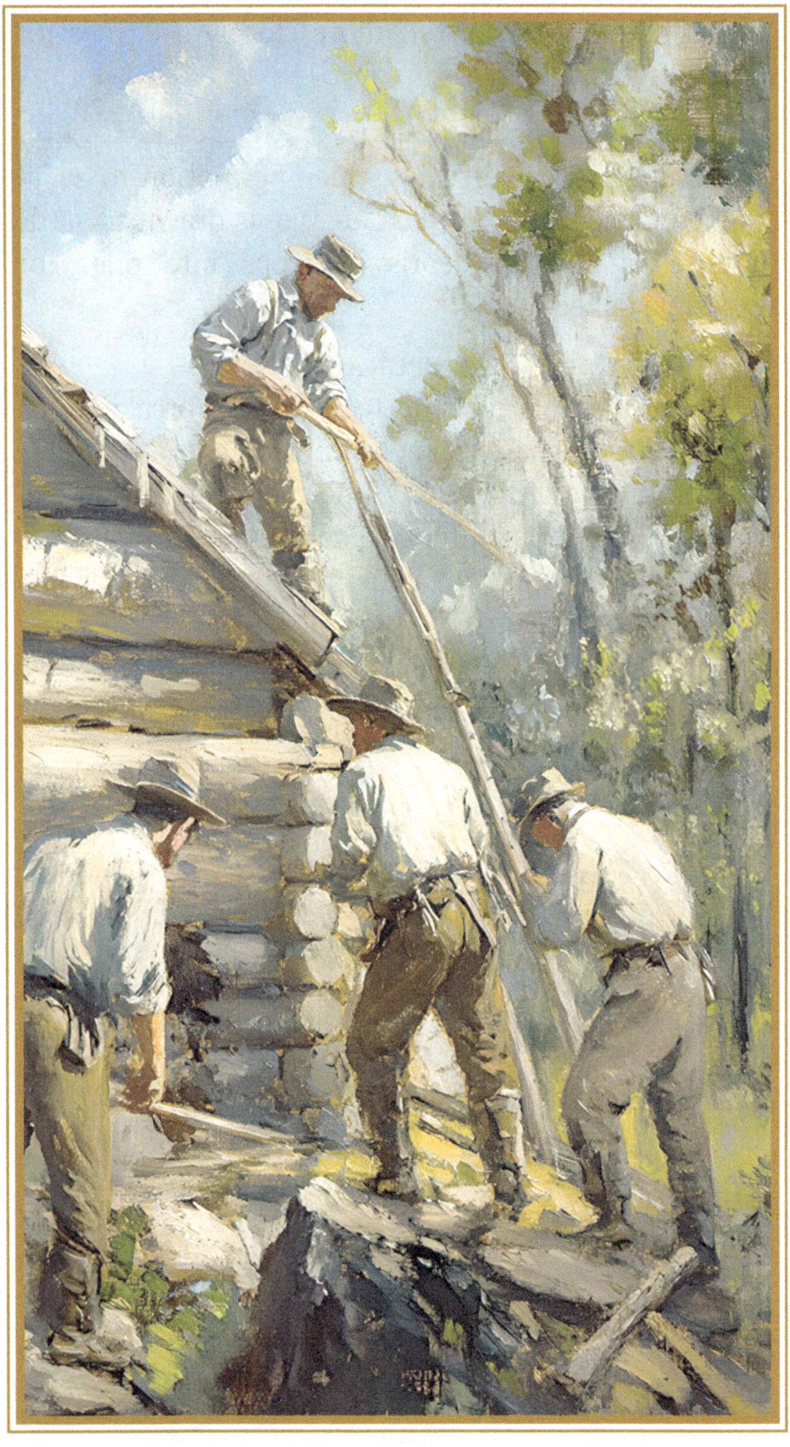

BUILDING AND CONSTRUCTION KNOWLEDGE

Shelter Building

It is essential that you possess the practical skills necessary to construct log cabins, barns, and other important structures using the materials at hand—wood, stone, and mud. A sound understanding of proper insulation methods and chimney construction is vital to endure the harsh winters that await.

LOG CABINS

Log cabins are the most common type of shelter among settlers, especially in regions where timber is abundant. These sturdy structures are practical, relatively swift to raise, and provide reliable protection against the elements.

SELECTING THE BUILDING SITE

Select slightly elevated ground to prevent flooding and ensure proper drainage. The cabin should be oriented with the front facing south, maximizing sunlight exposure during winter. This will naturally warm the interior, reducing the need for extra firewood.

TIMBER SELECTION AND FELLING

Trees like pine, oak, or chestnut are often chosen for their strength and resistance to decay. Pine is commonly preferred for its straight trunks and ease of splitting, while oak is prized for its exceptional durability. Felling the trees is done with axes and saws, trimming away branches and bark. It is wise to leave the logs to season or dry out before use, as this process lightens the wood and minimizes the risk of shrinking once the cabin is raised.

LOG CABIN CONSTRUCTION

A strong foundation is crucial to ensure that your cabin settles evenly and stands the test of time. Construct your cabin on stone piers or lay the first layer of logs atop flat stones, raising the structure off the ground to protect it from moisture and rot.

The logs are skillfully notched at the ends to interlock securely at the corners, forming a stable framework. Common styles include the saddle notch, the more secure V-notch, and the dovetail notch, which locks the logs tightly and resists shifting over time.

Logs are stacked horizontally to build the walls, each layer carefully aligned. Though the notches provide a tight fit, gaps between the logs are inevitable. These are filled with mud, clay, straw, and moss, known as chinking, to seal the cabin against drafts and pests.

The roof is generally constructed with a steep pitch to shed rain and snow. Split wooden shingles, called shakes or thatch, are often used as a roofing material. The roof's structure is supported by rafters secured to the topmost logs, ensuring that the cabin is well-protected from the elements.

THATCHED ROOFS AND SHINGLE MAKING

The resources at hand dictate the choice of roofing materials. In wooded regions, one may split logs to craft wooden shingles, which are layered over the roof supports to form a waterproof covering.

In areas where timber is scarce, grasses or reeds may be employed to fashion thatch. A thatched roof is constructed by tightly layering the plant material to effectively shed rain and provide insulation.

Whether fashioned from shingles or thatch, the roof's upkeep is a continual task, as damage from storms or the wear of time may result in leaks and drafts.

DOORS, WINDOWS, AND FLOORING

Doors are typically fashioned from split logs or planks and reinforced with wooden crossbars for added strength. Hinges are commonly made of wood or wrought iron. Windows are kept small to reduce heat loss and, when glass is unavailable, may be covered with greased paper or animal hides for protection. While most spartan cabins may have dirt floors, more permanent structures feature wooden plank flooring. These planks are laid atop a foundation of stones or logs and raised slightly above ground level to prevent dampness.

HEATING YOUR HOME

Insulation and Weatherproofing

Insulating your home is vital to retaining heat, reducing the need for constant fuel replenishment.

Chinking involves filling the gaps between the logs with mud, clay, straw, and moss. Once this is done, daubing follows—where a finer layer of clay or lime is applied over the chinking to create a smoother, more weather-resistant seal.

To further insulate the cabin, settlers often hang animal hides or quilts along the walls, particularly near the sleeping area, to retain heat. A thick layer of straw or dried grass is commonly spread on the floor, providing extra warmth against the cold ground. In some cases, the roof is also insulated with a layer of straw or thatch beneath the shingles, further helping to retain warmth and protect the cabin from harsh weather conditions.

Chimney Construction

The chimney is the most essential feature of your pioneer cabin. It will serve as both the heart of your home for cooking and the source of warmth during the long, cold months while safely carrying the smoke away from your living quarters.

STONE CHIMNEYS

Stone is the favored material for constructing chimneys, owing to its strength and resistance to fire.

You must gather stones from the surrounding land, carefully selecting and stacking them to form a solid chimney stretching from the hearth inside your cabin up through the roofline. This will provide safety from fire and ensure longevity, as the stone is less likely to suffer from wear.

CLAY AND STICK CHIMNEYS

Should you find yourself in an area where stone is scarce, you may need to rely on a "stick and clay" chimney. Though less durable, this method calls for crafting a chimney from a mix of sticks coated in clay. While easy to construct with the materials on hand, be mindful that this type of chimney will require more frequent maintenance and may not last as long as stone.

Fireplace Construction

Your fireplace will be built at one end of the cabin, with the hearth being lined with flat stones to protect the floor from the dangers of sparks and heat. It should be designed both broad and deep to accommodate the large logs necessary for a proper fire that will burn through the night, keeping you and your family warm.

See FIRE SAFETY for more details.

SMOKE VENTING AND DRAFT CONTROL

The chimney must be carefully designed to create a strong draft, pulling the smoke from the cabin while drawing fresh air into the fire. The proper height and shape of the chimney's interior are crucial for maintaining this draft, ensuring the fire burns efficiently without filling your home with smoke. Some pioneers install a damper within the chimney—a movable metal plate that controls airflow. When the fire is not in use, closing the damper will keep the precious warmth inside your cabin from escaping into the cold winter air.

BARNS AND OUTBUILDINGS

As you establish your homestead, constructing outbuildings beyond your main cabin will prove essential for managing both farming and livestock. These structures are vital for storing crops, providing animal shelter, and protecting tools and equipment from the elements.

Barn Construction

A barn is a central feature of any farm, serving various purposes. It will store your hay and grain, shelter your livestock, and house all your necessary tools. The needs of your farm will determine the size and layout of your barn, but its sturdiness and capacity are critical to the success of your operations.

FRAME CONSTRUCTION

Barns are commonly built using timber frame construction. This method involves assembling a framework of large wooden beams, expertly joined with mortise and tenon joints, then secured with wooden pegs. This method provides strength and ensures the barn's durability through years of use and exposure.

WALLS AND ROOF

The walls of your barn will be fashioned from sturdy wooden planks, while the roof will be covered with wooden shingles or thatch. These materials provide solid protection against the elements, while large doors allow easy access for your wagons, tools, and livestock.

Other Outbuildings

SHEDS AND WORKSHOPS

Smaller outbuildings like sheds and workshops are essential for storing tools, firewood, and other supplies. A workshop offers space for carpentry, blacksmithing, and other essential trades, allowing you to craft, repair, and maintain what your farm requires.

SMOKEHOUSES

A smokehouse is necessary for curing and preserving meat, especially as winter approaches. These structures are built to be airtight, save for a small chimney to vent the smoke. Inside, meat is hung, and a slow-burning hardwood fire is maintained for several days, infusing the meat with flavor while preserving it for future use.

ROOT CELLARS

Root cellars are indispensable for storing vegetables and fruits through the winter months. Typically dug into a hillside or underground, the earth naturally insulates these cellars, maintaining a calm, stable environment. A wooden door ensures protection from animals and cold air while your crops remain safely preserved within.

BUILDING WITH STONE, MUD, AND OTHER MATERIALS

While wood remains the primary building material for most settlers, there are regions where other natural resources prove more practical. In such cases, the environment offers an abundance of stone, mud, and even thatch to construct sturdy and lasting homes.

Stone Construction

STONE HOUSES

Where stone is plentiful, you may consider building your home entirely from it. Though it demands more effort and time, a stone house is unmatched in durability and insulation, providing warmth in winter and coolness in summer. The construction requires skilled craftsmanship, as each stone must be carefully placed and secured, often using lime mortar to bind the structure and ensure stability for many years.

STONE FENCES AND WALLS

Stones are also used to build fences and retain walls. These solid barriers manage livestock, protect crops, and prevent soil erosion on your farm. They are durable, require little maintenance, and can last generations if constructed carefully.

Mud and Adobe

MUD BRICK CONSTRUCTION

In regions with scarce timber, settlers often turn to mud bricks, also called adobe. These bricks are crafted from clay, straw, and water, formed into blocks, and then left to dry in the sun. Mud-brick houses are typical in dry climates where wood is less accessible, and while they demand regular upkeep, they provide good insulation against heat and cold.

PLASTERING

You might apply a mud or lime plaster layer to seal gaps in wooden or stone structures. This provides a smoother finish and offers protection from wind, rain, and pests.

Thatch and Sod

THATCH ROOFING

Where wood is scarce, thatch made from tightly bundled straw, reeds, or grass is a reliable roofing material. Thatch provides excellent insulation, keeping the cabin cool in summer and warm in winter while shedding rain effectively.

Sod Houses

On the Great Plains, where timber is scarce, some settlers construct homes from sod. These sod houses are built by cutting blocks of earth and stacking them to form thick, insulating walls. While these homes provide warmth in winter and coolness in summer, they require constant maintenance to prevent erosion and protect against moisture.

SEASONAL CONSTRUCTION CONSIDERATIONS

When it comes to harvesting timber, spring and early summer are ideal. During this time, the sap flow in trees is reduced, making the wood more straightforward to work with and less prone to warping as it dries. Timing your construction projects around the seasons will ensure the materials are more reliable and durable in the long run.

Spring and Summer Construction

TIMBER HARVESTING

Spring and early summer prove ideal for gathering timber. During these months, the sap flow in the trees is reduced, rendering the wood easier to cut and less likely to warp as it dries. This ensures your timber remains straight and sound for construction purposes.

FOUNDATION LAYING

With the warm, dry conditions of late spring and summer, it becomes the perfect time to lay the foundation of your cabin or barn. Whether you build upon stone, brick, or wooden piers, these favorable conditions ensure the foundation is set firmly, providing a stable base for any structure.

ROOFING

Roofing work is best undertaken during the summer when the threat of rain is lessened. Constructing the roof during this season helps to keep the building's interior dry and ensures the structure is secure well before the first snow arrives.

Fall and Winter Construction

INTERIOR WORK

As the exterior work nears completion, the cooler months of fall and winter present a suitable time for focusing on the interior. Finishing the floors, constructing the fireplace, and adding proper insulation become the primary tasks. These efforts ensure your dwelling is warm, comfortable, and ready for habitation.

WINTER PREPARATIONS

As winter draws near, you must ensure the house is adequately insulated. Every gap must be sealed tightly to keep out the chill, and firewood must be stacked close at hand to endure the season. Livestock barns are readied, providing shelter from the harsh weather and keeping the animals safe and warm.

Fencing

Fences are among the first structures you will likely construct after establishing your homestead. They serve a wide array of purposes, from securing livestock to protecting crops from wild animals and marking the boundaries of your property.

TYPES OF FENCES AND THEIR USES

The type of fence you will build depends on the specific needs of your homestead and the materials you have at hand. Each design offers its benefits and is suited to particular tasks.

Split Rail Fences

Split-rail fences are the most commonly used in regions where timber is plentiful. These fences are constructed by splitting logs lengthwise into rails and then stacked in a zigzag pattern. This method requires neither nails nor posts, making it a favored design among pioneers due to its ease of construction using simple tools and manpower.

These fences are ideal for marking property boundaries and enclosing pastures for livestock. Their sturdy design allows them to be built quickly, making them well-suited for large expanses of land. The zigzag pattern provides stability, particularly in rocky or uneven terrain where digging postholes is difficult.

The open design of split-rail fences ensures good visibility and airflow, essential for maintaining healthy pastures. The land stays well-ventilated, helping to keep the grass and soil in good condition. Furthermore, repairs are simple—if a rail becomes damaged, it can easily be replaced without dismantling the entire structure, making split-rail fences practical and durable for your needs.

Worm Fences

(Zigzag Fences)

A variation of the split-rail design, worm fences—also called snake or zigzag fences—are constructed without nails or fasteners. The rails are laid in a zigzag pattern, with each rail resting on the ends of two others. This method proves especially useful in regions where digging postholes is not feasible, such as on rocky ground.

Worm fences are commonly used to enclose large fields and pastures, as they can be assembled swiftly and cover vast areas with minimal materials. They are particularly effective in keeping out larger animals like deer and wild boar.

Much like split-rail fences, worm fences are easy to build and maintain. Their zigzag design offers stability without the need for posts, and the open structure provides flexibility on uneven ground, making this design an efficient choice for the homestead.

Post and Rail Fences

Post and rail fences are regularly built by setting vertical wooden posts into the ground, with horizontal rails attached. This design requires more materials and labor than a split-rail fence but offers greater strength and stability, making it well-suited for more permanent structures. Commonly used for corrals, livestock enclosures, and around gardens, post and rail fences also serve as boundary markers in more established areas where property lines are clearly defined.

These fences are long-lasting and more durable than split-rail varieties, ideal for places where a solid, lasting solution is necessary. Additionally, the design easily accommodates the inclusion of gates, making it versatile for many applications on the homestead.

Stone Fences

In regions where stone is plentiful, settlers often construct stone fences by stacking rocks without mortar, relying on the weight and shape of the stones to create a solid, stable barrier. These dry-stacked fences are commonly used to enclose fields, mark property boundaries, and protect crops from animals, particularly in rocky soil where the stones are easily sourced.

Stone fences are remarkably durable, often enduring for generations with little maintenance. Their strength makes them impervious to most animals, providing excellent protection for crops and livestock. Once built, these fences require minimal upkeep, making them a valuable, long-term solution for the homestead.

BUILDING FENCES TECHNIQUES AND CHALLENGES

Constructing a fence is a labor-intensive task that requires planning, skill, and often the cooperation of neighbors. Settlers frequently work together, sharing resources and labor to build fences efficiently.

Clearing the Land for Fences

Before building, the land must be cleared of trees, stumps, and rocks

TREE FELLING

Trees are felled with axes and saws, with the timber often repurposed for the fence. Clearing trees also opens space for crops and grazing.

STUMP REMOVAL

Removing stumps can be particularly challenging, as tree roots often run deep. Settlers use tools like grub hoes and draft animals to haul stumps from the ground. Some stumps are burned or left to rot over time.

ROCK CLEARING

In rocky areas, stones are cleared to prepare the ground for fencing. These stones are used to build or pile stone fences into walls around fields.

Erecting the Fence

MARKING THE BOUNDARY

Before construction begins, boundary lines are carefully measured to ensure the fence will enclose the intended area.

SETTING THE POSTS

For fences requiring posts, such as post and rail designs, posts are set into the ground regularly. Digging postholes is hard work, particularly in rocky or frozen ground, and requires robust tools like posthole diggers.

Assembling the Fence

Once the posts are set, rails or stones are added. Split-rail and worm fences rely on stacking and interlocking, while stone fences are built by carefully selecting and placing rocks for stability.

Building Gates

Gates are essential for accessing enclosed areas and are typically incorporated into post and rail fences, made from wooden planks and hung on sturdy wooden or iron hinges.

MAINTAINING FENCES

Fences require regular attention to remain effective. Weather, animals, and natural decay mean they must be inspected and repaired frequently.

Repairing Damaged Sections

REPLACING RAILS AND POSTS

Wooden rails and posts are vulnerable to rot or breakage, particularly in wet conditions. Settlers keep spare materials on hand to replace damaged sections as needed.

REBUILDING STONE FENCES

Stone fences may need rebuilding if sections collapse or are damaged by animals. Though labor-intensive, this task is necessary to maintain the fence's strength.

Protecting Against Weather and Decay

WEATHERPROOFING

To prolong the life of wooden fences, settlers treat them with oil or tar to prevent water damage and rot. This is especially important for posts set into the ground.

SNOW AND ICE MANAGEMENT

Winter brings the threat of snow and ice, which can cause fences to sag or collapse. Settlers clear snow from the base of fences and reinforce weak sections before winter arrives, ensuring the fences remain standing through the season.

Land Management

Beyond raising fences, you shall face the extraordinary task of managing the land, transforming it into fertile and productive farms. This labor involves clearing forests, removing stumps, carefully tending woodlots, and ensuring a steady, sustainable supply of firewood and timber.

CLEARING THE FOREST

Clearing the wilderness to make room for farmland is one of your first steps. The magnitude of this work cannot be overstated, often requiring years of steady effort.

Felling Trees

AXES AND SAWS

Your chief tools for felling trees will be axes and saws. A broad axe will bring down smaller trees, while larger ones demand the strength of crosscut saws to cut them into manageable lengths. Tree felling is often shared among neighbors, working together to clear vast tracts of land for planting and settlement.

SELECTIVE CLEARING

In your clearing, practice selectivity. Remove enough trees to create fields and pastures, but consider leaving some for future timber needs, shade, and protection against wind. A thoughtful balance will serve you well.

Stump Removal

GRUBBING AND PULLING

Removing stumps is, perhaps, the most laborious aspect of land clearing. Grubbing involves cutting the roots with axes or hoes and then digging the stumps out by hand. For the enormous stumps, oxen or horses will be your allies, pulling them free with chains and pulleys.

BURNING STUMPS

Where digging proves too arduous, you may resort to burning. Pile brush around the stump set it ablaze or bore holes and fill them with hot coals. While this method requires less effort, it takes time and careful management to avoid unintended fires spreading across the land.

Rock Clearing

STONE WALLS AND PILES

Boulders and stones must be removed from your fields, often with hand tools or the aid of draft animals. These stones are far from wasted; use them to build protective walls around fields or pile them at the edges of your property. These piles serve as homes for small creatures and barriers against erosion, safeguarding your land.

MANAGING FORESTS AND WOODLOTS

As a settler, your responsibility extends to managing the remaining forests on your property. The key to long-term prosperity is knowing how to care for these woodlots.

Timber Harvesting

SUSTAINABLE HARVESTING

You should practice the art of sustainable harvesting. Cut only the mature trees, leaving the younger ones to grow. This will guarantee a continuous supply of timber for building, fencing, and firewood, and preserve the health of your forest for years to come. Such careful management will also provide habitats for wildlife, supporting the delicate balance of nature on your land.

SEASONAL CUTTING

The best time to fell trees is late winter or early spring, when the sap flows slowly and the wood is less likely to rot. The logs will dry out during the warm months, making them far easier to work with when building and crafting.

With careful land management, you will secure your livelihood and future generations.

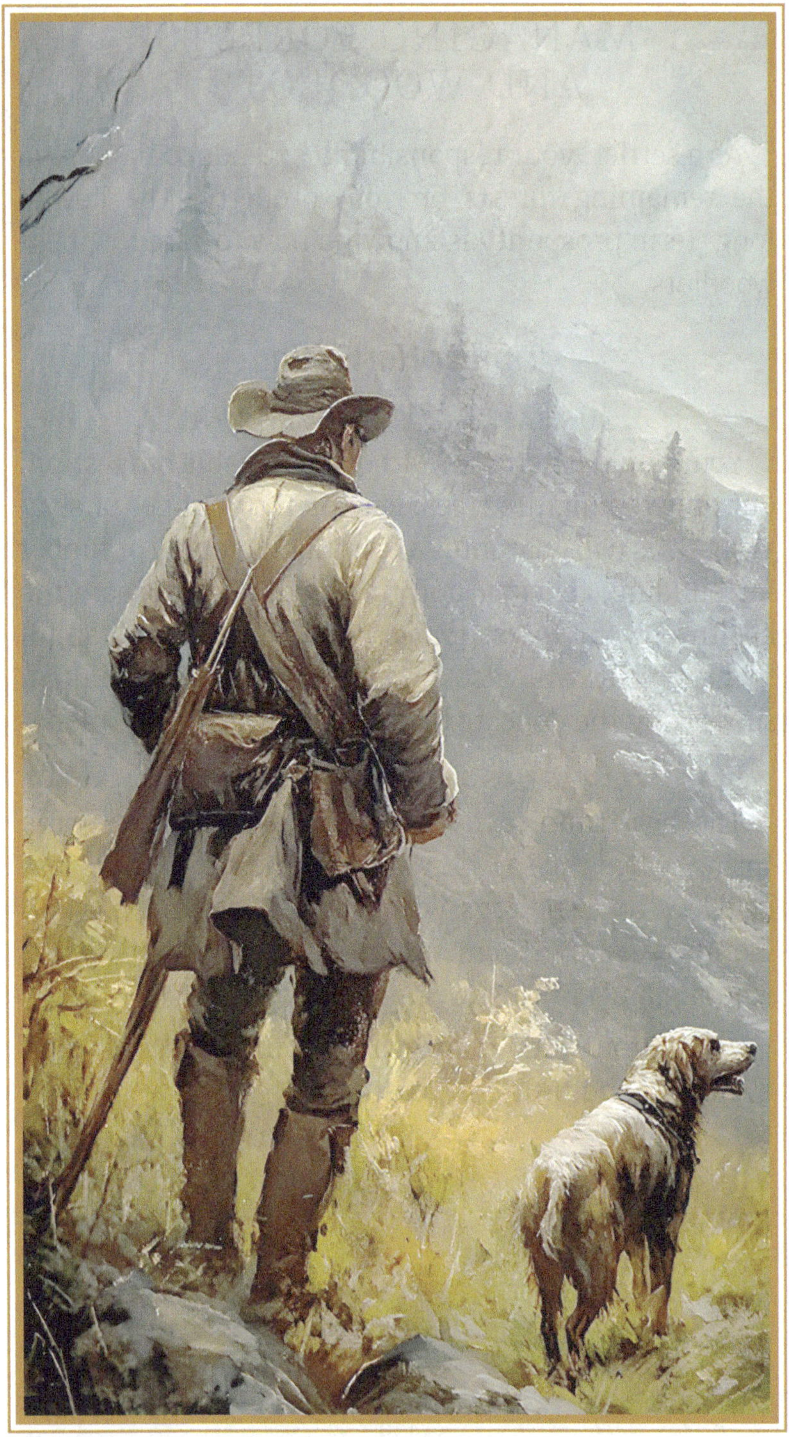

NATURAL RESOURCES AND THEIR USE

As you embark on your new life as a settler, it is vital to understand that while the wilderness offers many bountiful resources, you must also respect the delicate balance between utilizing and conserving nature. The natural world provides food, shelter, and material wealth, but unchecked exploitation can lead to ruin. Your success and survival will rest on your ability to live in harmony with the environment, managing it wisely for immediate needs and the future.

Sustainable Hunting and Trapping

SELECTIVE HUNTING PRACTICES

You should practice selective hunting, focusing on animals that directly threaten your crops or livestock while refraining from over hunting creatures vital to the local ecosystem. This measured approach ensures that wildlife populations remain robust and that the natural balance is not upset. For example, while wolves may occasionally prey on your animals, they also help regulate the number of deer, which, if unchecked, can devastate your crops.

Thus, the prudent management of hunting helps maintain a stable and healthy environment, allowing you to protect your homestead without diminishing future resources.

TRAPPING FOR FUR AND TRADE

In addition to hunting, trapping will play a key role in managing the land and supporting your household. Trapping not only controls nuisance animals but also provides valuable furs for trade. Beavers, foxes, and raccoons offer pelts of considerable worth, and trading them may grant you access to goods and tools otherwise challenging to obtain.

However, it is crucial to follow sustainable trapping methods. Trap only within the appropriate seasons, allowing the animal populations to recover. In doing so, you secure a lasting supply of fur and maintain the natural order, ensuring the resources endure for future generations.

Conservation of Natural Resources

MANAGING FORESTS AND WOODLANDS

The careful management of forests and woodlands will be vital to preserving a healthy environment and securing a steady supply of resources for years. Selective logging, where only mature trees are felled while younger ones are left to grow, is a practice you must embrace. This ensures the continued regeneration of the forest and maintains its overall vitality.

Beyond your immediate needs, there is great wisdom in preserving certain wilderness areas. These untouched lands serve as sanctuaries for wildlife and sources of vital food, fuel, and building materials. In safeguarding these spaces, you protect not only your livelihood but also the prosperity of future generations.

RESPECT FOR WILDLIFE

Though you may often need to defend yourself and your property from dangerous animals, you should always carry a deep respect for the wildlife that shares the land with you. Recognizing the vital role that animals play in the ecosystem, it would be wise to adopt practices of restraint and balance in your dealings with them.

You can learn much from Native American traditions, which teach a harmonious relationship with nature and stress the responsible use of resources. Aim to use every part of the animal in your hunting, leaving nothing to waste. Ensure that your actions do not jeopardize the survival of local species, for your success is tied to the delicate balance of the natural world.

Timber and Wood Resources

The forests of Orleans County stretch across the land, offering a wealth of timber, a precious gift to the pioneer. Yet, as with all natural resources, their wise use requires knowledge and skill. Timber is the backbone of pioneer life, serving in constructing homes, barns, and tools while also providing the fuel needed to warm hearths and cook meals. To thrive, you must learn where to find the finest timber and understand the distinct qualities of each type of wood.

Hardwoods and softwoods each have their place, and knowing which to use for a given task will ensure the longevity and strength of your structures. With careful stewardship, this vast resource will sustain your homestead for generations.

Identifying Prime Timber Locations

OLD GROWTH FORESTS

Some of the most prized timber resources lie within the region's old-growth forests. These ancient woodlands, untouched for centuries, contain mature trees ideal for logging. Their size, strength, and durability make them highly sought after for construction. Mature trees offer long, straight logs that are easier to work with and produce timber less prone to warping or cracking.

The dense, seasoned wood is naturally resistant to rot and pests, ensuring its use in building homes, barns, and other essential structures. As you venture into these forests, seek out these grand trees for their high-quality wood, but take care to be sparing in your cutting to preserve the resource for future needs.

WATERWAYS AS TIMBER TRANSPORT ROUTES

Rivers and streams are invaluable for moving heavy timber. When selecting timber, consider those trees that stand near these waterways, where felled logs can be floated downstream to nearby mills or markets. The convenience of transporting wood via water significantly reduces the labor and cost involved, making forests located near rivers far more valuable to you. This proximity will not only ease the burden of moving your timber but also allow you to profit by selling to those with greater distances to travel.

Clearing Land for Agriculture

Clearing land requires great strength and perseverance, but you can make the effort worthwhile using the timber you remove. The wood you gather from this work is a valuable byproduct, which can immediately serve in constructing your home, barns, and fences, or be stockpiled for future use. Each type of wood offers unique qualities, and you should evaluate the purpose for which each piece is best suited.

Whether for building or the market, a wise and thoughtful assessment will ensure that none of your labor goes to waste. Through careful management, you will maximize your return and make the most of the resources at your disposal.

TYPES OF WOOD AND THEIR USES

MATCHING THE MATERIAL TO THE TASK

It is imperative to understand the various types of wood available to make well-informed decisions about which species to use for specific purposes. This knowledge will ensure that you maximize the utility and longevity of the materials. Below is a list of standard trees in the area and their most suitable uses. A more detailed guide for identifying each tree is provided later in this volume.

Hardwoods

Durable and Versatile

OAK

Oak stands as one of the most valuable hardwoods for settlers. Its great strength and lasting durability make it ideal for constructing furniture, flooring, and structural beams. White oak is particularly prized for its resistance to moisture and decay, making it perfect for building barrels, ships, and outdoor structures. Though slightly less durable, red oak finds its place in interior work such as cabinetry and paneling.

MAPLE

Maple, known for its hardness and fine grain, is highly valued. Due to its strength and smooth finish, sugar maple is especially favored for furniture, tool handles, and flooring. Red maple, while softer and more plentiful, serves similar purposes. Maple is also commonly used for making spiles and buckets, essential in producing maple syrup.

HICKORY

Renowned for its toughness and resilience, hickory is often chosen for tool handles, wagon wheels, and items that demand shock resistance. It also burns hot and long, making it excellent firewood. Due to its tendency to warp, hickory is seldom used for construction, but its unique qualities render it indispensable for specialized tasks.

CHERRY

Cherry wood is cherished for its rich color and smooth finish, making it a popular choice for fine furniture and cabinetry. Though not as hard as oak or maple, cherry is still durable and easy to work with. Over time, it deepens in color, aging into a warm, rich hue. Settlers often reserve cherry wood for high-quality decorative pieces.

ASH

White ash is valued for its light weight and strength, and it is ideal for making tool handles, oars, and items that need flexibility and durability. Black ash, while rarer, is sought after for basket weaving due to its flexibility when wet.

Softwoods

Abundant and Easy to Work With

PINE

White pine is perhaps the most critical softwood for settlers, appreciated for its tall, straight trunks and soft, workable wood. It is widely used in building homes, barns, and various other structures, as well as in furniture and cabinetry. Easy to cut and finish, pine is a favorite for both rough and fine carpentry. Though less common, red pine is valued for outdoor uses due to its excellent durability.

HEMLOCK

Hemlock is another abundant softwood, often employed in construction framing and sheathing. While not as strong as pine, it boasts resistance to rot and insects, making it a suitable choice for barns, fences, and outbuildings. Though its coarse grain makes it less desirable for fine woodworking, its utility in rough construction is well-regarded.

SPRUCE

Spruce is a frequent choice for construction, mainly where pine is less available. It is lightweight, with a straight grain that makes it easy to work. Spruce is often used for rafters, joists, and structural elements. It is also valued for its resonance and is thus chosen for making musical instruments such as violins and pianos.

CEDAR

Northern white cedar is treasured for its natural resistance to rot and decay, making it ideal for outdoor applications. Cedar is often used for shingles, fence posts, and other items that must endure the elements. Its aromatic qualities also make it desirable for chests and closets, as it repels moths and pests.

TIMBER FOR CONSTRUCTION

Building the Pioneer Homestead

Constructing your home, barn, and other essential structures will require substantial timber. It is crucial to strategically use resources and select the suitable wood for each stage of the building process.

Log Cabins and Timber Frames

LOG CABINS

The log cabin remains the quintessential pioneer dwelling, crafted from the trunks of large trees, typically pine or oak. The logs are notched at the ends, interlocking to form a sturdy, weather-resistant structure. The type of wood will depend upon what is most abundant in your area. Pine is often favored for its straight trunks and ease of cutting, making it ideal for swift construction, while oak, though more challenging to work, offers added strength and durability, ensuring your home will stand for many years.

TIMBER FRAMES

Timber framing is often employed for more significant or permanent structures, such as barns or churches. This method involves constructing a framework from large hardwood beams like oak or ash. These beams are held together by wooden pegs rather than nails, creating a robust, flexible structure that can endure heavy loads and harsh weather. Timber-framed buildings are often clad with boards or shingles from softer woods like pine or cedar.

Roofing and Shingles

WOODEN SHINGLES

Roofing is a vital part of construction, and wooden shingles are the most common material. Cedar and pine are excellent choices due to their resistance to moisture and ease of splitting into thin, even pieces. Shingles are laid in overlapping rows to create a waterproof barrier, ensuring protection from rain and snow.

BOARD AND BATTEN SIDING

Another everyday use of timber is board-and-batten siding, where wide boards are nailed vertically to the frame, with narrower battens covering the gaps between them. This method is often used for barns and outbuildings, providing a durable, weather-resistant exterior. Pine, hemlock, and spruce are frequently employed for this purpose.

Flooring and Interior Work

HARDWOOD FLOORS

Hardwoods such as oak, maple, and cherry are typically used for flooring inside your home. These woods provide a durable surface capable of withstanding heavy use. The flooring is usually made from wide planks, nailed or pegged to the joists beneath.

INTERIOR PANELING AND TRIM

Hardwoods are also used for interior paneling, wainscoting, and trim work, adding warmth and elegance to your home. Cherry and maple are favored for decorative elements, while softwoods like pine are often used in less visible areas or where cost is a concern.

Fuel and Firewood

The Essential Energy Source

Beyond construction, timber serves as a primary fuel source. Firewood is essential for heating your home, cooking meals, and powering industries such as blacksmithing and baking.

Selecting Firewood

HARDWOODS FOR HEAT

Hardwoods like oak, hickory, and maple are prized for their high energy content and long burn times. These woods provide a steady, hot fire, ideal for heating your home through the cold winters. Hardwoods are precious for overnight fires, burning slowly and maintaining warmth for extended periods.

SOFTWOODS FOR KINDLING

Softwoods like pine and spruce are ideal for kindling, as they ignite quickly and burn hot. However, they burn faster and with more resin, leading to creosote buildup in chimneys if used as the primary fuel. It is best to start your fire with softwoods and add hardwood logs to maintain it.

SEASONING WOOD

To ensure firewood burns efficiently, it must be seasoned by allowing it to dry for several months before use. Freshly cut, or "green" wood, contains too much moisture, making it difficult to burn and produce excess smoke. Properly seasoned wood burns hotter and cleaner, reducing the risk of chimney fires.

Storing Firewood

WOODPILES AND SHEDS

Store your firewood in woodpiles or sheds near your home for easy access in winter. Stack the wood in a crisscross pattern to promote air circulation and prevent rotting. Cover the pile with a tarp or keep it in a shed to ensure the wood remains dry in wetter climates.

WINTER PREPARATIONS

Preparing enough firewood for winter is a monumental task. Spend the summer and fall months cutting, splitting, and stacking wood to ensure a sufficient supply. This requires careful planning and an understanding of how much wood is needed based on your home's size, the severity of winter, and the efficiency of your stove or fireplace. A wise settler knows it is better to have too much than too little when the cold winds blow. If you think you have enough, cut more—it is better to be prepared than to find yourself short in the dead of winter.

See FIRE MANAGEMENT for more details.

TIMBER FOR TOOLS AND IMPLEMENTS

Beyond its use for building and fuel, wood is indispensable for making tools, implements, and household items. As a settler, you will need to understand which types of wood are best suited for crafting durable, functional tools that will serve you well in daily life.

Tool Handles and Agricultural Implements

HICKORY HANDLES

Hickory is highly regarded for its exceptional strength and shock resistance, making it the preferred choice for tool handles. Axes, hammers, hoes, and other hand tools commonly feature hickory handles, as this wood can endure the repeated impacts and strains of daily labor. Its natural flexibility allows it to absorb force without breaking, ensuring a long-lasting, reliable tool.

PLOW BEAMS AND YOKES

For larger agricultural implements such as plow beams and yokes, ash or oak are the woods of choice. These hardwoods can withstand the weight and force required for plowing fields or harnessing livestock. Their resilience ensures they endure the harsh conditions of farm work, making them essential materials for these crucial implements.

BARREL STAVES AND HOOPS

Barrels are vital for storing and transporting goods, and the staves and hoops are typically crafted from oak. Oak's moisture resistance and flexibility make it ideal for crafting durable, watertight barrels. These barrels store liquids like water, whiskey, cider and dry goods like grain and flour. Oak's strength ensures the barrels maintain shape and function, providing settlers with dependable storage solutions.

Furniture and Household Items

CHAIR AND TABLE LEGS

Hardwoods such as maple and cherry are often employed for crafting sturdy furniture, particularly in making chairs, tables, and bed legs. These woods are prized for their strength, durability, and ability to hold detailed carvings, adding practical and decorative value to your household furnishings.

WOODEN UTENSILS AND CONTAINERS

Many essential household items, such as utensils, bowls, and storage containers, are fashioned from wood. Maple and birch, with their smooth and fine grain, are ideal for carving spoons, ladles, and bowls. Wooden containers are widely used to store foodstuffs like flour and grains and serve meals at the family table.

THE ENVIRONMENTAL IMPACT OF TIMBER USE

As you settle and harvest timber, be mindful of the effects your actions will have upon the land. The clearing of forests for wood and farming profoundly alters the landscape. Large-scale felling of trees disrupts wildlife habitats and can lead to soil erosion, as tree roots that once held the soil in place are removed. This, in turn, affects water flow and the health of the surrounding ecosystem.

SUSTAINABLE PRACTICES

A wise settler will heed the importance of sustainable forestry practices. Engage in selective logging—taking only what you need while leaving young trees to grow—and consider replanting to ensure future generations have access to this invaluable resource. Managing woodlots on your property by rotating harvested areas and allowing for regrowth is critical to maintaining a continuous supply of firewood and timber without exhausting the land.

TIMBER AS A CASH CROP

Timber is not only beneficial for your personal needs but is also a valuable commodity. The logging industry is growing in Orleans County, and settlers possessing large tracts of forested land can sell timber to local sawmills cut into boards, beams, and other products.

The presence of sawmills along rivers and streams has made lumber production more efficient, allowing settlers to profit from their timber lands.

EXPORT MARKETS

There is high demand for timber locally, throughout the East Coast, and beyond. Thanks to the Erie Canal and the Great Lakes, timber from Orleans County can be transported to distant markets where it is sought for shipbuilding, construction, and manufacturing. Settlers who harvest and sell timber can prosper by tapping into these larger markets.

BARTERING AND TRADE

Timber is often used as a form of currency in trade and barter. In areas where cash is scarce, you may find yourself trading firewood for a new plow or exchanging lumber for livestock. An abundant resource, Timber provides an excellent means for acquiring goods and services to aid your survival and success on the frontier.

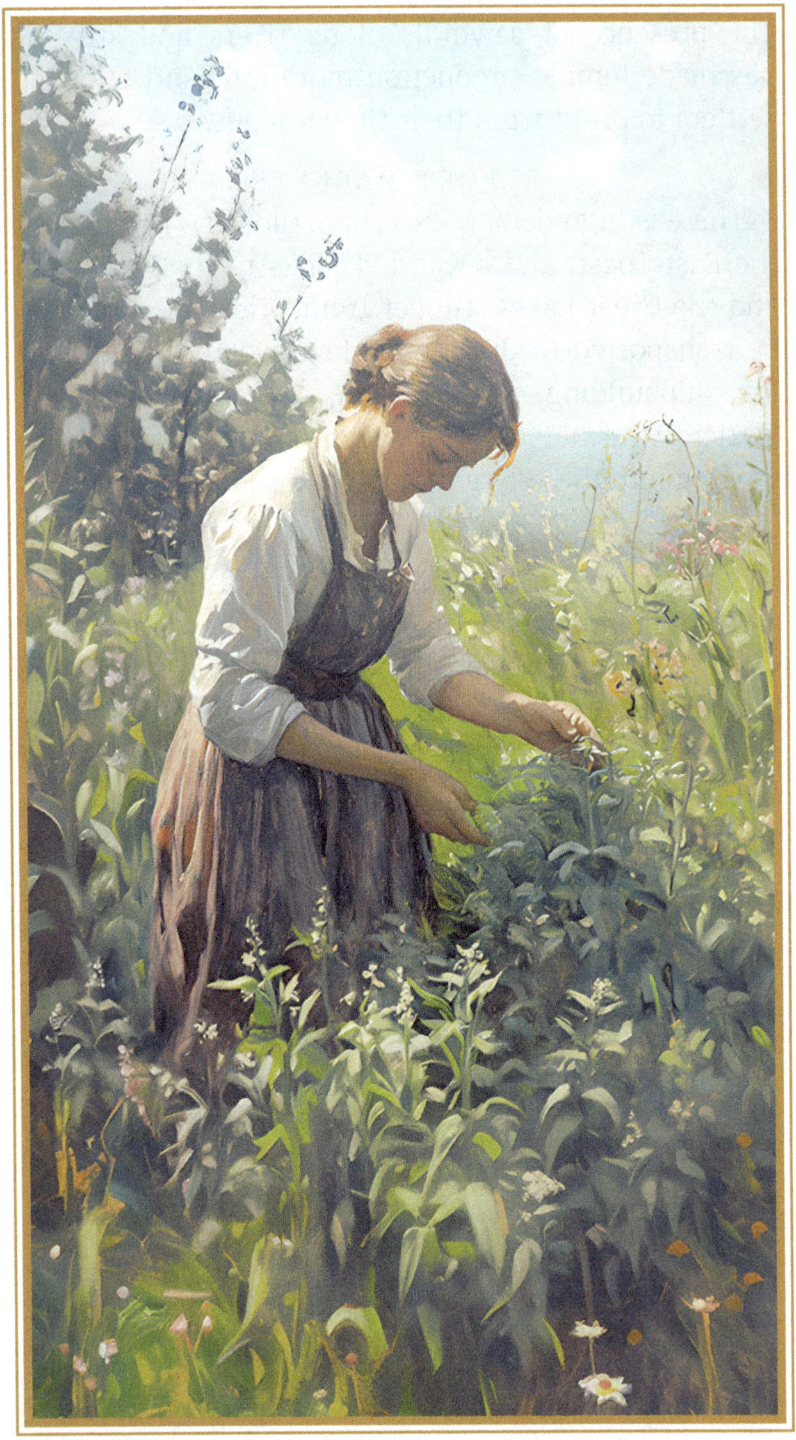

IDENTIFICATION OF COMMON PLANTS

As you make your way into this new land, it will become essential to distinguish the trees, plants, and other natural resources surrounding you. The forest has beneficial plants that can be foraged for food and medicine, and the trees provide shelter and materials necessary for your daily needs.

Familiarity with the different types of nuts and edible mushrooms can significantly aid in your sustenance. Yet, amidst these riches, you must also be wary of poisonous plants that could threaten your health or the safety of your livestock.

Your knowledge of the land will be one of your greatest assets, ensuring your well-being and success as you settle this wild frontier.

IMPORTANT
While every effort has been made to ensure accuracy, the authors are not responsible for any adverse effects resulting from the use of this information. Your safety is ultimately your own responsibility. Foraging for wild plants and mushrooms can be dangerous, as some species are highly toxic. Always use multiple resources when identifying plants—consulting an expert is highly recommended—as plant appearances can vary significantly depending on environmental conditions and lookalike plants can be poisonous.

Although we have noted known safety concerns, many species in this book have not been well studied, and scientific research is incomplete. Exercise caution and seek expert guidance before consuming any wild plants or fungi. The authors assume no liability for any illness, injury, or loss resulting from the application of this knowledge.

Common Trees

These towering sentinels of the forest provide wood for construction, fuel for warmth, and shade in the summer heat. They also play a critical role in the local ecosystem, offering food, shelter, and protection for wildlife. As you learn to recognize these trees, you'll discover how their unique characteristics can be harnessed to support your family and build a thriving homestead.

American Beech
(Fagus grandifolia)

The American beech is easily recognized by its smooth, pale gray bark and broad-spreading canopy. Its leaves are elliptical, with coarse teeth and pointed tips, often clinging to the tree well into the winter months. The long, narrow, pointed buds resemble small cigars. This tree is a major component of northern hardwood forests where it is often found with sugar maples. This tree provides excellent shade, making it a favored choice for resting areas or planting near your homestead. In late summer or early autumn, the beech produces a dry nut encased in a prickly husk, a favored food of bears.

See BEECH NUTS AND BEARS for more details.

Red Maple
(Acer rubrum)

The red maple is notable for its adaptability and stunning red autumn leaves. Its bark is smooth and gray in youth, becoming more furrowed as the tree matures. Red maple wood is versatile for furniture, tools, and flooring. Though its sap is not as sweet as maple sugar, it can still be used for syrup production.

Sugar Maple
(Acer saccharum)

    The sugar maple stands out for its vibrant autumn foliage, showing orange, red, and yellow hues. It has a straight trunk with rough, grayish-brown bark and a dense, rounded canopy. The leaves, with three to five lobes, feature smooth edges and U-shaped notches. In summer, the leaves are a deep green, turning brilliant in the fall. You will rely on this tree for its sweet sap and robust and durable wood, which helps build homes, craft furniture, and make tools. Wildlife, such as deer and squirrels, benefit from its twigs, buds, and seeds.

Hemlock

(Tsuga canadensis)

The eastern hemlock is a stately evergreen with fine, dark green needles and silver underneath. Its deeply furrowed, reddish-brown bark is often used to extract tannins for leatherwork. Hemlocks thrive in shaded, moist areas, providing shelter for various wildlife. While its wood is not as strong as hardwoods, it is often used for barns and outbuildings.

Basswood
(Tilia americana)

Also known as linden, the basswood is a large, broad-leaved tree with heart-shaped leaves and a broad crown. The bark is light gray and deeply furrowed with age. Its fragrant yellow flowers attract bees, producing a light, flavorful honey. The wood is soft and light, ideal for carving utensils, woodenware, and musical instruments, while the inner bark, or bast, is used for making ropes and mats.

Elm

(Ulmus americana)

Elms are tall, graceful trees with long, arching branches and rough, serrated leaves. They are commonly found in floodplains and along rivers. The robust, split-resistant wood is excellent for wagons, barrels, and flooring. While many elms have been affected by Dutch elm disease, they remain a valuable tree for settlers.

Black Ash
(Fraxinus nigra)

This medium-sized tree thrives in swampy areas. Its smooth bark and compound leaves, with 7-11 leaflets, are distinctive. The flexible wood of the Black Ash is traditionally used to weave baskets, furniture, and tool handles. Its seeds and foliage provide sustenance and habitat for wildlife.

Yellow Birch

(Betula alleghaniensis)

The yellow birch is a large, long-lived tree known for its shiny, yellow-bronze bark, which peels into papery strips. Its twigs emit a wintergreen scent when broken. Its hard, strong wood is ideal for making furniture, flooring, and tools. The seeds are an essential food source for wildlife, while its wood provides warmth and shelter.

White Oak
(Quercus alba)

Majestic in appearance, the white oak has deeply lobed leaves and rough, light gray bark. The acorns are an essential food source for wildlife, and settlers value the tree's wood for its strength, durability, and resistance to rot—making it ideal for building homes, barns, ships, and barrels.

White Pine

(Pinus strobus L.)

The eastern white pine is a tall, straight tree with clusters of five soft needles. The smooth, gray-green bark becomes rough and furrowed with age. Valued for its straight-grained wood, the white pine is ideal for constructing homes, barns, and ships, providing both timber and habitat for wildlife.

White Ash

(Fraxinus americana)

The white ash is a large, sturdy tree with compound leaves and distinctive diamond-patterned bark. Settlers prize its wood for its strength and versatility, using it to make tool handles, furniture, and sports equipment. The seeds provide food for birds and small mammals, while the tree supports the surrounding ecosystem.

Chestnut
(Castanea dentata)

Once a dominant species, the American chestnut was known for its tall, straight trunk and lance-shaped leaves. Its spiny burrs contain edible nuts, which were a crucial food source for settlers and wildlife alike. The wood's durability and resistance to decay made it valuable for building. Although the chestnut population was devastated by blight, efforts continue to restore this once-vital tree.

White Spruce
(Picea glauca)

The white spruce is a tall, stately tree with stiff, bluish-green needles about ½ to ¾ inches long. These needles are attached to the branches by woody pegs, giving the branches a distinctive rough texture when the needles are shed. White spruce is highly adaptable and is commonly found in well-drained soils, but climate change is expected to affect its distribution and growth. The wood is valued for construction lumber and pulp, and the tree is a popular choice for windbreaks.

Black Cherry
(Prunus serotina)

The black cherry is a tall, deciduous tree that thrives in the forests of Western New York. It is easily recognized by its dark, scaly bark and glossy, serrated leaves. In spring, the tree produces clusters of small white flowers, which later give way to dark, bitter cherries that are a food source for settlers and natives, birds and other wildlife. Black cherry wood is highly prized for its fine grain and rich color, making it sought after for furniture and cabinetry. This tree grows well in a variety of soil types but prefers moist, fertile environments.

Beneficial Plants

Gathering wild plants, berries, nuts, and other edible resources is essential to the pioneer diet. Foraging provides valuable nutrients and variety and ensures survival during lean times. However, the landscape holds both nourishment and danger, making knowledge of local plants critical to safe and successful foraging. Be mindful that some plants have deadly lookalikes, and proper identification is essential to avoiding harm.

Disclaimer: The information provided herein is for educational purposes only. While every effort has been made to ensure accuracy, the authors are not responsible for any adverse effects from using this information. Foraging for wild plants and mushrooms can be perilous, as some species are highly toxic. It is essential to seek guidance from an expert and exercise caution before consuming wild plants or fungi. The authors assume no liability for any illness, injury, or loss from applying this knowledge.

Cattails

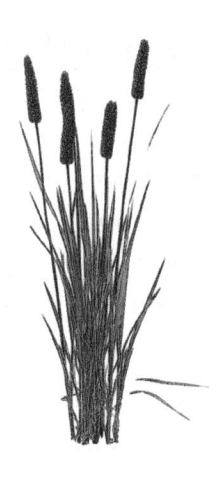

(Typha latifolia)

Cattails are tall, reed-like plants commonly found in wetlands and along the edges of ponds and streams. They have long, slender leaves and produce a distinctive brown, cylindrical flower spike.

Cattails are used extensively. The roots are edible when cooked, and the young shoots can be eaten, usually chopped and sauteed or steamed and served with fat and salt. The unripe flower heads and pollen are also edible. The fluffy seeds are used for stuffing pillows and blankets, while the leaves are woven into mats, baskets, and roofing materials.

Wild Ginger

(Asarum canadense)

Wild ginger is a low-growing plant with heart-shaped leaves and small, brownish flowers hidden near the ground. It thrives in shady, wooded areas.

The rhizome of wild ginger is used as a spice and for medicinal purposes, including treating digestive issues and colds. The plant is sometimes used as a substitute for actual ginger in cooking.

CAUTION: Wild ginger contains toxins that can be dangerous for people with kidney problems.

Yarrow

(Achillea millefolium)

Yarrow is a hardy perennial with feathery leaves and small, white to pink flower clusters. It grows in fields, meadows, and along roadsides. Yarrow is a versatile medicinal plant that stops bleeding, reduces inflammation, and promotes healing. It is also employed to treat colds, fevers, and digestive issues.

Yarrow leaves and flowers are often made into a poultice to stop bleeding and accelerate wound healing. For fevers or colds, a tea made from yarrow is consumed to induce sweating and help the body eliminate toxins. Yarrow is also used in baths to soothe skin irritations and promote relaxation.

EDITOR'S NOTE: Poison Hemlock can be mistaken for yarrow. Its toxin is deadly. Consult an experienced community member to identify the plants you gather.

Elderberry

Elderberry (Sambucus canadensis)

Elderberry is a hardy shrub with compound leaves and clusters of small, white flowers that develop into dark purple berries. It grows in moist areas, such as forest edges and stream banks. Valued for its immune-boosting properties, elderberry treats colds, flu, and respiratory ailments.

The berries, harvested in late summer, are made into syrups, wines, and jellies, while the flowers are used in making confections, "champaign," cordials, teas, poultices and more. Raw berries and flowers should be cooked before consuming, as they contain toxins. Stems must be fully removed before use as they are toxic.

Wild Strawberries

(Fragaria virginiana)

Wild strawberries are low-growing plants with trifoliate leaves and small, white flowers that produce tiny, sweet red berries. They are found in open fields and along forest edges.

The fruit is enjoyed fresh or dried. The leaves are used to make tea, which is believed to help treat digestive issues and boost overall health.

Dandelion

(Taraxacum officinale)

Dandelion is a widely recognized plant with bright yellow flowers and deeply toothed leaves, valued for its versatility and nutritional benefits. The leaves, rich in vitamins A and C, are harvested in early spring when tender and less bitter, used in salads, or cooked as greens.

The roots are dried, roasted, and ground as a coffee substitute, while the flowers can be made into dandelion wine. Dandelion is also used to treat liver and digestive issues, embodying the pioneer spirit of using every part of what nature provides.

Blueberry

(Vaccinium spp.)

Blueberries can grow as either highbush or lowbush shrubs. They have glossy green leaves and bell-shaped flowers that produce blue or blackberries. Commonly found in acidic soils, such as those in forests and bogs, blueberries are a staple food that can be eaten fresh or dried for winter.

They are valued for their flavor and nutritional content and are used in pies, jams, and preserves. The berries are also used in medicinal remedies to treat digestive issues and as a source of vitamins.

Goldenseal

(Hydrastis canadensis)

Goldeneeal is a low-growing woodland plant with large, lobed leaves and small, inconspicuous flowers followed by bright red berries. It has a thick, yellow root which is the part of the plant that is used.

Native Americans use the goldenseal as a powerful medicinal plant, particularly for treating infections, digestive disorders, and skin conditions. Settlers also use it for its antibacterial and anti-inflammatory properties, often incorporating it into homemade remedies.

Editor's note: in this modern day goldenseal is **significantly threatened and should not be removed from the wild.** *Roots can be purchased from trusted conservation sources like United Plant Savers to plant at home.*

Wintergreen
(Gaultheria procumbens)

Wintergreen is a low, spreading evergreen plant with glossy green leaves, small white flowers, and bright red berries. It thrives in acidic soils in forested areas. Wintergreen leaves are used to make a tea that relieves pain and reduces fevers. The plant's oil, extracted from the leaves, is used for its medicinal properties and as a flavoring agent in foods and candies.

Wild Mint

(Mentha arvensis)

Wild mint is a perennial herb with square stems, aromatic leaves, and clusters of small, purple flowers. It grows in moist areas like streambanks and wet meadows. Wild mint is used to make tea to treat digestive issues, colds, and headaches. The leaves are also a cooking flavoring agent and natural insect repellent.

Stinging Nettle
(Urtica dioica)

Stinging nettle is an herbaceous plant with serrated leaves and tiny, greenish flowers. It has fine hairs on its leaves and stems that release a stinging chemical when touched. The plant should be taller than knee high before harvesting. Despite its sting, the young leaves are cooked and eaten as a nutritious green, while the plant is used to make fiber for ropes and textiles. Nettle is used to treat various ailments, including arthritis, allergies, and skin conditions.

Fiddleheads

(Matteuccia struthiopteris)

Fiddleheads are the young, coiled fronds of the ostrich fern, recognizable by their tightly curled shape, resembling the scroll of a fiddle. These vibrant green shoots are harvested in early spring, typically along riverbanks, wetlands, and shaded woodlands. Fiddleheads are prized for their delicate flavor, often described as a cross between asparagus and spinach.

Not all fiddleheads are edible. Pick only the tightly coiled fronds before they begin to unfurl. They are a nutritious wild food, rich in vitamins A and C, iron, and fiber. Once harvested, they must be thoroughly cleaned and cooked before consumption to remove any potential bitterness or toxins. Fiddleheads are typically boiled or sautéed and can be enjoyed as a side dish or incorporated into soups, salads, and stir-fries, offering a unique and seasonal flavor to pioneer meals.

Jewelweed
(Impatiens capensis)

Jewelweed is a moisture-loving plant with succulent, translucent or yellow stems and orange-spotted flowers shaped like trumpets. It often grows in shady, wet areas. Jewelweed is a natural remedy for skin irritations, mainly poison ivy. The plant's juice relieves itching and inflammation when applied to the skin. It is also used as a general treatment for minor cuts and bruises.

Hops

(Humulus lupulus)

Hops are vigorous, climbing vines with lobed leaves and cone-shaped flowers. They grow in sunny, well-drained soils and are often cultivated. Hops are used primarily for their soothing properties, often in teas to promote sleep and reduce anxiety. Hops are also used in brewing beer, a practice that is important for both its nutritional and preservative qualities.

Wild Rose

(Rosa spp.)

Wild roses are shrubs with prickly stems, fragrant pink or white flowers, and red rose hips. They are commonly found in thickets, along roadsides, and at the edges of forests.

Wild rose hips are a valuable vitamin C source and are typically used for making teas, jellies, and syrups. The petals are also used in medicinal remedies and as a natural perfume. Settlers and Native Americans use the plant to treat various ailments, including colds and digestive issues.

Witch Hazel

(Hamamelis virginiana)

Witch hazel is a shrub or small tree with yellow, fragrant flowers that bloom in late fall. The bark and leaves treat skin conditions and inflammation and act as a general astringent.

Sassafras
(Sassafras albidum)

Sassafras is a small to medium-sized tree with aromatic leaves, bark, and roots. Native Americans and settlers use sassafras for their medicinal properties, including treating fevers, wounds, and respiratory ailments. The roots are also used to make tea, which is the base for traditional root beer. The dried and pounded leaves are used as a thickening agent called filé.

Cranberries
(Vaccinium macrocarpon)

Cranberries grow in bogs and wetlands and are an essential food source for Native Americans, who dry them for winter use. They are also used in pemmican, a high-energy food made of dried meat and fat. Settlers use cranberries for food and medicinal uses, particularly for treating urinary tract issues.

Juniper
(Juniperus communis)

Juniper is a coniferous shrub with needlelike leaves and berrylike cones. Native Americans use juniper berries for medicine, as well as in spiritual practices. Settlers use juniper berries in cooking, particularly in meat dishes, and as a flavoring for gin. The wood is also used for making tools and fences.

Editor's Note: Not all juniper are edible. J. communis or J. virginiana is advised.

Balsam Fir
(Abies balsamea)

The balsam fir is used for its fragrant needles, in bedding, or in traditional medicine to treat colds and respiratory issues. The resin, or "balsam," is used for sealing wounds and making poultices.

Wild Leeks (Ramps)
(Allium tricoccum)

Wild leeks, or ramps, are wild onions with broad, green leaves and a solid garlic-like flavor. They grow in moist, shaded forests and are among the first plants to emerge in spring. Taking only one leaf per plant is recommended when foraging for a meal, leaving the bulb to regrow more leaves.

When cows consume wild leeks, their milk will have a strong, unpleasant flavor, making it less desirable for drinking or butter production. You should keep livestock away from areas where wild leeks are abundant.

Purslane
(Portulaca oleracea)

Purslane is another common wild plant, often considered a weed, that is highly nutritious. Rich in omega-3 fatty acids, purslane is gathered throughout the summer and used in salads or cooked in soups and stews. Its slightly tangy flavor makes it a popular addition to various dishes.

Lambsquarters

(Chenopodium album)

Lambsquarters are a valuable wild green, often growing in disturbed soils. The leaves, which resemble spinach in flavor and texture, are harvested before the plant is used in soups, stews, or sautéed as a side dish. Rich in vitamins and minerals, lambsquarters are nutritious to the pioneer diet, especially in the early growing season.

Blackberries and Raspberries
(Rubus spp.)

These bramble fruits are gathered in late summer, often in thickets or along the edges of forests. Blackberries and raspberries are versatile ingredients used in everything from desserts to sauces and are usually preserved as jams or jellies. The seeds of blackberries and raspberries, rich in fiber, are also a healthful addition to the pioneer diet.

Crabapples

(Malus spp.)

Though small and tart, crabapples are a valuable foraged fruit, particularly for making preserves, jellies, and cider. Settlers often combine crabapples with other, sweeter fruits to create balanced flavors in preserves. The high pectin content in crabapples makes them ideal for jellymaking, ensuring that preserves are correctly set.

Wild Grapes
(Vitis spp.)

Wild grapes are another important foraged fruit growing along riverbanks and in forest clearings. Like cultivated varieties, wild grapes can be either sweet or tart, varying from vine to vine. Wild grapes are used to make juice, jelly, and wine. The tartness of wild grapes is often tempered by sweetening or blending with other fruits, creating a range of flavorful products that can be enjoyed throughout the year.

Common Foraged Nuts

Nuts provide essential fats and proteins, which are particularly important in a diet that might otherwise be heavy on carbohydrates and low on fresh produce. They are often stored for use throughout the winter.

Beech Nuts
(Fagus grandifolia)

Beech nuts are a highly nutritious food source, harvested in the fall. Settlers collect these small, triangular nuts, which are roasted or ground into flour for baking. Beech nuts are valued for their rich flavor and high-fat content, providing a crucial source of calories during winter.

Black Walnuts
(Juglans nigra)

Black walnut trees are native to the region and are known for their high-quality wood and edible nuts. These trees thrive in rich, well-drained soils and are often found in forests and along streams in the area. Black walnuts are valued for both their timber and their nuts, though the nuts can be challenging to harvest. The outer husks are tough, requiring careful removal, and the hard shells make cracking a labor-intensive task. Even once opened, extracting the nut meats is painstaking, as they are often embedded in tight, intricate chambers. Despite the effort required to harvest them, black walnuts reward the laborer with their uniquely rich, earthy flavor—bold and slightly bitter, yet sweetly aromatic—making them a prized addition to desserts such as cakes and cookies.

Hickory Nuts

(Carya spp.)

Hickory nuts are prized for their sweet, rich flavor. These nuts are gathered in the fall and used in various dishes, from breads to stews. Hickory nuts require careful cracking to extract the meat, but their high nutritional value makes them a worthwhile foraging target.

Chestnuts
(Castanea dentata)

Chestnuts are an important food source for wildlife and humans. They are high in carbohydrates and are used in a variety of dishes by Native Americans and settlers.

Acorns

(Quercus spp.)

Produced by oak trees, acorns are another high-calorie food source, rich in fats and carbohydrates. They are a staple food for Native Americans, who process them into flour, and are crucial for wildlife such as deer, squirrels, and wild turkeys. Acorns from White Oak trees are often preferred over those from Red Oaks, as they contain fewer bitter tannins and require less time to leach in water before they can be eaten.

Edible Mushrooms

Mushrooms and fungi are a valuable food source, that adds distinct flavors and hearty textures meals. However, use caution when harvesting as many edible varieties have poisonous counterparts.

Accurate identification is essential. Rely on careful observation and guidance from an experienced guide to determine edible varieties. When identifying mushrooms, pay close attention to their shape, color, gills, habitat in which they grow, and the season of their appearance. These details will safeguard your harvest and help you avoid deadly mistakes.

SAFE HARVESTING PRACTICES

Use baskets or cloth bags for gathering, as they permit the spores to disperse, encouraging the mushrooms to return the following season. Once collected, mushrooms are often best cooked immediately, though they may be preserved through drying or pickling, allowing you to extend their shelf life and enjoy them well beyond the harvest.

Editor's Note: Modern day foragers may store the mushrooms in paper bags in the refrigerator for a brief period of time to extend their shelf life

Morels

(Morchella spp.)

Morels are among the most prized wild mushrooms, known for distinctive honeycomblike caps and rich, earthy flavor. Found in the spring, often in forested areas, morels are sautéed, added to soups, or dried for later use. Morels are relatively easy to identify compared to some other wild mushrooms, making them a favorite among foragers.

Editor's Note: It is essential to consult with an expert and exercise caution before consuming wild plants or fungi.

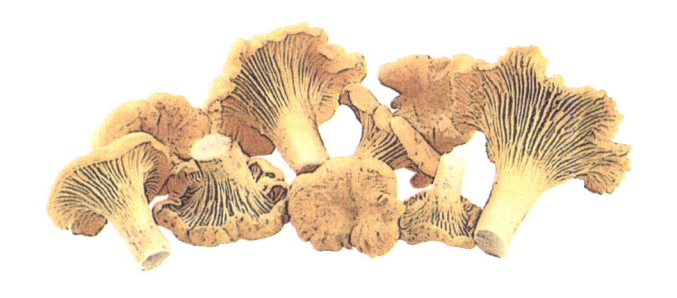

Chanterelles

(Cantharellus spp.)

Chanterelles have a golden yellow color and delicate, fruity floral fragrance. These mushrooms grow in the summer and early fall in mixed woodlands, and are often found near oak and pine trees. Chanterelles are used in various dishes, from sautés to soups.

Preservation of Foraged Foods

Preserving nature's bounty is paramount to ensure that the fruits of your foraging efforts may sustain you through the barren winter months. With the proper techniques, you can store and enjoy the harvest well after the growing season has passed.

Drying Berries and Herbs

Berries and herbs are often preserved by drying, a time-honored method. Berries should be spread on racks to allow the air to naturally dry them. Herbs, gathered and bundled, should be hung in a dry, well-ventilated space. Once dried, berries may be used in baking or eaten as a nutritious snack, while herbs are stored in jars or pouches, ready to flavor your meals or serve as medicines when needed.

Curing Nuts

To preserve various types of nuts, they are first cured by spreading them in a well-ventilated area to dry, reducing their moisture content and preventing spoilage. The duration of drying may vary depending on the type of nut, with harder-shelled varieties often requiring more time. Once dried, nuts can be stored in sacks, barrels, or jars, or if cracked and shelled immediately, the kernels are best kept in cool, dry places for convenient use during the colder months. This process extends their shelf life and ensures a steady supply of nourishment throughout winter.

Pickling and Fermenting

Wild vegetables such as ramps or fiddleheads are often preserved through pickling which maintains their flavor and nutritional value. Varying by recipe, the vegetables are packed into jars with vinegar, salt, and spices and left to sit for a period of time. Pickled vegetables are a welcome addition to the winter table, offering flavor and sustenance during the harshest months.

Poisonous Plants

As you settle the land, you must be ever mindful of the presence of poisonous plants, which pose a grave danger to both livestock and the safety of your food supply. These plants, often deceptive in appearance, must be identified with care and removed from pastures, fields, and any area where animals graze or forage. Vigilance in managing these threats is essential to the well-being of your homestead.

Poisonous plants, such as poison hemlock and water hemlock, are highly toxic and may cause serious harm if ingested by animals or humans. They often resemble harmless or beneficial plants, making identification particularly important. Removing these plants requires diligence, for even a tiny amount can cause sickness or death among livestock.

Regularly inspect your fields and pastures, and work to clear any suspicious or known toxic plants. In doing so, you protect your animals and food supply, ensuring that the crops and foraged goods you gather remain safe for consumption. If ever in doubt, consult with experienced neighbors or Native Americans, whose knowledge of the land and its dangers can be invaluable.

DANGEROUS ☠ TOXIC PLANT

Buttercups

(Ranunculus spp.)

DANGER TOXIC

Buttercups are bright yellow, cup-shaped flowers in meadows, pastures, and along roadsides. They are low-growing plants with glossy leaves.

Buttercups contain a toxin called protoanemonin, which can cause blisters in the mouth and digestive issues in humans and cattle if ingested in large quantities. Though generally unpalatable, cattle might eat them if better forage is unavailable, leading to health problems.

DANGEROUS ☠ TOXIC PLANT

Bracken Fern

(Pteridium aquilinum)

DANGER TOXIC

Bracken fern is a large, coarse fern with triangular fronds that grow in various habitats, including woodlands and open fields.

Bracken fern contains toxic compounds that can harm livestock, particularly if consumed in large amounts over time. It can cause a condition known as "bracken poisoning," leading to symptoms like weight loss, lethargy, and, in severe cases, internal bleeding. Settlers must manage pastures carefully to avoid overgrowth of bracken fern.

DANGEROUS ☠ TOXIC PLANT

Jimsonweed
(Datura stramonium)

DANGER TOXIC

Jimsonweed is an annual plant with large, trumpet-shaped flowers and spiny seed pods. It is typically found in disturbed soils, fields, and roadsides.

Jimsonweed is highly toxic to both humans and animals. If ingested by livestock, it can cause symptoms like dry mouth, dilated pupils, erratic behavior, and even death. Settlers must keep their fields and pastures free of this dangerous weed.

DANGEROUS ☠ TOXIC PLANT

Poison Hemlock
(Conium maculatum)

DANGER TOXIC

Poison hemlock is a tall, biennial plant with distinctive fern-like, bluish-green leaves and clusters of small, white, umbrella-shaped flowers.

A key feature for identification is its smooth, hairless stems, which are marked with purple blotches—resembling splashes of paint. The plant emits a foul odor, often compared to musty debris or mouse urine, primarily when its leaves are crushed. The leaves are deeply lobed, resembling parsley or ferns.

Poison hemlock is highly toxic to humans and livestock, affecting the nervous system and leading to respiratory failure, so it must be eradicated from homesteads to protect animals and people.

DANGEROUS ☠ TOXIC PLANT

Milkweed
(Asclepias spp.)

DANGER TOXIC

Common milkweed is a tall plant with broad leaves and clusters of pink to purplish flowers. It produces large seed pods filled with silky fibers.

While milkweed is a vital plant for monarch butterflies, it is toxic to livestock, particularly those that eat hay. Consumption can cause digestive distress, heart problems, and potentially death. Settlers must be careful when harvesting hay to ensure milkweed is not mixed with fodder.

Editor's Note: Common milkweed (Asclepias syriaca) is an important food plant for humans.

DANGEROUS ☠ TOXIC PLANT

Horsenettle

(Solanum carolinense)

DANGER TOXIC

Horsenettle is a perennial weed with spiny stems and leaves, small white or yellow flowers, and yellow tomatolike berries. It grows in fields, pastures, and along roadsides.

Horsenettle is toxic to livestock, particularly when the berries are ingested. The plant contains solanine, which can cause digestive upset, respiratory distress, and neurological issues. Settlers often find it difficult to eradicate due to its deep root system.

DANGEROUS ☠ TOXIC PLANT

Ragwort
(Jacobaea vulgaris)

DANGER TOXIC

Ragwort is a biennial or perennial plant with clusters of small, yellow flowers. It grows in fields, pastures, and along roadsides.

Ragwort contains toxic alkaloids that can cause liver damage in livestock, especially horses and cattle if consumed over time. Chronic ingestion leads to a condition known as "ragwort poisoning," characterized by weight loss, jaundice, and, eventually, liver failure. Managing pastures to keep them free of ragwort is essential for settlers.

DANGEROUS ☠ TOXIC PLANT

White Snakeroot
(Ageratina altissima)

DANGER TOXIC

White snakeroot is a perennial plant with clusters of small white flowers and grows in shaded areas, such as woodlands and along forest edges.

White snakeroot contains a toxin called tremetol, which can be passed into the cows' milk that graze on it. This toxin causes "milk sickness" in humans who consume contaminated milk or dairy products, leading to symptoms like nausea, vomiting, and even death. This is a significant concern for settlers, as milk sickness claimed many lives before the connection to white snakeroot was understood.

DANGEROUS ☠ TOXIC PLANT

Butterfly Weed
(Asclepias tuberosa)

DANGER TOXIC

Butterfly weed is a striking plant with bright orange flowers that attract butterflies and pollinators. It grows in dry, open areas like fields and prairies.

Like other milkweeds, butterfly weed contains toxic compounds that can harm livestock if ingested. The toxicity of butterfly weed (*Asclepias tuberosa*) is higher than that of common milkweed, and poses a risk to animals grazing in areas where it is abundant.

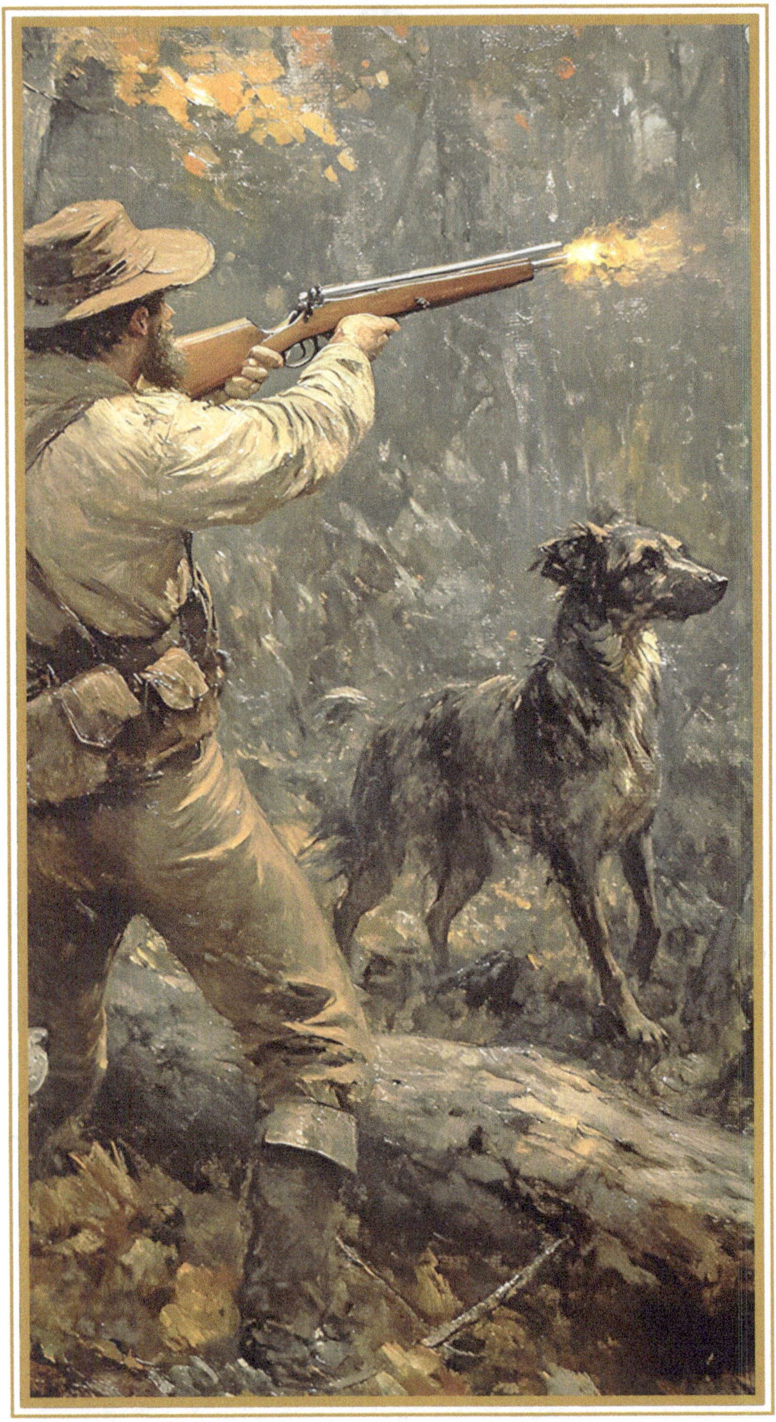

FISHING AND HUNTING

The ability to fish and hunt is indispensable for your survival and well-being. These pursuits will provide a substantial portion of your food, complementing what you gather, grow, raise, or swap for. To thrive in this land, you must learn the habits and habitats of the local wildlife and the necessary fishing and hunting techniques.

Success in these endeavors often requires keen observation, patience, and skill. The creatures of the forest and streams will not simply offer themselves up; you must know where and when to find them. Understanding their movements, breeding cycles, and feeding grounds is critical to ensuring a bountiful harvest from nature's larder.

Master these essential skills and secure a steady and reliable food source for yourself and your family. In times of scarcity, your ability to live off the land may prove the difference between hardship and plenty.

Fishing for Sustenance

HARVESTING THE BOUNTY OF RIVERS AND LAKES

Fishing offers settlers a dependable supply of fresh food, especially during the warmer months when fish are most active and plentiful. To be successful, however, you must know where to fish and which methods to employ.

Look for streams, rivers, and lakes where fish are abundant. Shallow, slow-moving waters often hold the most fish, particularly near rocks, logs, or vegetation where they seek shelter. Early mornings and late afternoons are the best times to fish, as fish are more likely to feed during these fantastic parts of the day.

The techniques you use will depend on the type of fish you seek and the equipment at your disposal. Simple lines, hooks, and bait will often suffice, though nets and traps can also prove effective, particularly in shallow waters. Using natural bait like worms, insects, or small fish will increase your chances of success.

Remember to be patient and observant, for fishing is a skill that rewards those who pay close attention to their surroundings. With experience, you will learn to read the waters and recognize the habits of the fish, ensuring a steady source of food to supplement your daily needs.

FISHING TECHNIQUES

Handlines and Poles

Handlines or fishing poles are the most straightforward tools when you set out to fish. Often crafted from horsehair or fibers drawn from local plants, the line is tied to a bone, wood, or metal hook. You will gather bait from the land—worms, insects, or even small fish will serve your purpose. Most of your fishing may be done from the shore, though if you have access to a small boat or canoe, you may venture into deeper waters to seek a more bountiful catch.

Nets and Traps

It will be of more excellent service if you aim to secure an enormous haul of fish, nets, and traps. A seine net, which is dragged through the water, will gather abundant fish. Alternatively, stationary traps made from woven branches or arranged stones are set in rivers and streams, funneling fish into confined spaces where they may be quickly taken. These methods prove particularly effective during spawning runs when the fish gather in great numbers as they journey upstream.

Ice Fishing

During the harsh winter months, when lakes and rivers are sealed by thick ice, ice fishing becomes essential for survival. You must cut holes in the frozen surface and drop baited lines into the waters below. Fish remain active beneath the ice, and this method allows you to continue securing food even when other sources are scarce. Be sure to exercise care in gauging the thickness of the ice before venturing out.

FISHING SEASONS

Spring Spawning Runs

In springtime, the waters brimming with life as fish, such as trout and bass, move into shallower streams and rivers to spawn. This season presents an ideal opportunity to secure a bountiful harvest. Set your nets, traps, and handlines in these waters, where fish will be abundant as they travel upstream.

Winter Ice Fishing

In the heart of winter, ice fishing will prove invaluable when the land offers little else to eat. You will focus on species such as pike and perch, which remain active under the ice. Pay heed to the thickness of the ice to ensure safe fishing, and with patience, you will gather enough to sustain you through the cold months.

PRESERVING THE CATCH

As a settler, preserving the bounty of your catch is essential to ensure a steady supply of food during the lean months when fresh fish is scarce. Several time-honored preservation methods passed down through generations allow you to store fish for extended periods without fear of spoilage.

Smoking

Smoking fish is one of the most reliable methods to preserve your catch. After cleaning and preparing the fish, they are hung in a smokehouse or placed over a low fire, where the smoke dries the flesh and imparts a rich flavor. This process allows the fish to be stored for months, ensuring it remains edible throughout the winter.

Salting

Salting is another staple of fish preservation. After cleaning, the fish are heavily salted and laid out to dry in the sun or a well-ventilated area. The salt draws out moisture, preventing the growth of bacteria and spoilage. Salted fish can be stored for many months and is an essential component of the pioneer diet, particularly when fresh food is scarce.

Drying

Drying is a simple yet effective way to preserve fish. The cleaned and filleted fish are laid on racks or hung from poles in a sunny, breezy spot. The air dries out the flesh, preventing spoilage and making it possible to store the fish for several months in a cool, dry location. Dried fish can later be rehydrated by adding it to soups or stews, providing a nourishing and hearty meal when fresh protein is complex.

Pickling and Brining

Pickling or brining is often used for smaller fish like herring or perch. The fish are cleaned and then packed tightly into barrels or jars with vinegar, salt, and a selection of spices. This method creates a preserved product with a tangy flavor that can be eaten as is or used in various recipes. Pickled fish adds variety to your meals and keeps you well, providing a welcome change from the more common smoked or salted fare.

Hunting Wild Game

Hunting is one of the most vital activities you will engage in as a settler, providing not only meat for sustenance but hides, bones, and other resources essential to daily life. Mastering the art of hunting and knowing the habits of local game is critical to ensuring your survival in Orleans County.

DEER HUNTING

White-tailed Deer

The white-tailed deer is a cornerstone of life in this region. The meat it provides can be smoked, salted, or dried to sustain your family through the harsh winter months. Beyond food, the hide is invaluable, used to craft clothing, moccasins, and other necessities.

See LARGE MAMMALS for more details.

HUNTING TECHNIQUES

Deer hunting requires not just strength but patience and skill. You must learn to track the deer by following signs such as footprints, droppings, and tree rubs where bucks have scraped their antlers. Many settlers practice still-hunting, moving silently through the forest, while others prefer to wait in blinds or stand near watering holes. Your rifle or musket will be your primary weapon, though some have adopted bows and arrows from Native American practices, which prove equally effective.

SMALL GAME HUNTING

Rabbits and Hares

When larger game proves elusive, rabbits and hares, especially the snowshoe hare, offer a steady source of meat and fur during the colder months.

See SMALL MAMMALS for more details.

SNARES AND TRAPS

Setting snares or traps is an effective way to catch small games while you tend to other tasks. A simple snare made from wire or cord can be placed along a well-worn rabbit path, ensuring the animal is caught as it passes through. Box traps and deadfalls, baited with food, are equally reliable. These methods allow you to harvest small games without expending too much energy.

WATERFOWL AND GAME BIRDS

Ducks, Geese, and Turkeys

Ducks, geese, and wild turkeys are another vital source of meat and feathers, especially in wetland areas and forests. Turkeys, in particular, are highly prized and provide a large quantity of meat.

See BIRDS for more details.

DECOYS AND CALLING

For waterfowl, decoys and calls are often employed to bring the birds within range. Set up decoys in open waters or fields and mimic their calls to draw them closer. For turkeys, imitating the gobble of a male turkey can lure the birds in. A shotgun is preferred for hunting birds, though some may still use rifles or bows.

PREDATOR CONTROL AND FUR TRAPPING

Wolves, Bears, and Coyotes

While predators are not hunted for food, it is essential to manage their numbers to protect your livestock and community. Wolf and bear pelts are valuable for clothing and trade, and their reduction helps to keep your cattle and other animals safe.

See PREDATORS for more details.

Trapping for Fur

Fur trapping is necessary for gathering warm clothing and securing trade goods. Beavers, foxes, and raccoons are commonly trapped along trails or near water. The pelts are cleaned and dried, then traded or used for clothing.

See FUR for more details.

SEASONAL HUNTING CYCLES

The success of your hunting and gathering efforts depends heavily on understanding the changing seasons and the habits of animals.

Deer Rutting Season

Fall is prime time for hunting deer, as the rutting season causes bucks to be more active and less cautious.

Plan your hunting trips around this time to ensure a successful hunt before winter.

Migratory Birds

Waterfowl hunting is most fruitful during migration in the spring and fall. Set blinds near wetlands or rivers to take advantage of the birds' resting stops along their journey.

PRESERVATION AND STORAGE

Once the hunt is successful, preserving the meat becomes your next task. Without proper preservation, the fruits of your labor will spoil.

Smoking and Curing Meat

Smokehouses are common on pioneer homesteads and used to preserve meat through smoking. The process involved hanging meat, such as venison or fish, in a smokehouse exposed to low heat and smoke for several days. This method not only preserves the meat but also adds flavor. Curing with salt, sugar, or a combination of both is another method to preserve meat, particularly pork, for long-term storage.

Drying Meat (Jerky)

Drying meat into jerky is an excellent way to store food that can be easily transported or kept for months. Thin strips of meat are salted and dried in the sun or over a low fire, producing a lightweight, nutritious source of protein that can sustain you during long journeys or times of need.

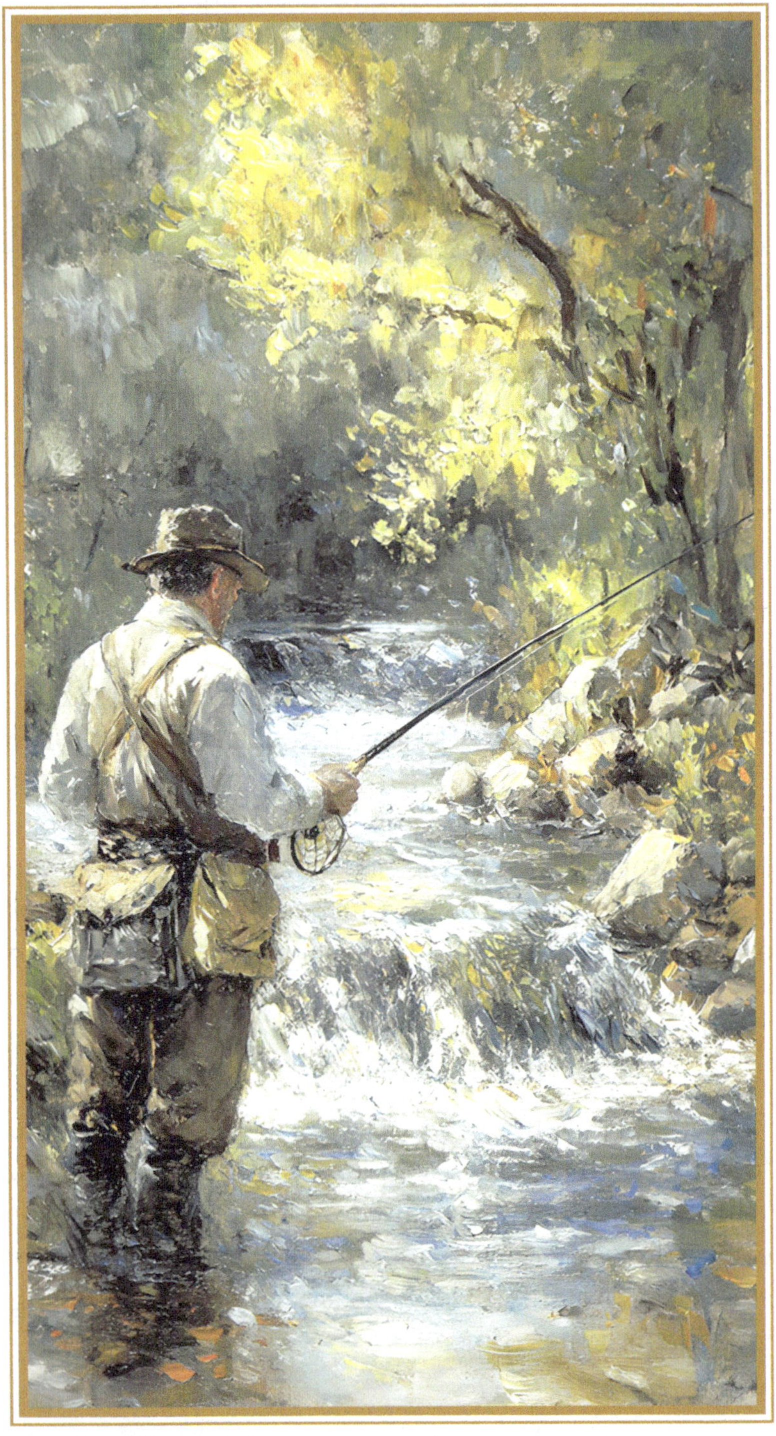

WILDLIFE IDENTIFICATION

Wildlife plays an essential role in your survival and the balance of the environment. Whether you're hunting for food, protecting your livestock, or simply observing the natural world, understanding the animals around you is vital. From the deer that roam the woodlands to the fish swimming in nearby streams, each creature serves a purpose in the ecosystem and offers opportunities for sustenance, trade, or protection. By learning to recognize these animals and understanding their behaviors, you will gain the knowledge needed to thrive on your land and coexist with the wild around you.

Fish

As you settle into life in Orleans County, you will come to rely on the rich waters that sustain both Native Americans and fellow settlers alike. Several fish species are important as a reliable food source and vital to the local economy and culture.

Lake Sturgeon

(Acipenser fulvescens)

50-70 INCHES (127-178 CM)

The lake sturgeon is a large, ancient fish species, often reaching lengths of 6 to 7 feet and weighing over 200 pounds. They have a distinctive long, torpedo-shaped body, bony scutes along the back, and a shovel-shaped snout.

Lake sturgeon are highly valued for meat, which is rich and flavorful. The fish's eggs are also used as a form of caviar. Sturgeons are sometimes caught using spears or nets. For settlers, the sturgeon is a valuable source of protein, and its roe is considered a delicacy. The fish's swim bladder also produces isinglass, a gelatin-like substance used for food clarification and as an adhesive.

Atlantic Salmon

(Salmo salar)

28-30 INCHES (71-76 CM)

Atlantic salmon are large, migratory fish reaching up to 30 inches long. They have a streamlined body, silver with dark spots, and are known for solid swimming ability, particularly during upstream migrations to spawn.

Atlantic salmon are abundant in the rivers and streams of Orleans County, including the Genesee River. Native Americans and settlers rely heavily on salmon as a seasonal food source, particularly during spawning runs. The fish is preserved by smoking or salting for use throughout the year.

EDITOR'S NOTE: Overfishing and habitat destruction eventually lead to the region's decline of Atlantic salmon populations.

American Eel
(Anguilla rostrata)

24–36 INCHES (61–91 CM)

The American eel is a long, snakelike fish that can grow up to 3 to 4 feet long. It has a smooth, slimy body, minor scales, and a preference for fresh and saltwater environments during its life cycle.

Eels are an important food source, often caught using spears, traps, or weirs. They are particularly valued for rich, oily meat, which can be smoked or dried for preservation. For settlers, eels provide a reliable source of protein, especially during the spring and fall when eels are more active in rivers and streams. Eels are also traded and sold in local markets.

Walleye

(Sander vitreus)

15–24 INCHES (38–61 CM)

Walleye are medium-sized predatory fish that can reach 20 to 30 inches long. They have long, slender bodies with olive or gold coloring and distinctive, reflective eyes that give them names.

Walleye are prized for tasty, white flesh. They are caught using various methods, including nets, spears, and fishing lines. Walleye are commonly found in rivers and lakes throughout Orleans County. Their abundance makes them a reliable food source, and they are often prepared by frying, baking, or smoking.

Northern Pike
(Esox lucius)

20-30 INCHES (51-76 CM)

Northern pike are large, predatory fish with long, streamlined bodies, pointed snouts, and sharp teeth. They are typically olive green with lighter, vertical stripes or spots and can grow up to 4 feet long.

Northern pike are valued for size and aggressive feeding behavior, which make them relatively easy to catch. The meat of the pike is eaten fresh or preserved by smoking or drying. Pike are also used in trading and are a popular target for sport fishing. Their presence in lakes and rivers makes them a significant part of the local diet.

Brook Trout

(Salvelinus fontinalis)

9-12 INCHES (23-30 CM)

Brook trout are small to medium-sized fish with a distinctive pattern of light spots on a dark background, a square tail, and a pinkish or reddish belly, especially during the spawning season. They are native to cold, clear streams and lakes.

Brook trout are an important food source, particularly in the colder, clear streams of Orleans County. They are often caught using nets, spears, or hooks, and delicate, flavorful meat is highly prized. Brook trout are also a popular target for early sport fishing, and their presence indicates clean, healthy water sources. They are commonly fried or baked, and bones are sometimes used for tools or crafts.

Yellow Perch

(Perca flavescens)

6–12 INCHES (15–30 CM)

Yellow perch are small to medium-sized fish with a distinctive yellow to golden body, dark vertical stripes, and a spiny dorsal fin. They are commonly found in lakes, rivers, and ponds.

Yellow perch is a staple food, providing a reliable source of protein throughout the year. They are relatively easy to catch in large numbers, particularly in winter, through ice fishing. The fish are often fried, baked, or smoked, and small bones can be used for needles or other small tools. Yellow perch is also essential in local trading and markets.

Largemouth Bass
(Micropterus salmoides)

12–15 INCHES (30–38 CM)

Largemouth bass are medium to large freshwater fish with a large mouth that extends past the eye, a greenish body with a darker horizontal stripe, and a slightly forked tail. They are known for strength and are popular among anglers.

Largemouth bass are prized for their fighting ability when hooked, making them a popular target for subsistence fishing and sport. Their white, flaky flesh is enjoyed by Native Americans and settlers alike, often prepared by frying or baking. Largemouth bass are commonly found in warm, slow-moving waters, such as ponds, lakes, and rivers, and are also important in trade and local markets.

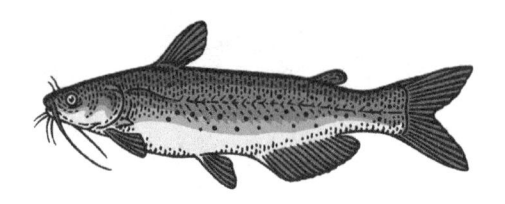

Channel Catfish

(Ictalurus punctatus)

16-24 INCHES (40-61 CM)

Channel catfish are medium to large fish with a smooth, scaleless body, whisker-like barbels around the mouth, and a forked tail. They are usually gray to olive in color with a light belly and can grow to over 3 feet in length.

Channel catfish are a popular food source due to their size and abundance in rivers and lakes. They are often caught using lines baited with worms or other bait, and meat is prized for its flavor, particularly when fried. Catfish are also a staple in trade and local markets. The fish's barbels and whiskers are sometimes used in Native American crafts.

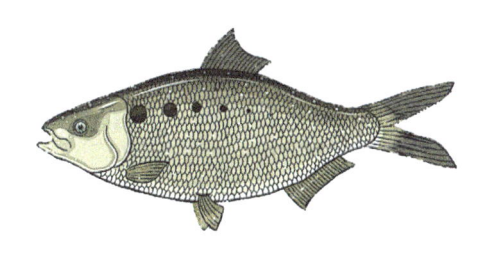

American Shad
(Alosa sapidissima)

20-24 INCHES (51-61 CM)

The American shad is a medium-sized fish with a laterally compressed body, silvery sides, and a deeply forked tail. They are known for strong migratory behavior, moving from saltwater to freshwater rivers to spawn.

Shads are highly valued, particularly during spawning runs in spring. The fish are caught in large numbers using nets and weirs, and oily, flavorful meat is often smoked, salted, or pickled for preservation. Shad roe is considered a delicacy. The arrival of shave in rivers is a significant event, marking a time of abundance and celebration.

Bluegill

(Lepomis macrochirus)

6-10 INCHES (15-25 CM)

Bluegill is a small freshwater fish with a deep, laterally compressed body, a dark spot at the base of the dorsal fin, and a bluish tint on the lower parts of the body. They are commonly found in ponds, lakes, and slow-moving rivers.

Bluegill is an important food source for its abundance and ease of catching, particularly by children and novice anglers. They are often seen with simple fishing gear, such as poles or hand lines, and are typically fried or baked. Bluegill are also important in local ecosystems, serving as prey for larger fish and birds.

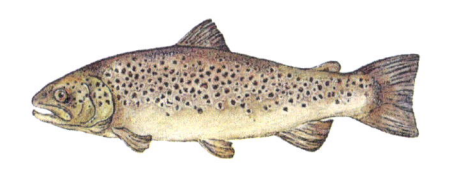

Brown Trout

(Salmo trutta)

14–24 INCHES (35–61 CM)

Brown trout are medium to large fish with a brownish body covered in black and red spots and a more robust build than brook trout. They are not native to North America but were introduced in the 19th century and quickly established.

Although introduced later in the 19th century, brown trout quickly became an important species for subsistence and sport fishing. Their larger size and adaptability make them a popular target for anglers, and their presence contributed to developing early sport fishing culture in the region. Brown trout are often baked, fried, or smoked and are important in local trade and markets.

Smelt

(Osmerus mordax)

7-9 INCHES (18-23 CM)

Smelt are small, slender fish with silvery bodies and a slight greenish tint along the back. They are known for their distinctive cucumber-like smell and are typically found in cold freshwater lakes and rivers.

Smelt is an important seasonal food source, particularly during spring spawning runs when it is caught in large numbers. Native Americans and settlers used nets and baskets to capture frozen, dried, or smoked smelt.

BIRDS

In the wild lands of Western New York, birds play a vital part in the lives of Native peoples and settlers alike. They provide food and feathers and serve as indicators of the seasons, contributing to local customs and beliefs. You will find that knowledge of these birds, their habits, and their uses will greatly aid you in establishing a thriving homestead.

Ruffed Grouse

(Bonasa umbellus)

The ruffed grouse is a medium-sized game bird, much sought after by hunters for its delicate meat. It is a common sight in the forests of this region, and you'll often hear the distinctive drumming sound made by the males during the breeding season, a rhythmic beating that echoes through the woods. Its presence provides a reliable source of food for your table.

Wild Turkey
(Meleagris gallopavo)

The wild turkey, with its dark, iridescent plumage, fan-shaped tail, and bald head, is a large, ground-dwelling bird of great significance. The males, known as toms, are larger and more vibrant than the hens. Turkeys are omnivorous, feeding on nuts, berries, insects, and even small reptiles. These birds, though heavy, are strong fliers and often roost in trees for protection at night. Wild turkey is highly prized for its meat, especially in the colder months, and their feathers serve various uses. However, you should be mindful of overhunting, for turkeys are important to both the native peoples and your fellow settlers.

Bald Eagle

(Haliaeetus leucocephalus)

The bald eagle, majestic in its appearance with a white head, dark brown body, and powerful wings, is often found near rivers and lakes where it fishes for its meals. It builds large nests, or eyries, high in trees or on cliffs, which are used year after year. This bird holds deep symbolic value for the Native peoples, representing strength and a connection to the spirit world. Settlers respect the eagle for its majesty, though there are occasional conflicts when it is seen as a threat to livestock.

Great Horned Owl
(Bubo virginianus)

The great horned owl is a powerful predator known for its large, ear-like tufts of feathers, yellow eyes, and deep, resonant hoot. It hunts by night, feeding on small mammals, birds, and reptiles. The owl's silent flight and deadly accuracy make it formidable in the wilderness. Native peoples often revere the owl as a symbol of wisdom and mystery. At the same time, settlers appreciate its role in controlling rodents and other tiny pests, though they must oversee their poultry.

Northern Cardinal
(Cardinalis cardinalis)

The northern cardinal, with its bright red plumage, is a welcome sight, especially in winter when the landscape turns bleak. Males are striking in their vivid red, while females bear more subdued hues. Cardinals are known for their beautiful songs, which can be heard year-round. Their cheerful presence in gardens and orchards helps keep insect populations in check, and they are often seen as symbols of vitality and perseverance.

Pileated Woodpecker
(Dryocopus pileatus)

The pileated woodpecker, one of the largest of its kind, is recognized by its black body and bold red crest. It is often found in mature forests, where it drills large, rectangular holes in trees, searching for insects like ants and beetle larvae. These woodpeckers are industrious creatures, respected by Native peoples for their hard work. Settlers also value their presence, as they help control insect pests in the forest and farm.

American Crow

(Corvus brachyrhynchos)

With their all-black plumage and raucous calls, crows are intelligent and social birds often seen in large flocks. They feed on various foods, from insects and small animals to grains and carrion. Crows are helpful and troublesome, as they clean up waste and control pests, but they are also notorious for raiding crops, particularly cornfields. In some Native American traditions, crows are seen as tricksters, and settlers often use scarecrows to keep them at bay.

Wild Goose
(Branta canadensis)

The Canada goose, with its black head and neck and distinctive honking call, is a familiar sight along rivers and lakes. These geese migrate in V-formations and are highly social, feeding on grasses, grains, and aquatic plants. Settlers rely on them as a food source during migration, using their feathers for bedding and their meat for sustenance. Be aware, though, that large flocks can damage crops when they feed in your fields.

Eastern Bluebird
(Sialia sialis)

The eastern bluebird, with its brilliant blue back and rust-colored chest, is a small bird of great cheer, heralding the arrival of spring. These birds feed on insects and fruits, and their presence in gardens and fields helps keep pest populations in check. Their bright colors and melodious songs make them a symbol of joy and renewal, often welcomed near homes as good omens.

American Robin

(Turdus migratorius)

The American robin, easily recognized by its red breast, is common in gardens and forests. Feeding on earthworms, insects, and fruits, robins are often seen hopping across lawns for food. Their arrival in early spring signals the end of winter, making them a cherished symbol of the season's renewal. Though beneficial in controlling insects, robins may challenge fruit crops if not managed carefully.

Barred Owl
(Strix varia)

The barred owl, a large and round-headed creature of the night, is easily recognized by its dark, soulful eyes and a pattern of horizontal bars across its chest, with vertical streaks upon its belly. Deep and haunting, its call echoes through the forest and sounds like it asks, "Who cooks for you? Who cooks for you all?" This bird prefers the quiet of mature woodlands, especially near water, where it hunts silently, gliding through the night air in pursuit of small mammals, birds, and amphibians.

Among the Native peoples, the barred owl holds a place of reverence as a symbol of wisdom and mystery, often thought to be connected with the spirit world. You will come to value this owl for its role in controlling the rodent population and helping to protect your food supplies from these pests. Though its eerie call may send a shiver through the night, rest assured that it is a guardian of balance in the wilderness.

Red-tailed Hawk

(Buteo jamaicensis)

The red-tailed hawk, with its broad, rounded tail colored in a striking shade of red, is a formidable sight as it soars high above the fields and forests in search of prey. Its piercing cry cuts through the air, and its sharp eyes are ever watchful for the movement of small mammals, birds, and reptiles. With its brown body and white chest marked by a dark belly band, this noble bird of prey is frequently seen along roadsides and in open lands.

The Native peoples hold this hawk in high esteem, admiring its strength and hunting prowess, and often use its feathers in rituals. As a settler, you will appreciate the red-tailed hawk's ability to keep rodents in check, safeguarding your crops from these vermin. However, be mindful that hawks may sometimes threaten your poultry, a challenge that all who live close to nature must face.

Northern Flicker
(Colaptes auratus)

Unlike most others, the Northern Flicker, a woodpecker, can often be found foraging on the ground rather than pecking at trees. It is a medium-sized bird with a brown body dotted with black spots, a red nape at the back of its neck, and bright yellow underwings visible as it flies. Flickers feed primarily on ants and insects, making them valuable allies in managing pests.

This bird's dynamic drumming on trees as it seeks food or prepares a nesting site will familiarize you. The Native peoples hold the flicker in respect for its role in controlling insect populations, and settlers like yourself will come to rely on it for the same reason. However, flickers can sometimes be a nuisance when pecking at wooden structures, but their usefulness far outweighs the trouble.

Mallard Duck

(Anas platyrhynchos)

The mallard duck, a common sight in ponds and rivers, is a medium-sized waterfowl known for the male's striking green head and chestnut-brown chest. Females are more plainly dressed in mottled brown feathers, offering excellent camouflage as they nest and care for their young. Both sexes have a distinctive blue patch, or speculum, on their wings.

Mallards feed on aquatic plants, insects, and small fish, often gathering in large flocks, particularly during migrations. For both Native peoples and settlers, these birds provide an essential food source. Their feathers are prized for stuffing, bedding, and clothing, and their meat is a welcome addition to any meal. Beyond their utility, mallards play a vital role in maintaining the balance of wetlands by controlling aquatic vegetation.

Common Raven
(Corvus corax)

The common raven, with its thick neck, black feathers, and strong, wedge-shaped bill, is a considerable size and intelligent bird. Its deep croak is a sound you will likely recognize quickly, as ravens are known for their cleverness and resourcefulness. These birds feed on various foods, from small animals and insects to grains, fruits, and carrion, making them highly adaptable to any environment.

Ravens are significant in Native American mythology, often seen as messengers or symbols of transformation. As a settler, you will witness their cunning in raiding crops and livestock feed and in their ability to solve problems. While they may be viewed cautiously for the trouble they can cause, their intelligence and presence are remarkable, earning them both admiration and wariness.

Reptiles

These reptiles play various roles in the lives of Native Americans and settlers in Western New York. While some are feared or considered pests, others are valued for their contributions to controlling pest populations or as a source of food and materials.

SNAKES

Eastern Massasauga Rattlesnake
(Sistrurus catenatus catenatus)

The Eastern Massasauga rattlesnake is a modest-sized serpent, typically growing to lengths between 18 and 30 inches. It bears a stout body with a gray or light brown hue, adorned with darker, saddle-shaped blotches along its back. You will find a slight rattle at the tip of its tail, which the snake shakes as a warning when threatened.

This rattlesnake often inhabits rocky areas, fields, and places near water, where it preys upon small mammals and birds. As a settler, you must exercise caution while working in such areas, especially when the snake is most active in warm weather. A bite from the Massasauga can be dangerous if not treated swiftly. Though bites are rare, the risk remains significant, and one must be prepared to act quickly in case of an encounter.

    Among Native peoples, the Massasauga rattlesnake is feared and respected for its potent venom. While some Indigenous tribes use the venom in small doses for medicinal purposes, settlers often seek to avoid or kill these snakes for the safety of themselves and their livestock.

Northern Copperhead

(Agkistrodon contortrix mokasen)

The Northern Copperhead is another venomous snake that settlers should be wary of. It is a medium-sized snake, 24 to 36 inches long, with a stocky body. Its most striking feature is its copper-colored head, and its body bears hourglass-shaped bands in copper, brown, and tan shades.

Copperheads favor rocky, wooded hillsides and areas near streams and rivers. They are ambush hunters, waiting silently for small mammals, birds, or amphibians to pass by. Encounters with copperheads are often by accident, as their coloration allows them to blend in with the leaves and rocks. Though a bite from a copperhead is seldom fatal, it can cause considerable pain and swelling. Settlers must tread carefully when working in fields or clearing land, and Native Americans are well aware of the need to be vigilant when foraging or hunting in areas where copperheads may be present.

Common Garter Snake
(Thamnophis sirtalis)

    The common garter snake is a small, nonvenomous serpent, typically growing to lengths between 18 and 26 inches. It is slender and easily recognized by the three long, light-colored stripes that run along its back, usually yellow or white, set against a darker background.

    These snakes are found in many habitats, from meadows and woodlands to wetlands and even near homes and gardens. They are active during the day and feed on small prey such as earthworms, amphibians, and fish. Unlike venomous species, garter snakes are viewed favorably by Native peoples and settlers alike, as they help control pests like insects and rodents. Children often capture them for amusement because they pose no threat to humans. Many settlers welcome their presence near the home and garden, knowing the benefits they bring.

Eastern Milk Snake

(Lampropeltis triangulum triangulum)

The Eastern milk snake is a medium-sized, nonvenomous snake, often reaching 24 to 36 inches long. Its body is smooth and glossy, covered with striking red or brown blotches bordered in black, set against a background of gray or tan.

These snakes inhabit woodlands, fields, and farm areas, where they are most active at night. They primarily hunt rodents but will also eat birds and their eggs. The milk snake is often mistaken for a venomous species because of its colorful markings, sometimes leading to unnecessary fear and the snake being killed.

Northern Water Snake
(Nerodia sipedon sipedon)

The Northern water snake is a large, nonvenomous creature that may grow as long as four feet. Its thick body is adorned with dark bands or blotches against gray, brown, or reddish hues. As the snake ages, its color often deepens and darkens, making older snakes appear nearly black.

These snakes are highly aquatic and thrive in lakes, rivers, ponds, and wetlands. They are strong swimmers, feeding on fish, amphibians, and the occasional small mammal. Unfortunately, their appearance often makes them mistaken for venomous serpents, which stirs unnecessary fear among settlers. Their aggressive nature, when cornered, can heighten these concerns, especially when encountered near water sources.

While they may appear threatening, water snakes serve a valuable purpose in keeping the populations of fish and amphibians in check. Though their presence sometimes conflicts with settlers, they pose no real danger, and their role in the ecosystem should be respected.

Eastern Hognose Snake
(Heterodon platirhinos)

The Eastern hognose snake is a medium-sized, nonvenomous snake that grows to lengths between 20 and 33 inches. It is easily recognized by its upturned snout and variable color patterns, which range from yellow to brown or even black, often with darker blotches along its body.

Hognose snakes favor loose, sandy soils and are often found in woodlands, fields, or forest edges. They are best known for their dramatic and unusual defensive behaviors, including flattening their heads, hissing loudly, and even pretending to be dead to deter threats. Their primary diet consists of amphibians, particularly toads, which they catch with great skill.

Despite their intimidating displays, hognose snakes are entirely harmless to humans. Unfortunately, their threatening postures lead many to mistakenly believe they are venomous. However, they are beneficial to the land, as they help control the population of amphibians.

TURTLES

Painted Turtle
(Chrysemys picta)

The painted turtle is a small to medium-sized creature with a smooth, flat shell, olive to black, adorned with bright red and yellow markings along the edges. Its dark skin is streaked with yellow stripes on the head and limbs.

These turtles are highly aquatic, often found basking on logs in ponds, lakes, and marshes. Omnivorous by nature, they feed on aquatic vegetation, insects, and small fish. Active during daylight hours, they retreat to the mud for hibernation in winter.

Admired for their bright colors, painted turtles are sometimes kept as pets by both Native Americans and settlers. They also serve as a minor food source. Their presence in wetlands is a sign of a healthy environment, and their peaceful nature makes them a welcome sight near homesteads.

Snapping Turtle
(Chelydra serpentina)

The snapping turtle is a fearsome, large creature with a rough shell, a powerful beak-like jaw, and a long tail ridged like a saw. These turtles can grow up to 18 inches in length and weigh over 30 pounds.

Primarily aquatic, snapping turtles dwell in ponds, rivers, and marshes, feeding on fish, amphibians, birds, and aquatic plants. They are well-known for their aggressive behavior when encountered on land, making them creatures to approach cautiously.

Feared and respected alike, snapping turtles provide a valuable food source. Their meat is often used in soups and stews, particularly prized for its richness. However, their powerful bite makes them dangerous to handle, and they can threaten livestock or pets. Additionally, their shells are sometimes used in traditional crafts or tools.

Eastern Box Turtle
(Terrapene carolina carolina)

The Eastern box turtle is small to medium-sized, easily recognized by its domed shell, often brown with vibrant yellow or orange patterns. Unique to this species is its ability to close its shell tightly, offering protection from predators.

Box turtles prefer the moist floors of forests and meadows, usually near streams or ponds. Their diet varies: insects, worms, berries, mushrooms, and other plant material. Slow-moving yet long-lived, these turtles may survive for several decades.

Often captured as pets, Eastern box turtles are valued for their bright appearance and docile nature. Occasionally used as a food source, they are also regarded as symbols of endurance and wisdom, particularly by Native Americans. Their slow movement and colorful shells make them a common sight in the forests.

Wood Turtle
(Glyptemys insculpta)

The wood turtle is a medium-sized, semi-aquatic species with a sculpted, rough shell, brown in color, and marked with yellow or orange on the neck and limbs. They typically reach a length of about 6 to 9 inches.

Found near streams, rivers, and ponds in forested areas, wood turtles feed on plants, insects, and small animals. Known for their intelligence, they are often seen moving actively on land, displaying curious behaviors.

Both Native Americans and settlers admire the wood turtle for its resilience and sharpness. They are sometimes kept as pets or used as a food source, though their vulnerability to habitat loss due to land clearing for agriculture makes them increasingly scarce. The presence of these turtles is often seen as a marker of a healthy ecosystem.

Amphibians

Amphibians are indispensable to the natural balance of the land you will soon inhabit, playing a crucial part in controlling the insect population, offering signs of the environment's health, and marking the transition of the seasons.

American Bullfrog
(Lithobates catesbeianus)

North America's most enormous American bullfrog is a common sight near water. These creatures can grow to nearly 8 inches long, with backs ranging from green to brown and bellies from white to yellow. One can easily recognize them by the large round eardrums behind their eyes.

These frogs are highly aquatic and favor the calm waters of ponds, lakes, and marshes. Voracious in their appetite, they prey on insects, small mammals, birds, fish, and other frogs.

For both Native Americans and settlers, the bullfrog offers a prized source of food, particularly the legs, which are valued for their tender meat. Their presence is also a boon in controlling insects near water sources, helping to ease the burden of pestilence around your homestead. However, be prepared—their loud calls may become unwelcome near your dwelling, especially on warm nights.

Spring Peeper
(Pseudacris crucifer)

The spring peeper is a small, modest frog, rarely exceeding an inch in length. Its tan or brown body bears a distinctive dark "X" mark across its back. Though humble in appearance, these tiny frogs are known for their loud, high-pitched calls that fill the air come springtime.

Spring peepers are often found in wetlands, marshes, and the wooded lands surrounding ponds and streams. They are nocturnal and spend much time hidden beneath leaves or vegetation, only emerging to sing their chorus when the warmer weather returns.

The song of the spring peeper is among the first signs that winter's grasp is loosening, heralding the coming of spring. Though too small to be used as food, they are highly beneficial in reducing the number of insects, a service of great value to your crops, and overall comfort. Their chorus will become familiar and comforting as the cold season gives way to warmth.

Wood Frog

(Lithobates sylvaticus)

The wood frog, a creature of moderate size, often measures two to three inches in length and is easily recognized by the dark "mask" around its eyes. Its hue varies from tan to deep brown, allowing it to blend seamlessly with the forest floor. Primarily a land-dwelling species, these frogs are often found in forested areas, particularly near vernal pools, where they gather to breed in early spring.

Feeding mainly on insects and small invertebrates, they contribute to controlling the insect population. For Native Americans and settlers, the wood frog's early breeding season marks the welcome transition from winter to spring, a sign of the changing seasons. Their eggs and tadpoles also serve food for other wildlife, highlighting their importance in the ecosystem.

Northern Leopard Frog
(Lithobates pipiens)

The northern leopard frog is another of moderate size, typically reaching two to four inches in length. It is distinguished by its green or brown body, marked with large dark spots, each outlined in yellow or white. Its belly is white, and its long legs make it a powerful jumper.

These frogs favor wet habitats such as marshes, ponds, and wet meadows, where they remain active during daylight hours, feeding on insects, spiders, and other small creatures.

Native Americans and pioneers prize these frogs, particularly for their legs, which make a fine meal. Additionally, their role in reducing insect populations is invaluable, helping to keep pests in check around homesteads and fields. The presence of northern leopard frogs in wetlands signifies clean water and a healthy environment.

American Toad
(Anaxyrus americanus)

The American toad, a stout amphibian, grows to about two to four inches in length. Its skin is rough and warty, varying in color from brown to gray or olive. Its short legs and stocky build make it easily recognizable.

Often found in gardens, forests, and fields, the American toad is primarily active at night, feeding insects, slugs, and other small invertebrates. During the spring breeding, they gather in ponds and wetlands to lay their eggs.

To both settlers and Native Americans, toads are highly beneficial, as they help control garden pests, especially insects and slugs. Their distinctive call in spring is familiar and often welcomed. Many settlers encourage these helpful creatures to dwell near their homes, as they provide a natural means of pest control.

Green Frog
(Lithobates clamitans)

The green frog, growing to about three to four inches, is easily recognized by its green or brown body, prominent ridges along its back, and a white or yellow belly. Its call, often compared to the sound of a banjo string, is distinctive in the wetlands.

Living in ponds, lakes, marshes, and slow-moving streams, these frogs feed on insects, small fish, and other aquatic creatures.

Green frogs are a vital part of the water-based ecosystems in Western New York, helping to manage the insect population. Some settlers consider Their legs a delicacy, and they serve as prey for larger animals. Their call is commonly heard near water sources, reminding Native Americans and pioneers of their presence.

Gray Treefrog
(Hyla versicolor)

Though small at just one and a half inches, the gray treefrog is remarkable for its ability to change color, shifting from gray to green to match its surroundings. With large, sticky toe pads, it is well-suited for climbing trees and other vegetation.

Dwelling in forests and woodlands near wetlands, the gray treefrog is primarily nocturnal, feeding on insects and other small invertebrates. Its melodious trill can be heard during the warmer months of spring and summer. These frogs play an essential role in keeping insect populations under control, especially in wooded areas. Their presence is a sign of a thriving forest, and their song, which is heard on warm nights, is a welcome sound to those living in the area.

Pickerel Frog
(Lithobates palustris)

The pickerel frog, measuring about two to three-and-a-half inches, has a tan or brown body, with rectangular dark spots running along its back. Its underbelly is white, and the underside of its thighs is marked with a bright yellow or orange color.

Pickerel frogs are commonly found near streams, ponds, and wetlands. They are active daily, feeding insects, spiders, and other small invertebrates.

These frogs are well-known to both Native Americans and pioneers for their role in controlling insects, especially near water. However, their skin secretes a mild toxin, which can irritate predators and humans, so they must be handled carefully.

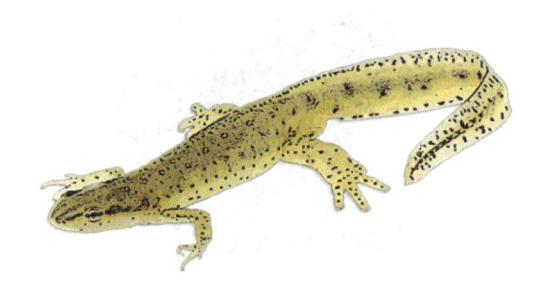

Eastern Newt

(Notophthalmus viridescens)

The Eastern Newt is a small but brightly colored creature known for its two distinct life stages. In its aquatic adult form, it appears olive green with a yellow belly adorned with red spots, while in its terrestrial "eft" stage, it dons a striking orange or red hue.

You will often find these newts in ponds, small lakes, and forested wetlands, where they make their home. Feeding on small invertebrates, they play a vital role in controlling insect populations.

Native Americans and settlers have taken note of the Eastern Newt's distinctive appearance, often observing it in the local wetlands. Though they do not serve as food, their presence is a clear indicator of a healthy aquatic environment and a benefit to agriculture through their role in pest control.

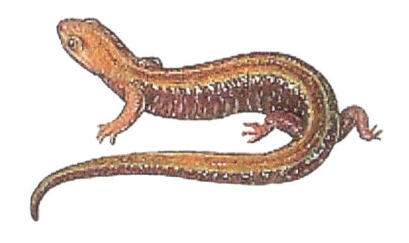

Eastern Redback Salamander
(Plethodon cinereus)

The Eastern redback salamander is a small, lungless creature, typically 2.5 to 4 inches long. It comes in two forms—one displaying a red or orange stripe running down its back (known as the redback phase), and the other completely dark (leadback phase).

These salamanders dwell on land, favoring moist, forested areas, often hiding beneath logs, rocks, or leaf litter. They are most active at night, feeding on insects, spiders, and other small invertebrates. Unlike many amphibians, the redback salamander has no aquatic larval stage, spending all its life on land.

A healthy forest is often home to abundant redback salamanders, and their presence is a sure sign of a well-balanced ecosystem. Native Americans and settlers frequently encounter them while gathering firewood or clearing land, noting their importance in controlling pest populations.

Spotted Salamander

(Ambystoma maculatum)

The spotted salamander, a large and stout creature, grows about 6 to 9 inches long. Its dark gray or black body is covered in bright yellow or orange spots, making it a striking sight in the forest. With smooth skin and mostly nocturnal habits, it remains hidden during the day.

These salamanders prefer moist, deciduous forests, emerging during the rainy nights of early spring to breed in vernal pools. After laying their eggs, which hatch into aquatic larvae, the adults return to their underground caves, where they spend most of their time.

Spotted salamanders are crucial to the woodland ecosystem, helping control insect populations. Their annual breeding migration is a notable event each spring, observed by Native Americans and pioneers as a signal of the changing seasons. Their presence is a clear sign of the health of the forest, marking them as an important part of the land you are about to inhabit.

Mammals

Small game animals like rabbits, squirrels, and raccoons are an essential daily food source and are abundant in the Orleans County area. Deer are plentiful and highly prized for their meat. Beavers, mink, and foxes are highly valued for their fur, an essential commodity for trade. Farm animals must be protected from predators – large mammals including wolves and cougars. Understanding these animals' behaviors, habitats, and uses will enhance your hunting skills and aid in sustaining your homestead.

ESSENTIAL FOOD SOURCE

Eastern Gray Squirrel
(Sciurus carolinensis)

The Eastern gray squirrel is a lively creature you will often see darting about the trees, its bushy tail and sleek gray fur catching the light. Some of these squirrels may even sport brown or black fur. Agile climbers spend much of their time in the branches, gathering food and leaping from tree to tree.

Gray squirrels are omnivorous, though they favor nuts, seeds, fruits, and fungi. They are known for caching food in preparation for winter, burying nuts in the ground to sustain them through the colder months. These squirrels are most active at dawn and dusk, scurrying to gather their stores.

To Native Americans and settlers alike, squirrels are a valuable food source. Their fur is used for clothing, but these little creatures can also become quite the nuisance, raiding grain stores and orchards when the opportunity presents itself.

Eastern Chipmunk
(Tamias striatus)

The Eastern chipmunk is a small, ground-dwelling rodent with reddish-brown fur and a white belly. Its most distinctive feature is the black and white stripes along its back. Watch for these busy little creatures, always on the move, cheeks puffed with food, for they gather seeds, nuts, fruits, and insects to store in their underground burrows.

Though chipmunks tend to be solitary and do less harm than larger pests, they can still pose a minor inconvenience by raiding gardens and food stores. Their burrows, though modest, can sometimes undermine the foundations of buildings or walls, so it is wise to keep an eye on their comings and goings.

Snowshoe Hare
(Lepus americanus)

The snowshoe hare is a familiar sight in the forests of this land, easily recognized by its large, fur-covered hind feet, which enable it to travel effortlessly across the snow. Its fur changes with the seasons, from brown in the summer to snowy white in the winter, making it nearly invisible to predators.

These hares survive on grasses, twigs, and bark, particularly in the lean winter months when food is scarce. For settlers, the snowshoe hare is a vital source of sustenance during the colder months. Though they may cause trouble by nibbling on garden plants and young trees, their abundance makes them an easy and reliable hunt. However, their speed and agility make capturing them a challenge worthy of any hunter.

Eastern Cottontail Rabbit
(Sylvilagus floridanus)

The Eastern cottontail rabbit is a small, brownish-gray creature with large ears and a fluffy white tail, resembling a cotton ball, which gives it its name. These rabbits blend well into their surroundings, whether in open fields or forest edges.

They are herbivores, feeding on grasses, herbs, and various crops. Known for their rapid breeding, cottontails can quickly become numerous, creating challenges for settlers trying to protect their vegetable gardens and crop fields. Yet, their meat and fur make them valuable for food and clothing, and Native Americans also prize these animals for trade and practical use. While they may be a nuisance at times, they are a plentiful and reliable source of sustenance for both pioneers and natives alike.

Raccoon

(Procyon lotor)

The raccoon is a medium-sized creature, easily recognized by the black "mask" across its eyes and its ringed tail. Its front paws are notably nimble, allowing it to open containers and explore with great curiosity. Raccoons are cunning and quick to adapt, foraging by night and often lingering near water sources.

As omnivores, raccoons feed on whatever they can find—whether fruits, nuts, small animals, or even scraps left behind by settlers. Though they can be a valuable source of fur, commonly fashioned into clothing or traded, and their meat is occasionally eaten, raccoons often prove a nuisance. They are known to raid crops, steal poultry, and rob food stores, making them an unwelcome visitor at many homesteads.

Opossum
(Didelphis virginiana)

The opossum, North America's sole marsupial, is about the size of a house cat. It possesses a grayish-white coat, a long prehensile tail, and a narrow snout. One curious trait of the opossum is its tendency to "play dead" when threatened, lying still as though lifeless to deter predators.

Opossums are nocturnal and omnivorous, feasting on fruits, insects, small animals, and even carrion. Though they are hunted for both their fur and meat, their habit of raiding chicken coops, gardens, and garbage often leads to conflict with settlers. Nonetheless, their resourcefulness allows them to thrive even as settlements grow.

Muskrat
(Ondatra zibethicus)

The muskrat is a medium-sized, semi-aquatic rodent, distinguished by its stout body, short legs, and long, scaly tail. It is often found near ponds, wetlands, and rivers, where its dense brown fur provides warmth in the colder months. Muskrats are industrious builders, constructing dome-shaped lodges from mud and vegetation in shallow waters.

Though primarily nocturnal, they are sometimes active during the day, feeding on aquatic plants, small fish, and shellfish. Muskrats are highly valued for their fur, often sought after for trade. However, their burrowing habits can damage dikes and pond banks, posing a challenge for settlers who depend on stable water systems for their crops and livestock.

Weasel

(Mustela spp.)

Weasels are small, slender animals with long, curved bodies, sharp teeth, and claws, known for their agility and ferocity as hunters. Depending on the season, their fur may be brown or white, helping them blend into their surroundings.

Weasels are carnivorous, preying on small mammals, birds, and eggs. Though they can be troublesome to settlers due to their tendency to raid poultry, they also serve a useful role by controlling rodent populations, which can otherwise devastate grain stores. While not as prized as other furs, weasel pelts are sometimes used in clothing or trade.

Woodchuck (Groundhog)

(Marmota monax)

The woodchuck, or groundhog, is a large rodent with a stout, chunky body and short legs. Its fur is typically brownish-gray and is well known for its burrowing abilities. Woodchucks dig extensive tunnels for shelter and hibernation and are active during daylight hours.

Woodchucks are herbivores, feeding on grasses, clover, and garden crops. Though they are occasionally hunted for their meat and fur, their burrowing can cause considerable damage to gardens, fields, and even the foundations of buildings. Both Native Americans and settlers must take care to manage the woodchuck population, lest their agricultural endeavors suffer.

Porcupine

(Erethizon dorsatum)

As you settle into these new lands, you'll soon become familiar with the porcupine. Slow-moving and small, it is well-guarded by sharp quills across its back and tail. Its sturdy, dark-colored body allows it to forage efficiently, and it is often seen climbing trees for bark, leaves, and twigs, which it favors as food. Active mostly at dusk and dawn, it may seem harmless, but its habit of gnawing on wood can cause damage to your trees and structures.

Be wary of its quills, as they pose a real danger to livestock or pets that get too close. While porcupines may seem a nuisance, their quills are often used by Native Americans for intricate decorations, adding some value to this troublesome creature.

VALUED FOR FUR

Red Fox
(Vulpes vulpes)

You will undoubtedly encounter the red fox in your travels—a clever and agile predator with a reddish coat, sharp ears, and a bushy white-tipped tail. It is most active in the early hours of dawn and dusk, quietly hunting small animals, birds, insects, or even scavenging fruits and carrion. Red foxes adapt quickly to forests and open fields, even wandering near your settlements in search of food.

Highly sought after for its fur, trappers hunt the red fox, yet it is also a pest, prone to raiding poultry coops or small livestock pens. You'll need to remain watchful, as this wily creature will challenge your efforts to protect your animals, but its pelt, when captured, is highly prized in trade.

American Mink
(Neovison vison)

If you settle near rivers or streams, the American mink is a creature you must know. Sleek and swift, with a dark brown coat, the mink is as skilled a swimmer as a hunter. It lives a solitary life, coming out mostly at night to hunt small creatures like fish, birds, and amphibians. Its fur is precious, making it a favored animal among trappers, but take care—minks will occasionally raid your poultry or small livestock, causing you trouble. Trapped by Native Americans and settlers alike, the mink offers lucrative fur, yet it can be a nuisance near your water sources.

Striped Skunk
(Mephitis mephitis)

While the skunk may seem an unassuming little creature, its black-and-white striped coat should serve as a warning. Known for its powerful spray, which it uses to fend off threats, the skunk is a nocturnal forager, feeding on insects, small animals, and even plants or fruits it may find in your fields. You must be cautious around skunks, as their spray is no minor inconvenience. Yet their fur is quite valuable; despite the risks, some choose to hunt them. Skunks are also known to raid chicken coops and gardens, so you must remain alert if they wander near your homestead.

Gray Fox
(Urocyon cinereoargenteus)

The gray fox is among the most elusive creatures in these lands. Smaller than the red fox and distinguished by its salt-and-pepper coat and bushy black-tipped tail, the gray fox is one of the few canines that can climb trees. This trait allows it to avoid capture and hunt in the forests, where it finds small animals, birds, fruits, and nuts. It creeps at night or in the twilight, making it harder to spot. Like the red fox, the gray fox is a hunter's prize for its fur and a pest for its predation on poultry or small animals. Keep watch, for its ability to climb trees, may surprise you, and it is far more elusive than its red cousin.

Beaver

(Castor canadensis)

The beaver is a remarkable creature, easily recognized by its stout body, webbed hind feet, and the unique flat, scaly tail it uses to great effect in its work. With dense brown fur and sharp teeth suited for gnawing through wood, the beaver is well-known for its industry. It builds dams and lodges from trees and mud, creating ponds that foster an array of wildlife.

Beavers are nocturnal, meaning they do much of their work and feed—on bark, leaves, and aquatic plants—under the cover of night. The beaver's pelt is of great value in the fur trade, and many a settler finds it an essential resource. Yet be warned: their dams may flood areas of land you've labored to clear for crops. Though a useful creature, the beaver can bring challenges as it reshapes the landscape around you.

VALUED FOR MEAT AND HIDES

White-tailed Deer
(Odocoileus virginianus)

The white-tailed deer, a common sight in these parts, is an invaluable resource for the pioneer. With a reddish-brown coat that turns grayish-brown in winter, this medium-sized ungulate is easily recognized by the white underside of its tail, which it raises as an alarm signal. The males, or bucks, grow antlers each year, which they shed come winter.

These adaptable creatures feed on leaves, twigs, fruits, and nuts and roam in forests, meadows, and near settlements. All parts of the deer are used—meat for sustenance, hides for clothing, bones, antlers for tools, and sinew for binding. While the abundance of deer makes them a staple of the pioneer diet, they can become a nuisance when grazing on your crops.

Eastern Elk
(Cervus canadensis canadensis)

The Eastern elk is a grand and majestic creature, standing around five feet tall at the shoulder and weighing up to 1,000 pounds. With a reddish-brown coat and lighter rump, the males boast large antlers stretching several feet across. Grazing on grasses, leaves, and bark, these elk travel in herds, especially during the fall mating season, favoring open woodlands and meadows near water.

For Native Americans and pioneers alike, the elk was a vital resource, providing meat, hides for clothing and shelter, and antlers for tools and trade. However, the elk population has suffered as settlement expands and hunting increases. By the mid-19th century, the once-abundant Eastern elk has largely disappeared from the region, a testament to the cost of unchecked expansion.

Moose
(Alces alces)

The moose, a truly towering beast, is the most prominent member of the deer family, with bulls, or males, standing up to seven feet tall at the shoulder and often weighing over a thousand pounds. Their long legs, humped back, and broad, bulbous noses make them easily distinguishable, and the antlers of a bull, when grown to full size, are a sight to behold—massive and wide-spreading. These solitary creatures prefer the wet, forested regions, where they feed on aquatic plants, shrubs, and the bark of trees. Moose are also remarkable swimmers, often wading into ponds and lakes for food.

While moose are not as common in Western New York as some other large animals, they are still prized by both Native Americans and settlers for their substantial meat, durable hides, and impressive antlers. The size and strength of a moose make it a formidable animal to hunt, yet the reward of such a hunt, in terms of food and materials, is significant.

Bison

(Bison bison)

Known to many as the American buffalo, the bison is a genuinely immense creature with a large hump over its shoulders, dark, shaggy fur, and curved horns. These animals can weigh as much as two thousand pounds and stand around six feet tall at the shoulder. Bison are naturally grazers, feeding primarily on the grasses of the plains. They once roamed in great herds, stretching across the plains and into parts of the Eastern United States.

By the time settlers began establishing themselves in Western New York, the bison had already started to disappear from the region, and their numbers were significantly reduced by hunting and environmental changes. For Native Americans, the bison was a cornerstone of life, providing not just meat but hides for clothing and shelter and bones for tools and weapons. Though they are no longer a common sight in these parts, the memory of their presence and importance to trade and survival remains.

PREDITORS

Eastern Mountain Lion
(Puma concolor cougar)

Commonly referred to as cougars or panthers, these large, solitary cats are easily recognized by their tawny coats and long, black-tipped tails. Their robust, muscular frames allow them to weigh anywhere from 70 to 170 pounds, with the males generally more significant than the females. Cougars are stealthy and highly territorial, often roaming over vast areas in search of prey.

Their primary diet consists of deer, smaller mammals, and birds, but they have been known to attack livestock, and though it is rare, they can pose a danger to humans. These predators are most active during the dawn and dusk, moving silently through the wilderness. Native Americans hold the cougar in high esteem, often considering it a spirit animal of great power. Take precautions; the mountain lion's stealth and strength make it a formidable foe.

Eastern Wolf
(Canis lupus lycaon)

Known as the timber wolf, the Eastern wolf bears a coat ranging from gray to reddish-brown. With a bushy tail and long legs, these wolves, though slightly smaller than their western relatives, still weigh between 50 and 100 pounds. Wolves are pack hunters, relying on their numbers and coordination to bring down larger prey such as deer or elk.

Their presence is both feared and respected, for while wolves typically avoid direct conflict with man, they are cunning hunters of livestock. A pack of wolves, especially under the cover of night, can decimate a farmer's cattle, sheep, or other domestic animals in a single attack. The loss of livestock is not merely an inconvenience but a severe blow to their survival, as it impacts food stores and economic stability. Wolves roam far and wide, so vigilance is critical, especially after dusk when these predators are most active. Be prepared, and always watch over your animals closely.

American Black Bear
(Ursus americanus)

Black bears are common in Orleans County forests and pose a significant threat to settlers, particularly when food is scarce. Bears are attracted to settlements by the smell of livestock, crops, and stored food, leading to potentially dangerous encounters. While black bears generally avoid humans, they can become aggressive if threatened, particularly if they are surprised or if a mother bear is protecting her cubs. Settlers have to be cautious, especially in the fall when bears are preparing for hibernation and are more actively foraging for food.

The black bear is a formidable, large, robust creature with a thick black or dark brown coat, a short tail, and a distinctive snout. These animals can weigh anywhere from 200 to 600 pounds, with the males generally being the larger of the two. Solitary in nature, black bears are often seen foraging alone, except for mothers who protect their cubs.

As omnivores, these bears consume a wide variety of food, including berries, nuts, insects, small mammals, and even carrion. Their adaptability and strong climbing abilities allow them to thrive in forests and other wild areas. However, their occasional forays into pioneer fields and livestock pens cause the most trouble. To both Native Americans and settlers, the black bear offers valuable resources. They are hunted for their meat, particularly prized in the fall when the bears have fattened in preparation for winter. Their thick fur is used for warmth, and the bear's fat is rendered into grease, which serves many purposes—cooking, lubricating machinery, and waterproofing clothing and gear. Yet, with all their uses, black bears can become a great nuisance, raiding crops and livestock. It is common for settlers to defend their homesteads against these incursions, as a single bear can cause great loss.

Be mindful of their presence; while they offer much, they also bring considerable risk to your livelihood and safety.

PROTECTING LIVESTOCK AND PROPERTY

As you venture into this new land, a chief concern will be safeguarding your livestock and property from the many predators that roam the wilderness. Wolves, bears, and even hawks and owls pose a constant threat, and it is essential that you prepare well to protect your animals from harm.

Building Fences and Enclosures

The first defense is constructing solid and durable fences and enclosures. For larger animals like cattle and sheep, you'll need to build tall and robust fences to withstand attacks from wolves or bears. Wood or stone are often the materials of choice, depending on what is available, and some settlers even reinforce their fences with thorny hedges or other natural barriers. Chickens and smaller animals will require even more care, as aerial predators such as hawks and owls can quickly swoop down. Cover their enclosures with a roof or wire to shield them from such dangers.

Using Guard Dogs

You should also consider employing guard dogs to watch over your livestock. Breeds such as the Great Pyrenees, Mastiff, or Collie are favored for size, strength, and loyalty. These dogs are vigilant and brave, standing their ground against wolves and bears, alerting you at the first sign of danger. A well-trained dog is an invaluable companion on any farm, capable of saving you from considerable loss by keeping predators at bay.

Nightly Vigilance

Take special care at night, for it is then that the greatest threats arise. Wolves and bears are most active after dark, and you must remain watchful. Bringing livestock into secure pens or barns at night is common practice, and many settlers burn fires around the homestead to discourage prowling predators. Some go so far as to stand guard or take turns keeping watch through the night, for a single unchecked attack could cost you dearly. Your livestock is your livelihood, and protecting them from harm is worth the extra effort.

DEALING WITH PREDATOR ATTACKS

Hunting and Trapping

Should predators persist in attacking your livestock, you may need to take more direct action. Hunting wolves and bears is no small task, requiring both skill and courage. It is often done with the help of neighbors, for tackling such a formidable foe alone is perilous. Trapping is another option. Set traps along paths you know the predators frequent or near places where your livestock have been attacked. These traps can either capture or kill the predator, but be mindful not to set them where they might accidentally harm your own animals or family.

Scare Tactics

In some instances, scare tactics can be enough to keep predators away. Loud noises, such as banging pots, firing a gun into the air, or even setting off firecrackers, may frighten away a bear or a wolf. You can erect scarecrows or other effigies near your barns or pens to serve as visual deterrents. While these methods may not always work, they can provide additional protection for your homestead when combined with sturdy fencing and guard dogs.

With these precautions, you can better defend your farm and family from the dangers lurking in the untamed wilderness. Preparedness and vigilance are your greatest allies on the frontier.

Of Bears and Beech Trees

The American beech tree (Fagus grandifolia) plays a crucial role in the ecosystem of Orleans County, particularly in its relationship with black bears (Ursus americanus). The production of beechnuts, often referred to as "bear superfood," is directly linked to female black bears' reproductive patterns and overall health. Beechnuts are highly nutritious, rich in fats, and contain double the protein of acorns, making them an essential food source for bears as they prepare for hibernation.

Beechnuts and Bear Behavior

Beechnut production varies yearly, with some years producing an abundance of nuts, known as "mast years." During these mast years, black bears are particularly active in beech forests, where they can be seen foraging for these calorie-dense nuts.

Bears rely heavily on beechnuts in the fall to build up fat reserves for the winter months when they enter hibernation. The availability of beechnuts can influence the reproductive success of female bears, as a plentiful supply of this food allows them to produce and sustain more cubs.

You can often tell where a bear has been feasting on beechnuts by the signs they leave behind in the forest. Bears will climb beech trees to access the nuts, leaving distinctive claw marks on the bark. They may also break lower limbs or create a scramble of branches in the upper limbs that resemble nests as they move about in search of nuts. These signs are clear indicators of bear activity and highlight the importance of beech trees in supporting bear populations.

The Role of Beech Trees in the Ecosystem

Beech trees are vital for black bears and support many other wildlife. Their nuts provide food for various species, including deer, squirrels, and birds, particularly during the fall and early winter when other food sources are scarce. The dense canopy of beech trees offers shelter for numerous animals, while the trees' strong wood has historically been valued for furniture and toolmaking by both Native Americans and Settlers.

Bears and the Environment

Black bears are keystone species in many ecosystems, including Orleans County. Their foraging habits can influence the distribution of seeds, such as those from beechnuts and acorns, helping to shape the composition of forests. By feeding on carrion and other animals, they also help maintain the balance of populations within the environment.

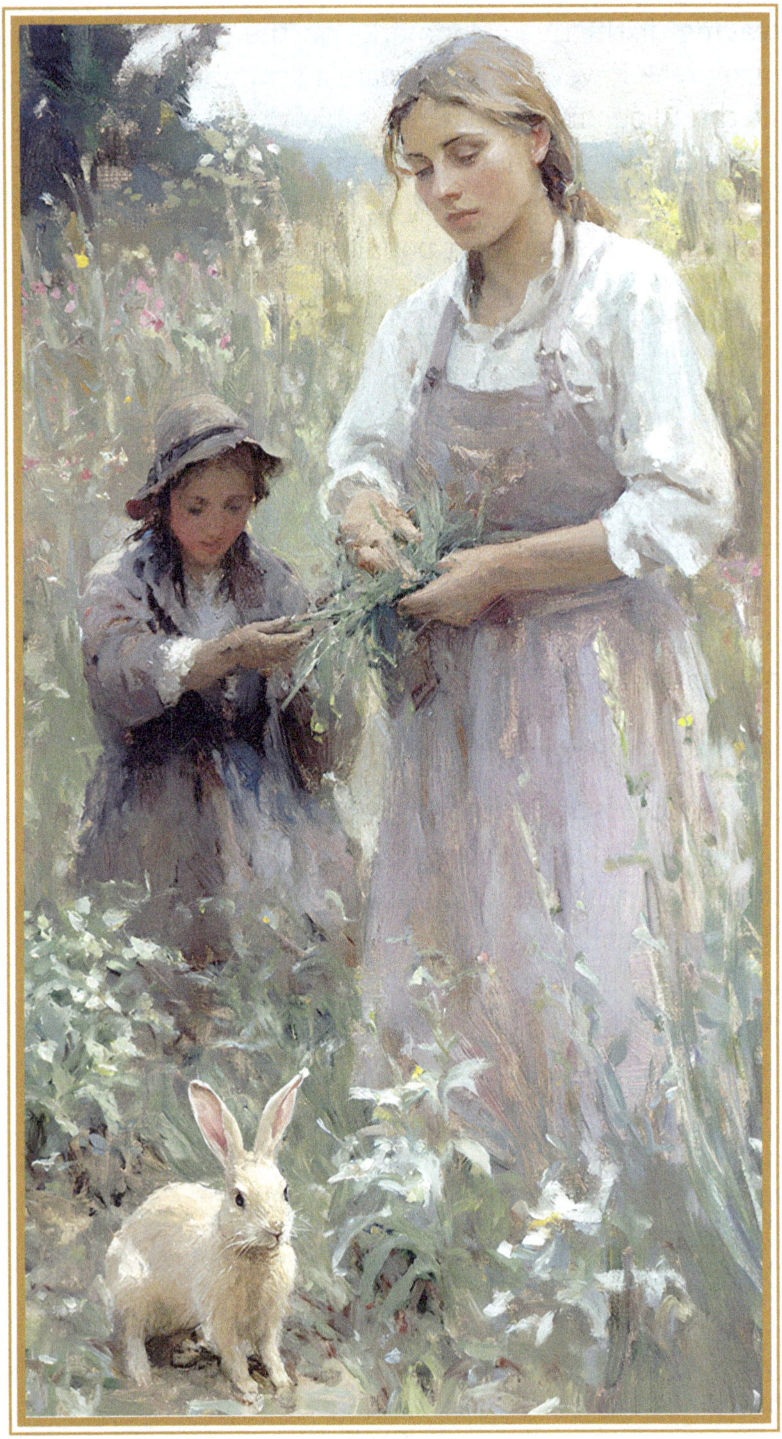

PEST CONTROL

Understanding how to manage pests, such as rodents, insects, and birds, that can damage crops, stored food, and buildings is essential for maintaining a stable food supply and healthy living conditions.

In addition to large predators, settlers faced constant threats from more minor pests, such as rodents, insects, and birds, that could damage crops, spoil stored food, and undermine buildings. Effective pest control is essential for maintaining a stable food supply and ensuring the health and safety of the pioneer homestead.

Rodents

(Mice, Rats, and Squirrels)

You will quickly learn that rodents are among the most troublesome pests you shall face on the frontier. Mice and rats are relentless in invading your granaries, pantries, and barns, gnawing through sacks of grain, chewing on wooden beams, and leaving droppings contaminating your food supplies. Their presence is dangerous to your provisions and health, for these creatures are known disease carriers.

While less likely to go indoors, squirrels can still be a nuisance. They may nest in the attics of your home or steal food from your gardens and storage areas, causing frustration and loss. It is vital that you remain vigilant, sealing up any small holes or gaps where these rodents may gain access to your stores and employing traps where necessary to keep them at bay.

Birds
(Crows, Pigeons, and Sparrows)

You will find that birds can be as much of a pest as any rodent when protecting your crops. Crows, pigeons, and sparrows are notorious for raiding fields and devouring seeds, berries, and young plants, which can significantly reduce your harvest. These birds are especially troublesome during planting and harvest seasons when your crops are most vulnerable. It will be essential for you to take measures to guard against their depredations if you hope to bring in a full yield.

INSECT PESTS AND THEIR IDENTIFICATION

(Locusts, Weevils, and Termites)

The threat posed by insects is no less severe than that of rodents. Locusts and grasshoppers, in particular, can lay waste to your fields in a shockingly short amount of time, devouring entire crops and leaving you with little to harvest. This scourge can be devastating, for your survival depends on a successful crop. Weevils and other grain pests are equally dangerous, as they infest stored food, spoiling the supplies you've carefully laid by to last through the long winter months.

Your hard work may come to naught if these pests take hold in your stores. Though not as widespread, termites are yet another enemy to watch for. These insidious creatures burrow into wooden structures, undermining the strength of your home and barns. Termites can weaken the very beams that support your roof without timely intervention. To protect your livelihood, you must act swiftly against any signs of insect infestation in your crops, food stores, or structures.

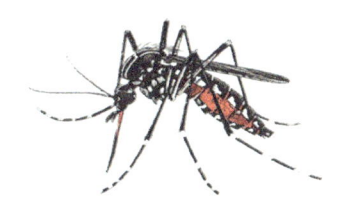

Mosquitoes
(Culicidae family)

Among the many trials you shall face, mosquitoes will likely be among the most irritating. These tiny, bloodsucking pests swarm in great numbers, especially in the summer months near wetlands, rivers, and any area with standing water. Their bites are more than a mere irritation; mosquitoes are known to spread ailments such as the dreaded "Ague and Fever" (malaria) and, in some cases, other disorders like West Nile fever. Their constant buzzing and biting make them a torment, driving people to seek relief by any means available. You will find that many protect themselves with long clothing, smoky fires, and herbal salves to ward off these nuisances. Their impact on health and daily life is no small matter; you must remain vigilant.

Black Flies

(Simuliidae family)

Black flies will become another enemy of your peace in the spring and early summer. These small, biting insects are particularly fierce, and their bites leave painful, itchy welts. In great numbers, they can torment both you and your livestock, causing severe discomfort. Like mosquitoes, black flies are often found near rivers and streams, where they breed in abundance. Many settlers and Native peoples will avoid outdoor work during the worst black fly season or resort to smoke and herbal remedies to keep these pests at bay. You would do well to follow suit.

Like mosquitoes, black flies are a significant nuisance, especially near rivers and streams where they breed. People often avoid being outdoors during peak black fly seasons and use smoke or herbal repellents to ward them off.

Deer Ticks
(Ixodes scapularis)

Though not as numerous as mosquitoes or black flies, deer ticks pose a more hidden danger, particularly if you venture often into the woods or grassy meadows. The bites of these small, flat insects may lead to severe illness, though such afflictions, like Lyme disease, are poorly understood. Still, the consequences of a tick bite can be severe. Therefore, it is wise to scrutinize yourself and your animals after time spent outdoors, and many turn to herbal repellents to fend off ticks before they bite. You cannot afford to be careless, for ticks are insidious in their ways.

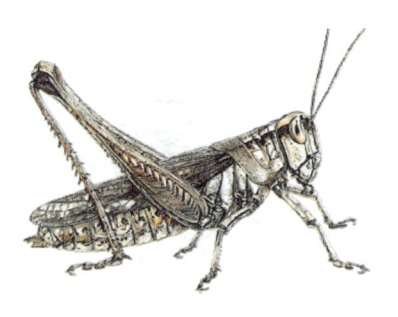

Locusts/Grasshoppers
(Acrididae family)

Should you take up farming, as most pioneers must, you will soon learn to fear the coming of locusts and grasshoppers. These ravenous insects can strip a field bare in hours, devouring crops and leaving nothing behind but barren stalks. A single swarm has brought Entire communities to the brink of starvation. While some farmers create barriers, burn smoke, or remove the insects by hand, such methods often prove futile against the overwhelming numbers of a true locust swarm. These pests can turn a season of hope into a year of famine, so prepare yourself for the challenge.

Cabbage Worms
(Pieris rapae larvae)

In your garden, cabbage worms will prove to be an unrelenting foe. These tiny, green caterpillars feed on cabbage, kale, and other vital vegetables, often ruining crops before you realize the danger. Your winter provisions may depend on the success of these very crops, so diligence is required. You may need to handpick the worms from your plants, use natural repellents, or plant companion crops to discourage the butterflies from laying eggs. These tiny pests can ruin a gardener's efforts if not swiftly addressed.

Gypsy Moth

(Lymantria dispar)

The gypsy moth has become a scourge upon our forests, having been introduced to the northeastern U.S. Its caterpillars devour vast expanses of foliage, threatening not only the natural beauty of the woodlands but also the timber upon which we settlers depend. The loss of trees due to this infestation affects everything from firewood supplies to the wood needed for building our homes and barns. While some efforts are made to destroy the moth's egg masses and apply insecticides, these measures often fall short in the face of large outbreaks.

Corn Earworm
(Helicoverpa zea)

Corn, the staple crop of many settlers, is often plagued by the corn earworm, an insidious pest that feeds on the very ears of the maize. These worms can devastate entire harvests, significantly losing the corn your family may rely on. Farmers endeavor to control the pest through crop rotation, handpicking the worms, and planting varieties of corn that are less susceptible to this blight. However, despite their best efforts, the corn earworm often causes considerable hardship by reducing the yield of this vital crop.

Cutworms
(Noctuidae family)

Cutworms present another grave threat to your crops. These caterpillars sever young plants at the base, making short work of seedlings before they even have a chance to grow. Corn, tomatoes, and other vegetables are particularly vulnerable. Farmers place collars around the plants, till the soil to expose the larvae to predators and employ natural repellents to combat this menace. Even so, cutworm infestations can wreak havoc on a garden, undoing much of your hard labor.

Houseflies
(Musca domestica)

Houseflies are a constant nuisance within the homestead, and their presence extends beyond mere annoyance. These insects spread dangerous illnesses like typhoid fever, dysentery, and cholera, as they contaminate food and water with filth. The best defense against them includes hanging sticky flypaper, swatting them with diligence, and maintaining cleanliness within the home. Yet, despite these precautions, houseflies remain a frequent cause of disease in pioneer settlements.

Weevils

(Curculionidae family)

Weevils are infamous for destroying stored grains, flour, and dry goods. They burrow into your food stores, rendering much of it unfit for consumption. Settlers must take great care to store grain in sealed containers to protect it from infestation. Even then, some weevils manage to invade. While the infested grain can be sifted and salvaged to some extent, the losses are often heavy, threatening your ability to sustain yourself through winter.

Bedbugs

(Cimex lectularius)

Bedbugs are a persistent problem for many settlers. These tiny insects infest bedding, furniture, and even the cracks in walls, leaving itchy bites and causing much discomfort. Regular cleaning, using herbs like tansy or wormwood, and airing out bedding are common remedies, but once these pests have taken hold, they are challenging to eradicate. You must remain ever vigilant to keep these parasites from overwhelming your home.

Termites

(Isoptera order)

Termites pose a grave threat to the integrity of your buildings. These tiny insects can chew through wooden structures, undermining homes, barns, and fences. If left unchecked, their activity may lead to the collapse of buildings, costing both time and money to repair. Settlers often choose hardwood for construction, as it is more resistant to termite damage, and regularly inspect the buildings to catch infestations early. However, should termites take hold, they can inflict great economic damage upon your homestead.

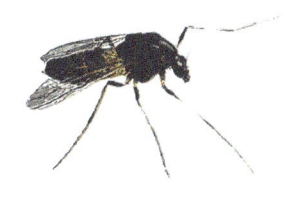

Midges
(Ceratopogonidae family)

Midges, particularly the biting kind often referred to as "noseeums," are a constant vexation for those living near wetlands or other bodies of water. Though these tiny creatures are scarcely visible, their bites cause no small measure of discomfort, often resulting in irritation and swelling. When they gather in large swarms, settlers and livestock may find them intolerable. Much like mosquitoes and black flies, midges are difficult to escape, and while using smoke, long garments, and herbal remedies offers some relief, these pests will undoubtedly trouble you during the warmer months.

STRATEGIES FOR PEST CONTROL

Traps and Poisons

One common way to handle pests, particularly rodents, is through traps. You will likely need to set traps in your granary, pantry, and barn to catch mice, rats, and other small creatures before they do much harm. Traps range from simple spring-loaded devices to more complex designs that capture several simultaneously. Some settlers also use poisons, though these must be handled with care, for they pose a risk to children, pets, and even non-targeted wildlife. Poisoned bait can be placed where rodents are active, to stop infestations before they get out of hand.

Natural Predators

Another excellent method of controlling pests is to encourage the presence of their natural enemies. Keeping cats on your homestead is a time-honored tradition for controlling mice and rats. A good cat will not only reduce the number of pests but also serve as a deterrent to others. Birds of prey, such as owls and hawks, are likewise valuable allies, hunting down rodents and smaller birds that threaten your crops. Many settlers attract these beneficial birds by building nesting boxes or leaving parts of their land wild, where these predators can thrive.

Crop Protection Techniques

You must employ several tactics to protect your crops from crows and sparrows. The Scarecrow is a tried-and-true device that frightens away birds by creating the illusion of human presence. You can dress the figure in old clothes, and adding flapping materials or shiny objects will increase its effectiveness. Noisemaking devices like clappers or wind chimes can also scare off birds and other pests from your fields.

Storing Food Safely

Once your crops are harvested, the battle isn't over. Protecting your stored food is just as important. You'll want to keep your supplies in secure containers, preferably metal or thick wood, to guard against rodents and insects. Granaries should be built with raised floors and tightly fitting doors to keep pests at bay. Inside the home, your pantry must be kept clean and well-organized to minimize the risk of infestation. Frequent inspections are also necessary to catch the first signs of pest activity.

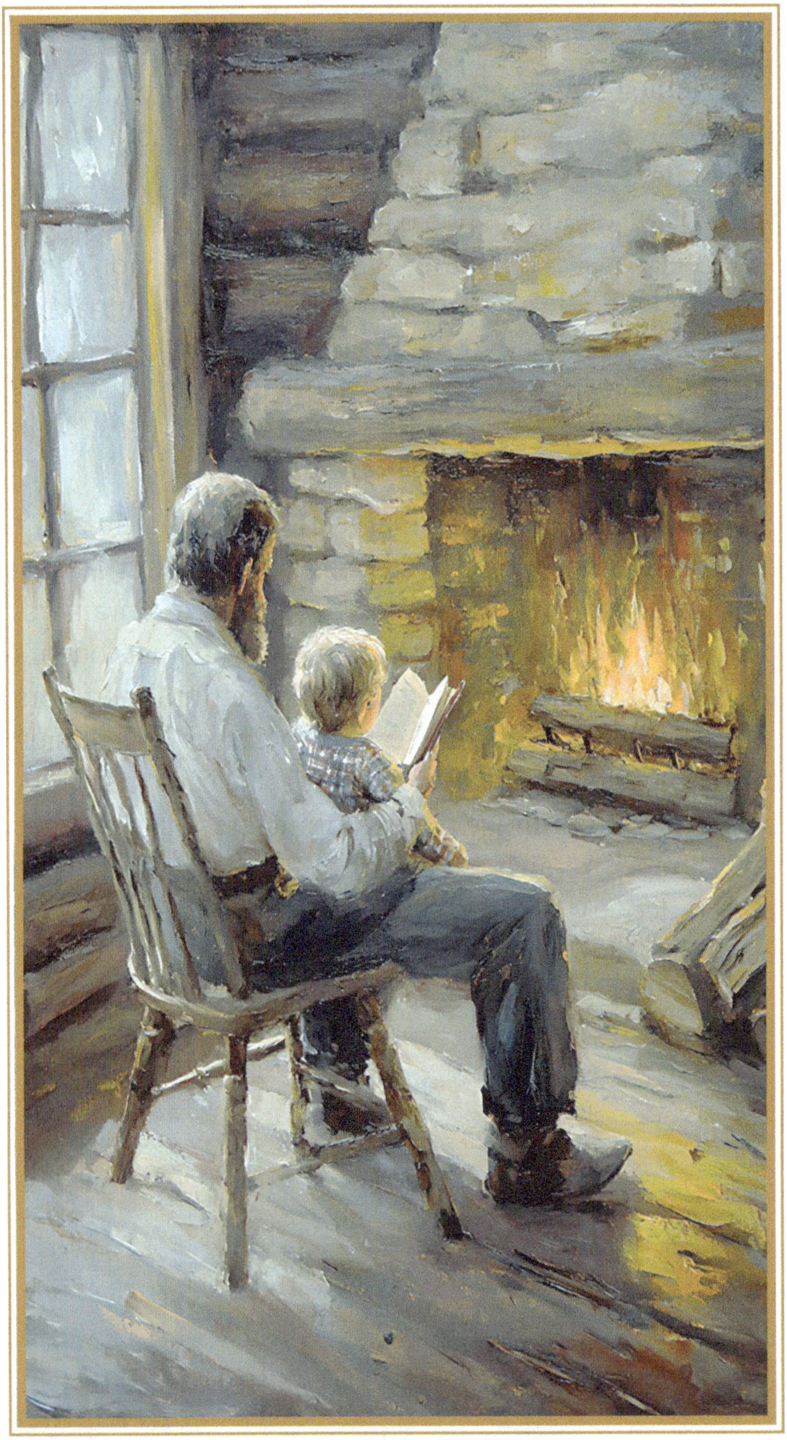

FIRE MANAGEMENT

Fire is a constant companion on the frontier, and understanding its management is essential for every pioneer. It provides warmth, food, and protection, but must be handled with skill and caution.

Mastering the art of building, maintaining, and controlling fire will be central to your survival here. You must know how to use different types of wood, kindle a flame in any weather, and, most importantly, safeguard your home and land from the ever-present danger of a fire getting out of control.

Fire Building

You will need to know how to build a proper fire daily. Fire serves not only for cooking your meals and warming your home but also for protection against the wild creatures that roam these woods.

TYPES OF FIRES AND THEIR USES

COOKING FIRES

The fire built for cooking should be small and manageable to off steady heat without wasting wood. Hardwood, such as oak or hickory, is ideal for these fires because it burns long and evenly. Fires for cooking are often made in a hearth or outdoors, with pots and pans hung over the flames or placed on grates to control the temperature of the food inside the vessel.

HEATING FIRES

During the long, cold winters, your hearth will need a larger, more enduring fire. To achieve this, you'll want to start with softwood kindling like pine or birch, which lights quickly, and then add hardwood logs to keep the fire going throughout the night. A well-tended fire in a stove or fireplace will heat your home, but it must be fed continuously in the harshest months to keep the chill at bay.

SIGNAL AND PROTECTIVE FIRES

A smoky fire made with damp or green wood is best for signaling over long distances or warning of danger. Burning a small fire throughout the night will help ward off wild animals if you're camping or out in the wilderness.

SELECTING AND PREPARING FIREWOOD

UNDERSTANDING WOOD TYPES

Understanding your wood is vital. Hardwoods like oak, maple, and hickory are your best choices for long-lasting heat. These woods burn hot and slow, with little smoke. Softwoods such as pine or fir are good for starting a fire but burn out too quickly for extended use.

SEASONING WOOD

Cut your firewood well in advance and allow it to dry for several months. Fresh from the tree, green wood is too wet to burn well and will produce smoke without much heat. Stack your wood in a dry, airy place so it can season appropriately before the winter comes.

CUTTING AND SPLITTING WOOD

Once your logs are cut to the correct length, they must be split to fit into your stove or hearth. A sharp axe or maul will help you split the wood, and it dries faster once split, making it ready for use when the cold sets in.

FIRE STARTING TECHNIQUES

Starting a fire is an art. You may need flint and steel to strike a spark into some fuel, such as dry leaves or bark. Once you have a spark, the small flame is carefully nurtured with kindling until it is strong enough to burn logs

USING FLINT AND STEEL

This is the most common fire-starting method, requiring a steady hand and patience. You strike the flint to create sparks, aiming them at fuel, and with luck, the tinder catches. Once it does, you must coax it into a flame with small twigs and gradually more significant pieces of wood.

TINDER AND KINDLING

Tinder, like birch bark or dry grass, catches fire quickly. Once the fuel is alight, add kindling—small, dry twigs or sticks—to get the fire going.

FIRE PISTONS AND BOW DRILLS

You may sometimes rely on older methods to kindle a flame without flint and steel, such as the fire piston or the bow drill. Though more laborious, these methods can prove effective when other tools are scarce.

FIRE PISTONS

A fire piston works by using the force of air compression to ignite a small piece of fuel. The piston is quickly forced into a tightly fitting cylinder, creating enough pressure and heat to ignite the fuel placed at the end. Once the ember is formed, it must be carefully transferred to your kindling to grow into a flame. Though it requires practice, this tool is highly valued for its efficiency in varying conditions.

BOW DRILLS

The bow drill is another ancient method, requiring only wood and determination. A wooden spindle is spun rapidly against a fireboard using a bow, creating friction and eventually enough heat to form an ember. This glowing ember can then be nurtured into a flame by adding it to a nest of dry tinder. Though it demands patience and strength, the bow drill will serve you well if no other means are available.

Both methods require skill and perseverance but offer reliable alternatives when more modern fire-starting tools are unavailable. In the wilderness, mastering these techniques can make the difference between a cold night and a warm fire.

Fire Safety

While fire is a vital tool, it also poses significant risks. Understanding fire safety is crucial for preventing accidents and managing emergencies, especially in an environment where homes and forests are highly flammable.

PREVENTING HOUSE FIRES

Your fireplace must be built of stone or brick to withstand the high temperatures of a fire. The chimney must be tall enough to draw smoke away from the house. It's wise to inspect and clean it regularly to prevent soot buildup, which could cause a fire

BUILDING FIREPLACES AND CHIMNEYS

Properly constructing fireplaces and chimneys is essential to venting smoke safely and preventing house fires. Fireplaces are typically built with stone or brick, which can withstand high temperatures. Chimneys must be tall enough to create a strong draft, pulling smoke up and out of the home while burning the fire efficiently. Regular maintenance, such as cleaning out soot and creosote, is necessary to prevent chimney fires, a common cause of house fires.

FIREPROOFING MEASURES

Settlers often took additional measures to fireproof homes, especially in kitchens and near stoves. Hearths are built with stone or brick, and wooden walls are sometimes protected with metal sheets or plaster. Keeping flammable materials like curtains, wooden furniture, and dry goods away from open flames is a crucial safety practice. In addition, maintaining a bucket of water or sand nearby is a standard precaution in case the fire spreads beyond the hearth.

SAFE STORAGE OF FIREWOOD

Firewood must be stored safely in the home to prevent accidental ignition. Settlers typically stack wood in a dry, covered area away from open flames, sparks, or the home's exterior walls. Properly stacked wood also reduces the risk of pest infestations and allows air to circulate, keeping the wood dry and ready for burning.

PREVENTING AND CONTROLLING WILDFIRES

CLEARING BRUSH AND FIREBREAKS

The first line of defense against wildfires is to keep your land clear of brush, dead leaves, and other materials that can easily catch fire. By creating firebreaks—those strips of bare land between your homestead and the surrounding woods or fields—you can stop or slow the spread of any blaze that may approach. These firebreaks act as barriers, allowing you to fight the fire before it reaches your crops or dwelling. To reduce the risk, maintain these cleared paths regularly, especially in dry weather.

CAMPFIRE SAFETY

Do so safely when building a campfire, whether for cooking or warmth. Clear away all flammable material around the fire and encircle it with stones or dirt to contain the flames. Never leave the fire unattended; ensure it is fully extinguished when you're finished. Douse the fire with water and stir the ashes, ensuring no embers are smoldering, for even the slightest spark can ignite a wildfire. It is best to avoid lighting a fire during dry spells unless necessary.

FIREFIGHTING TECHNIQUES

If a wildfire does break out, time is of the essence, and every able body will be needed. Beating out the flames with wet blankets or branches is a common way to snuff out smaller fires. For more enormous blazes, digging trenches or creating new firebreaks can help to contain the fire's spread. Some settlers have used controlled burns, deliberately setting fire to the land ahead of the wildfire to burn off the fuel in its path. This method, though risky, can be effective when appropriately managed. Remember, when fire strikes, the swift and coordinated efforts of the community often make a difference.

EMERGENCY PREPAREDNESS

FIRE DRILLS AND EVACUATION PLANS

Though we don't have formal fire drills like in later times, every family should have a clear plan for what to do in the event of a house fire. It's wise to decide how to evacuate the house, which doors or windows to use, and where the family will gather once outside. Keep your most important belongings—documents, money, and valuables—within reach so they can be grabbed quickly if you need to swiftly exit.

BUCKET BRIGADES

When a fire breaks out, the neighbors and the community unite to fight it. Without modern equipment, we rely on bucket brigades. This involves forming a line of people from the nearest well or water source to the fire, passing buckets to douse the flames. It's a time-honored method that depends on everyone's cooperation. When the alarm is raised, everyone able-bodied must respond, as these brigades are often the only way to prevent a fire from spreading and consuming all in its path.

MANAGING AND MAINTAINING FIRE TOOLS

Fire Tongs, Shovels, and Pokers

Proper tools and maintenance are essential for building and controlling fires, whether for daily use or emergencies.

USING FIRE TOOLS

You will need tongs, shovels, and pokers to safely tend to your fires. Fire tongs are used to move and adjust burning logs without risking getting too close to the flames. A shovel allows you to clear away ashes and embers, while a poker is necessary for stirring the fire and keeping it burning evenly. These tools are typically forged from iron to endure the heat.

MAINTAINING TOOLS

To ensure your fire tools serve you well, they must be adequately maintained. After each use, clean them to remove soot and ash, which can lead to rust. Store them in a dry place, and if you notice any damage, such as a bent poker or a loose handle, repair it quickly. A well-kept tool is vital for both safety and efficiency in managing your fires

Fire Starters and Fuel

STOCKING KINDLING AND TINDER

To make fire-starting easier, you'll need to keep a steady supply of both kindling and fuel close at hand. Dry twigs, pine needles, and bark work well as kindling, helping to catch the flame and build up your fire. For fuel, you might use dried grass, moss, or wood shavings—light, dry materials that ignite easily. It's wise to store these in a dry place, perhaps near your hearth, so they're always available when needed.

MAINTAINING FIRE STARTERS

Whether you rely on flint and steel or more primitive means like a bow drill, keeping your fire-starting tools in good order is vital. Flint should be kept dry and free from cracks, while your steel needs protection from rust. Many settlers carry their fire-starting materials in a small, waterproof pouch to shield them from moisture. In this way, you'll ensure that whenever you need to light a fire, your tools are in prime condition and ready for use.

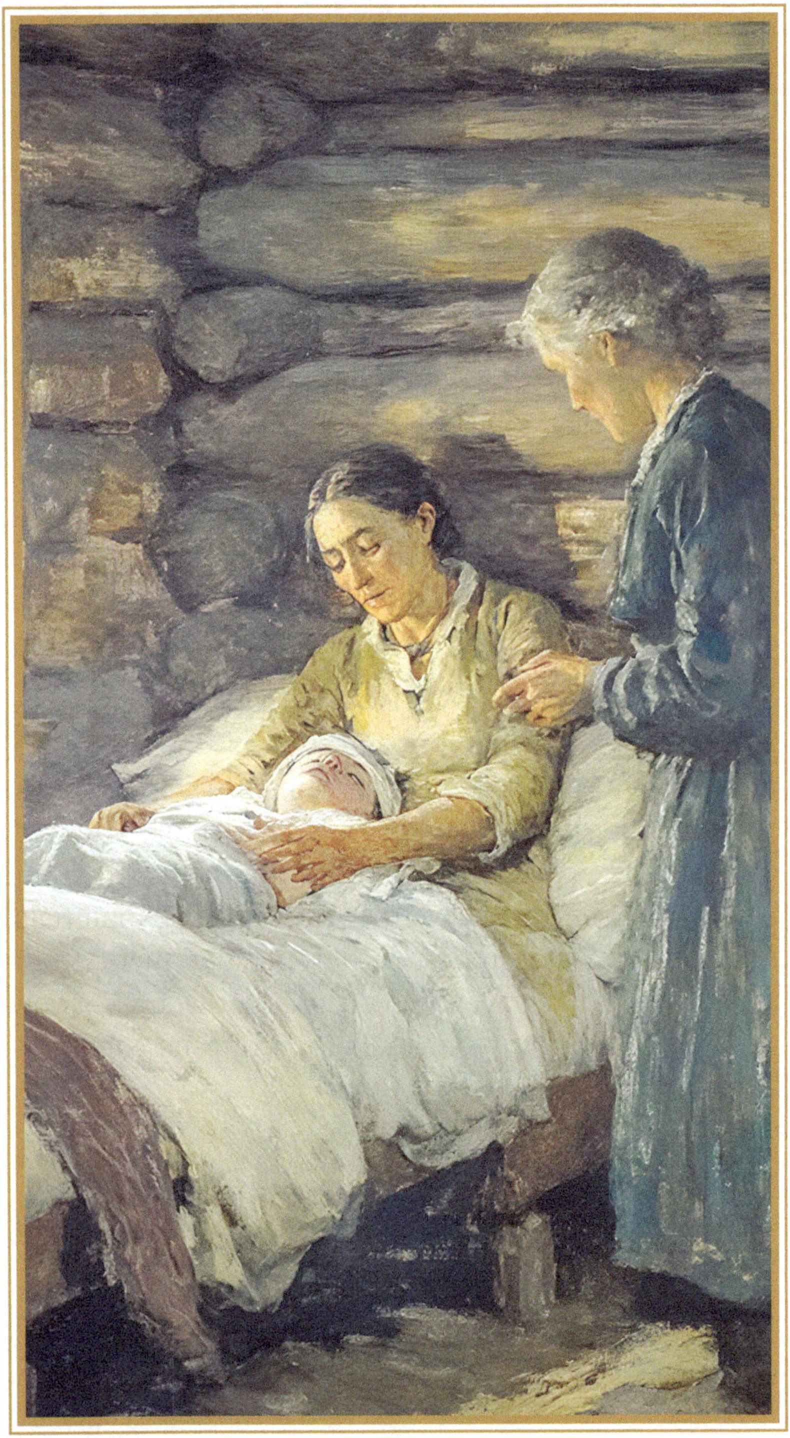

COMMON AILMENTS AND CAUSES OF DEATH

When embarking upon life in these wild and untamed lands, it is vital that you be well-acquainted with the means to tend to injuries, burns, common ailments, and the many dangers that accompany frontier life. With no doctor nearby and often little aid to be had, settlers must equip themselves with the knowledge of first aid, the ability to assist with childbirth, and the care of infants, for their very survival may depend upon it.

Common Ailments

Ague and Fever (Malaria)

"Ague and Fever" is an old term commonly used to describe what is now understood as malaria. It can be debilitating and sometimes fatal, especially in areas where malaria is endemic. The disease influences settlement patterns, health practices, and daily life, particularly in regions near wetlands and rivers where mosquitoes are abundant.

AGUE

"Ague" refers specifically to the recurring chills, shivering, and sweating that characterize malaria.

These symptoms typically occur in a cyclical pattern, often coinciding with the release of parasites into the bloodstream during the malaria infection cycle.

The age is marked by sudden onset chills, shaking, and coldness, followed by a fever and then a sweating period. These symptoms often repeat every few days, depending on the type of malaria parasite causing the infection.

FEVER

The "Fever" part of "Ague and Fever" refers to the high temperature accompanying the chills and sweating. This fever is usually intense and can last several hours before subsiding, only to return with the next cycle of chills.

The fever typically follows the chills and can be accompanied by headaches, muscle pain, fatigue, and a general feeling of illness. This cycle of chills, fever, and sweating can leave individuals feeling very weak.

Malaria is caused by parasites of the genus Plasmodium, transmitted to humans through the bites of infected Anopheles mosquitoes. The term "Ague and Fever" was coined before discovering the parasitic cause of malaria and the role of mosquitoes in its transmission.

Malaria is more widespread in temperate regions, including parts of North America like Orleans County, due to the presence of mosquito habitats. Wetlands, rivers, and areas with stagnant water are common breeding grounds for mosquitoes, contributing to the spread of the disease.

Treatments are largely based on herbal remedies, such as quinine derived from the cinchona tree's bark, which is used to reduce the severity of symptoms.

Smallpox

Smallpox is a highly contagious and often deadly viral disease characterized by fever, body aches, and a distinctive rash that turns into pus-filled sores. Survivors are usually left with severe scarring. Smallpox is a serious threat, leading to widespread illness and death.

Smallpox outbreaks are devastating, especially among Native American populations, who have no prior immunity to the disease brought by European settlers. Smallpox epidemics can decimate entire communities.

EDITOR'S NOTE: *The introduction of the smallpox vaccine in the early 19th century began to reduce the impact of the disease.*

Cholera

Cholera is a bacterial infection caused by Vibrio cholerae, which leads to severe diarrhea and dehydration. It is spread through contaminated water or food.

Cholera epidemics were common in the 19th century, particularly in areas with poor sanitation and contaminated water supplies. In frontier settlements, where sanitation infrastructure is rudimentary, cholera can spread rapidly, leading to high mortality rates. The disease often strikes during the summer months and can wipe out entire families or communities.

Tuberculosis (Consumption)

Tuberculosis, also known as "consumption" in this era, is a bacterial infection caused by Mycobacterium tuberculosis. It primarily affects the lungs, leading to a chronic cough, chest pain, fever, night sweats, and weight loss.

Tuberculosis was a leading cause of death in the 19th century. The disease is highly contagious and spreads through airborne droplets when an infected person coughs or sneezes. Tuberculosis can linger for years, slowly debilitating the affected person. Poor living conditions, malnutrition, and close quarters in frontier communities contribute to the spread of the disease.

Dysentery

Dysentery is an intestinal infection that causes severe diarrhea with blood and mucus. It is usually caused by bacteria, such as Shigella or amoebas, and is spread through contaminated water or food.

Dysentery is a common and often deadly illness, particularly in areas with poor sanitation. Outbreaks are frequent during warm months when water sources are more likely to become contaminated. Both Native Americans and settlers are vulnerable to dysentery, which can cause rapid dehydration and death, especially in children and the elderly.

Typhoid Fever

Typhoid fever is a bacterial infection caused by Salmonella typhi. It is spread through contaminated food and water and is characterized by prolonged fever, weakness, abdominal pain, and sometimes a rash.

Typhoid fever is a significant health concern in the 18th and 19th centuries, particularly in crowded or unsanitary conditions. Settlers often face typhoid outbreaks due to the lack of clean water and proper waste disposal. The disease can incapacitate individuals for weeks and is frequently fatal without appropriate treatment.

Rheumatism

Rheumatism is a term used to describe various painful conditions affecting the joints and muscles, including arthritis. Symptoms include chronic pain, stiffness, and swelling in the joints.

Rheumatism is a common affliction among settlers due to the hard physical labor and exposure to harsh weather conditions. The damp, cold environment of Orleans County can exacerbate symptoms. Without effective treatments, individuals with rheumatism often live with chronic pain, which can limit their ability to work.

Malnutrition and Scurvy

Malnutrition, including specific nutrient deficiencies like scurvy (caused by a lack of vitamin C), is a common issue, especially during the winter when fresh produce is scarce. Scurvy leads to symptoms such as weakness, swollen and bleeding gums, and skin issues.

Malnutrition is a significant problem for settlers, particularly during the early years of settlement when food supplies are limited, and preservation methods are rudimentary. Scurvy is particularly common when fresh fruits and vegetables are unavailable during long winters. Native Americans, who have more knowledge of local food sources, are less affected by scurvy but can still suffer from malnutrition in difficult times.

Pneumonia

Pneumonia is an infection of the lungs that bacteria, viruses, or fungi can cause. Symptoms include cough, fever, chest pain, and difficulty breathing.

Pneumonia is a common cause of death, particularly in the winter months when cold weather and weakened immune systems make individuals more susceptible. Both Native Americans and settlers face high mortality rates from pneumonia, especially in the absence of effective antibiotics or treatments.

Measles

Measles is a highly contagious viral disease characterized by fever, cough, runny nose, inflamed eyes, and a red, blotchy skin rash.

Measles is a significant threat to Native American populations, who have little immunity to European diseases. Outbreaks can quickly spread through communities, causing high mortality rates, especially among children. Settlers also face measles outbreaks, which can be deadly, particularly for the young and vulnerable.

Whooping Cough
(Pertussis)

Whooping cough is a bacterial infection that causes severe coughing fits, followed by a "whooping" sound when the person breathes in. It primarily affects children.

Whooping cough is a significant cause of illness and death among children in the 18th and 19th centuries. The lack of vaccines and effective treatments meant that outbreaks can be deadly, particularly in crowded frontier settlements. The disease is highly contagious and can spread rapidly through families and communities.

Influenza
(The Flu)

Influenza is a viral infection that affects the respiratory system, causing fever, body aches, sore throat, and cough. Influenza outbreaks can be highly contagious and spread rapidly through communities.

Influenza outbreaks are common and often deadly, particularly during the winter months. Both Native Americans and settlers are vulnerable to the flu, which can lead to severe complications, especially in the absence of modern medical care. Influenza is particularly dangerous for the elderly, young children, and those with weakened immune systems.

Common Causes of Death

Several causes of death common in the 18th and 19th centuries are relatively easy to manage or prevent with modern medical knowledge and technology.

Childbirth Complications

Childbirth is a leading cause of death for women in the 18th and 19th centuries. Complications such as bleeding, infection (puerperal fever), and obstructed labor are common and often fatal due to the lack of adequate medical interventions and the absence of antibiotics.

EDITOR'S NOTE: *Modern prenatal care, sterile delivery practices, and access to emergency medical interventions like cesarean sections and antibiotics have significantly reduced the maternal mortality rate. Deaths from childbirth complications are now rare in developed countries.*

Infections
(Bacterial and Viral)

Infections like strep throat, pneumonia, and skin infections can quickly become life-threatening due to ineffective treatments. Sepsis, a severe response to infection, is often fatal.

EDITOR'S NOTE: *The advent of antibiotics, vaccinations, and improved hygiene practices have dramatically reduced infection deaths. Once fatal conditions, like strep throat or a minor wound infection, can be easily treated with antibiotics.*

Injuries and Trauma

Injuries from accidents falls, or animal attacks can lead to death, particularly if they result in severe bleeding, infection, or bone fractures. Lack of proper medical care and sanitation often means that even minor injuries can become deadly.

EDITOR'S NOTE: Modern trauma care, including first aid, surgery, and antibiotics, allows for effective treatment of injuries that have been fatal in the past. Emergency medical services, advanced surgical techniques, and rehabilitation have greatly improved survival rates for trauma patients.

Malnutrition and Vitamin Deficiencies

Malnutrition and vitamin deficiencies, such as scurvy (vitamin C deficiency) and rickets (vitamin D deficiency), are common and can lead to death, especially during long winters when fresh food is scarce. Poor diet and lack of nutrition knowledge exacerbated these issues.

EDITOR'S NOTE: With a better understanding of nutrition vitamin deficiencies are rare in most parts of the world.

Diarrheal Diseases

Diarrheal diseases, often caused by contaminated water or food, are a significant cause of death, especially among children. Dehydration and electrolyte imbalances from prolonged diarrhea can be fatal.

EDITOR'S NOTE: Modern sanitation practices, access to clean water, and oral rehydration therapy (a simple mixture of salt, sugar, and water) have greatly reduced deaths from diarrheal diseases. Antibiotics and antiparasitic medications also help treat the underlying infections.

Appendicitis

Appendicitis, or inflammation of the appendix, is often fatal if the appendix ruptures, leading to peritonitis (a severe abdominal infection). Without surgical intervention, the condition typically results in death.

EDITOR'S NOTE: Appendicitis is now routinely treated with surgery (appendectomy), and deaths from the condition are rare. Early diagnosis, access to surgical care, and antibiotics to prevent infection have made this once-deadly condition manageable.

Dental Infections

Dental infections, such as abscesses, can lead to severe pain, systemic infection (sepsis), and death if the infection spreads to the bloodstream or vital organs. Poor dental hygiene and ineffective dental care make these infections common.

EDITOR'S NOTE: Regular dental care, improved oral hygiene practices, and the availability of antibiotics make dental infections easy to treat. Root canals, extractions, and other dental procedures can prevent diseases from becoming life-threatening.

Heatstroke and Hypothermia

Exposure to extreme temperatures without adequate shelter or clothing can lead to heatstroke in summer or hypothermia in winter, both of which can be fatal. Settlers and Native Americans, particularly the elderly and young children, are vulnerable to extreme weather conditions.

EDITOR'S NOTE: Modern climate control, appropriate clothing, and improved shelter have made deaths from exposure much less common. Knowledge of first aid for heatstroke and hypothermia, along with access to emergency medical care, has dramatically reduced mortality from these causes.

Tetanus
(Lockjaw)

Tetanus is a bacterial infection that causes severe muscle spasms and can be fatal if it leads to respiratory failure. It is often contracted through wounds contaminated with soil or animal waste, making it a common risk for settlers working with tools or farming.

EDITOR'S NOTE: *The widespread use of the tetanus vaccine and proper wound care have made deaths from tetanus extremely rare.*

Influenza

Influenza (flu) is often deadly, particularly during pandemics. Without antiviral treatments or vaccines, the flu can lead to severe complications such as pneumonia, especially in vulnerable populations like the elderly and infants.

EDITOR'S NOTE: *Annual flu vaccines have reduced the severity and mortality of influenza. While still a concern, especially in specific populations, the flu is much more manageable.*

Parasites
(Worms and Lice)

Parasitic infections, including intestinal worms and lice, are common due to poor sanitation, close living conditions, and limited medical knowledge. These parasites can cause malnutrition, anemia, and other health problems that sometimes lead to death.

EDITOR'S NOTE: *Improved sanitation, personal hygiene, and the availability of antiparasitic medications have greatly reduced the incidence and impact of parasitic infections.*

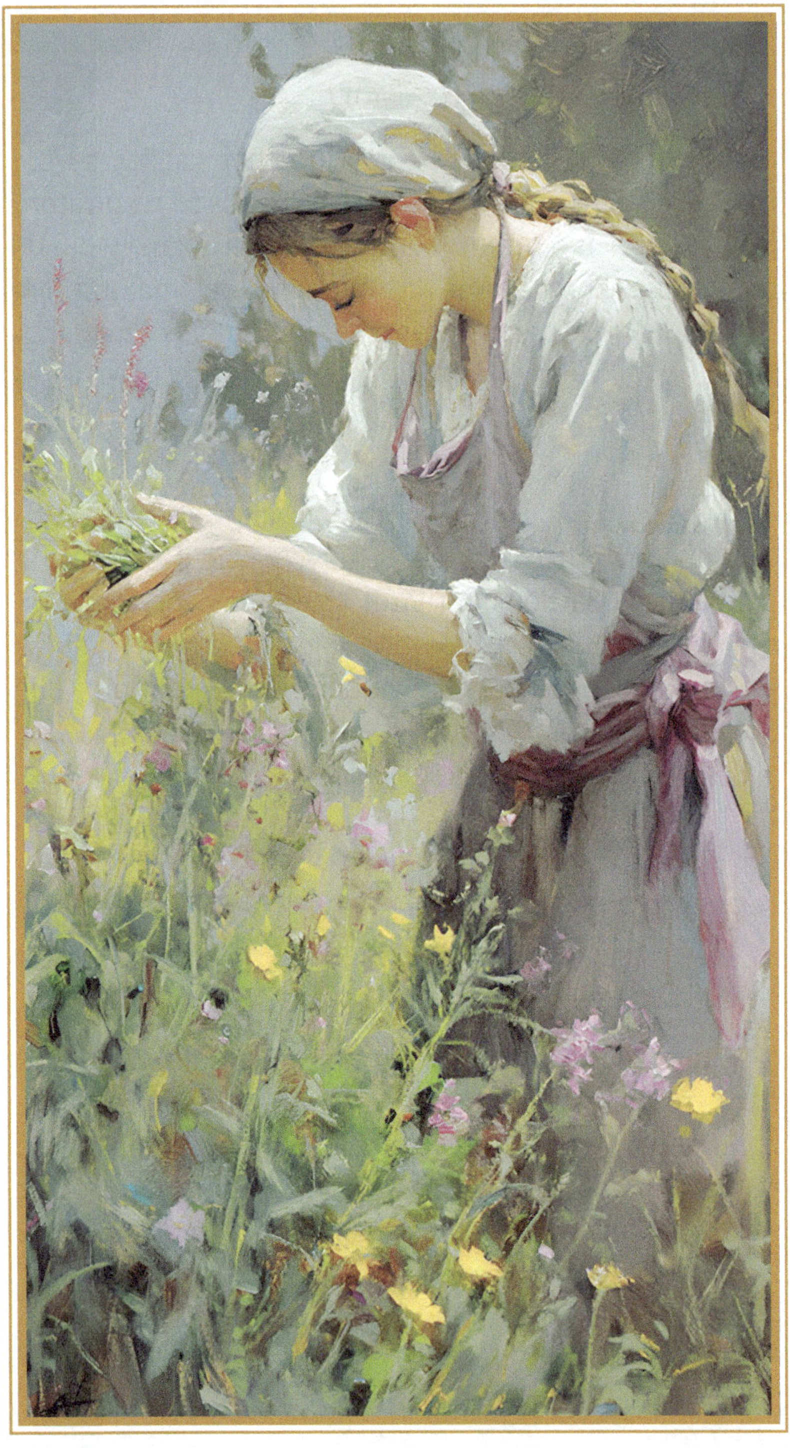

REMEDIES AND PIONEER HEALING PRACTICES

Access to formal medical care is often limited in the wilderness, making self-reliance in healthcare a necessity. Herbal remedies, derived from local plants and knowledge passed down through generations, are a crucial part of pioneer medicine.

Disclaimer: The information in this book is provided for educational purposes only. While every effort has been made to ensure the accuracy of the information, the authors and publishers are not responsible for any adverse effects that may result from using this information. Foraging for wild plants and mushrooms can be dangerous, and some species are highly toxic. It is essential to consult with an expert and exercise caution before consuming any wild plants or fungi.

Folk Medicine Home Remedies

Much of the medical knowledge of settlers is based on folk medicine, a blend of European traditions, and the local knowledge acquired from Native Americans. Home remedies are often passed down through families, with each generation adding to the collective understanding of effective treatments.

COLLABORATION WITH NATIVE AMERICANS

EXCHANGE OF KNOWLEDGE

The relationship between settlers and Native Americans is complex, but one area where collaboration is often mutually beneficial is the exchange of medicinal knowledge. Native Americans have a deep understanding of the medicinal properties of local plants, which they have gained through centuries of experience. Pioneers, eager to learn how to survive in a new environment, often seek out this knowledge, sometimes forming alliances or friendships that facilitate sharing herbal remedies.

NATIVE AMERICAN HEALING PRACTICES

Native American medicine is holistic, treating the mind, body, and spirit as interconnected. This approach resonated with pioneers who adopted certain practices and remedies that complemented their own. Commonly shared knowledge included using specific plants for teas, poultices, and salves, as well as techniques for preparing and applying these remedies.

COMMON MEDICINAL PLANTS AND THEIR USES

Settlers in Orleans County have access to a rich variety of medicinal plants. Identifying, harvesting, and preparing these plants is essential for treating various ailments.

Echinacea
(Echinacea purpurea)

Echinacea, or coneflower, is widely used to boost the immune system and treat infections, particularly respiratory infections and colds. The roots and leaves are commonly made into teas or tinctures.

To make an echinacea tea, settlers would steep the dried roots or leaves in hot water for several minutes. This tea is often consumed at the first sign of a cold or infection to help ward off illness. Echinacea tinctures are made by soaking the roots in alcohol for several weeks and then straining the liquid for use as needed.

Willow Bark
(Salix spp.)

Willow bark is known for its pain-relieving and anti-inflammatory properties, thanks to its high content of salicin, a precursor to modern aspirin. It is commonly used to treat headaches, fevers, and pain associated with injuries or rheumatism.

Willow bark is typically prepared as a tea, with the bark being boiled in water to extract the active compounds. The tea is consumed as needed to relieve pain or reduce fever. A poultice made from ground willow bark is sometimes applied directly to sore joints or muscles.

Goldenseal
(Hydrastis canadensis)

Goldenseal is a powerful medicinal herb that can be used as a natural antibiotic and immune booster. It is particularly effective for treating infections, digestive issues, and inflammation.

The roots of the goldenseal plant are dried and ground into a powder, which can be used in teas, tinctures, or capsules. Settlers often use goldenseal to treat respiratory infections, digestive problems, and skin conditions. It is also applied topically to wounds to prevent infection.

Peppermint
(Mentha piperita)

Peppermint is valued for its soothing effects on the digestive system and its ability to relieve headaches and respiratory issues. It is commonly used to treat indigestion, nausea, and colds.

Peppermint leaves are made into tea and consumed to ease digestive discomfort or help clear the sinuses during a cold. The essential oil of peppermint, extracted by distilling the leaves, is used in inhalations for respiratory relief or applied topically for headache relief.

Plantain
(Plantago major)

Plantain is a typical "weed" with potent healing properties. It is used to treat wounds, insect bites, and skin irritations. Plantain is also known for its ability to soothe digestive issues and respiratory conditions.

Fresh plantain leaves are often crushed and applied directly to wounds, insect bites, or rashes to reduce inflammation and promote healing. Plantain leaves can be brewed into tea to treat coughs, colds, and digestive problems. Plantain is also used in salves and ointments for its soothing effects on the skin.

Elderberry
(Sambucus nigra)

Elderberries are often cooked and made into syrups, consumed to prevent or shorten the duration of colds and flu. The flowers are used to make teas or infusions that help alleviate symptoms of respiratory infections and fever. Elderberry is also known for its antioxidant properties, which support overall health.

Valerian
(Valeriana officinalis)

Valerian is known for its calming effects and is commonly used as a natural remedy for anxiety, insomnia, and nervousness. It is also used to relieve pain and muscle tension.

The valerian plant's roots are dried and made into teas or tinctures. Valerian tea is consumed before bedtime to promote restful sleep or during the day to calm anxiety. The tincture is often taken in small doses to relieve stress or muscle pain. Valerian is also used in bath preparations for its soothing effects.

Preparing and Using Herbal Remedies

The effectiveness of herbal remedies depended not only on the plants themselves but also on the methods used to prepare and apply them. Settlers must know various techniques to make the most of the medicinal properties of their harvest plants.

HARVESTING AND DRYING HERBS

TIMING OF HARVEST

The timing of harvest is crucial for ensuring that herbs retain maximum potency. Leaves are typically harvested in the morning after the dew has dried, while roots are often dug up in the fall when the plant's energy is concentrated underground. Flowers are picked at peak bloom, and bark is harvested in early spring or late fall when sap flows lower.

Disclaimer: The information provided herein is for educational purposes only. Foraging for wild plants and mushrooms can be perilous, as some species are highly toxic. It is essential to seek guidance from an expert and exercise caution before consuming wild plants or fungi.

DRYING METHODS

After harvesting, herbs are usually dried to preserve them for later use. This is done by hanging bundles of herbs in a warm, dry, and well-ventilated area, away from direct sunlight. Some settlers also used drying racks or screens to spread the herbs, ensuring even drying. Properly dried herbs retained color and aroma, which indicated that medicinal properties are preserved.

Teas and Infusions

MAKING HERBAL TEAS

Herbal teas, or infusions, are one of the simplest and most common ways to use medicinal plants. To make an herbal tea, settlers steeped the dried or fresh herb in hot water for several minutes, allowing the beneficial compounds to dissolve into the liquid. Teas are typically consumed warmly and treat various conditions, from colds and fevers to digestive issues and anxiety.

INFUSIONS FOR EXTERNAL USE

In addition to drinking, herbal infusions are sometimes used externally as washes or compresses. For example, an infusion of chamomile or calendula might be applied to the skin to soothe irritations or wounds. These infusions are made by steeping the herbs in boiling water, then straining and cooling the liquid before applying it to the affected area.

Tinctures and Extracts

ALCOHOL BASED TINCTURES

Tinctures are concentrated herbal extracts from soaking herbs in alcohol or vinegar for several weeks. This process extracts the active compounds from the herbs, creating a potent liquid that can be stored for long periods. Tinctures are typically taken in small doses, diluted in water or tea, and are especially useful for treating chronic conditions or when a more potent remedy is needed.

GLYCERIN AND VINEGAR EXTRACTS

For those who prefer to avoid alcohol, glycerin or vinegar can be used as a base for tinctures. Glycerin extracts are viral for children or those sensitive to alcohol, as they are sweeter and gentler. Vinegar-based tinctures are often used for digestive issues, as vinegar itself has health benefits and helps preserve the extract.

Poultices and Compresses

APPLYING POULTICES

Poultices are a common method for treating wounds, infections, and inflammations. A poultice is made by crushing or grinding fresh herbs into a paste and applying it directly to the skin, usually on a cloth or bandage to keep it in place. The herbs in the poultice would draw out infection, reduce inflammation, and promote healing. Common poultice ingredients include comfrey, plantain, and yarrow.

HOT AND COLD COMPRESSES

Compresses are cloths soaked in herbal infusions and applied to the body to relieve pain, reduce fever, or soothe sore muscles. Hot compresses are often used for muscle aches, while cold compresses help reduce swelling and inflammation. The herbs chosen for compresses varied depending on the treatment condition—chamomile and lavender for relaxation, or mint and eucalyptus for cooling and stimulating effects.

Salves and Ointments

MAKING HERBAL SALVES

Salves and ointments are made by infusing herbs into oils, then mixed with beeswax to create a semisolid product that can be applied to the skin. These preparations treat cuts, burns, rashes, and other skin conditions. Calendula, comfrey, and St. John's wort are popular herbs for making healing salves.

APPLICATION AND STORAGE

Herbal salves are applied directly to the affected area and often covered with a bandage to protect the skin and allow the herbs to work more effectively. These salves are stored in small jars or tins and can last several months if kept in a cool, dark place.

Understanding the Risks and Limitations of Herbal Medicine

While herbal remedies are essential to pioneer healthcare, they are not without risks. Settlers need to understand the limitations of herbal medicine and be cautious in its use.

POTENTIAL SIDE EFFECTS AND TOXICITY

KNOWING SAFE DOSAGES

One of the main challenges in using herbal remedies is determining the correct dosage. While most herbs are safe in moderate amounts, some can be toxic if misused. For example, plants like foxglove (Digitalis purpurea) have powerful medicinal properties but are highly toxic in large doses. Settlers rely on traditional knowledge, experience, and caution to avoid poisoning.

ALLERGIC REACTIONS

Some individuals are allergic to certain herbs, and using these plants can cause adverse reactions. Settlers have to be aware of potential allergies and be prepared to treat symptoms like rashes, swelling, or difficulty breathing if they occur. In some cases, these reactions can be severe and require immediate attention.

INTERACTION WITH OTHER TREATMENTS

HERBS AND MEDICATIONS

As formal medical practices became more available, settlers sometimes combined herbal remedies with conventional treatments. However, this can lead to interactions between herbs and medications, potentially reducing the effectiveness of either or causing harmful side effects. Settlers need to be aware of these risks, mainly if they use herbs alongside treatments obtained from a doctor.

COMBINING HERBS

Some herbs have synergistic effects when used together, enhancing each other's benefits. However, others can counteract each other or cause unwanted side effects when combined. Settlers often experimented with different combinations of herbs but relied on established recipes and traditional knowledge to guide practices.

Disclaimer: The information provided herein is for educational purposes only. While every effort has been made to ensure accuracy, the authors are not responsible for any adverse effects from using this information. Foraging for wild plants and mushrooms can be perilous, as some species are highly toxic. It is essential to seek guidance from an expert and exercise caution before consuming wild plants or fungi. The authors assume no liability for any illness, injury, or loss from applying this knowledge.

RECOGNIZING THE LIMITS OF HERBAL MEDICINE

SERIOUS ILLNESSES AND INJURIES

While herbal remedies are effective for many common ailments, they have limitations, especially regarding serious illnesses or injuries. Conditions like broken bones, severe infections, or chronic diseases often require more intensive treatment than herbs alone can provide. In such cases, settlers sought out professional medical care when possible or turned to other methods, such as surgery or the use of more robust, sometimes dangerous, home remedies like mercury or opium.

THE ROLE OF EXPERIENCE

Herbal medicine is as much an art as a science, and the effectiveness of treatments often depends on the knowledge and experience of the person administering them. Experienced herbalists, whether among the pioneer settlers or Native Americans, are highly valued in communities for diagnosing conditions and recommending appropriate remedies.

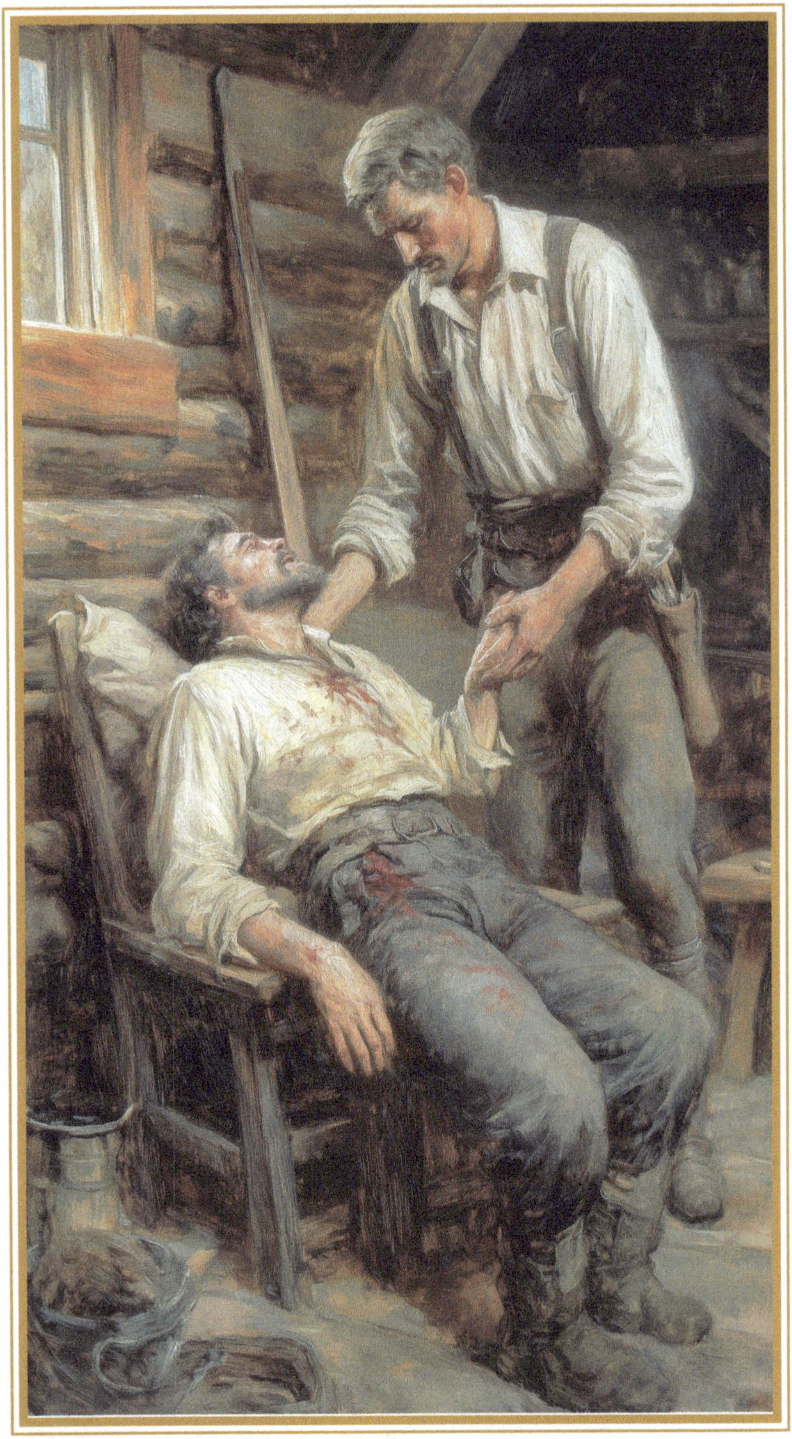

FIRST AID AND EMERGENCY CARE

In this wild and untamed land, far removed from the ready aid of doctors and hospitals, you must be prepared to handle health emergencies independently. The knowledge of first aid and emergency care is not a mere convenience—it is a necessity for survival. As a settler in Orleans County, you will face injuries, burns, and illnesses, and must also be ready to manage childbirth and care for infants. These basic medical skills often mean the difference between life and death for you and your family.

Treating Injuries

Injuries are a part of life in this rugged wilderness. Whether from an accident with an axe, a fall from a horse, or a mishap with farming tools, you must be prepared to treat anything from minor scrapes to severe wounds.

WOUND CARE

CLEANING AND DISINFECTING WOUNDS

The first task in treating a wound is cleaning it thoroughly, for infection is dangerous in these parts. Use boiled water, if possible, or herbal infusions such as yarrow or calendula tea to wash away dirt and debris. Should you have spirits or alcohol on hand, it may serve as a disinfectant. Once the wound is cleansed, dry it carefully and cover it with a clean cloth or bandage to keep it protected.

USING POULTICES AND SALVES

After the wound is clean, apply a poultice made from healing herbs. Plantain, comfrey, or goldenseal are common choices, as they help to draw out infection and ease inflammation. Once the poultice is applied, wrap the wound with a cloth bandage to keep it clean and promote healing.

STITCHES AND SUTURES

Stitching the wound closed may be necessary for deeper cuts that will not heal independently. Settlers often use a needle and thread, sewing the wound shut with steady hands. If proper medical sutures are not available, you may need to improvise with materials on hand. However, you must not cause further harm— this is delicate work, requiring knowing how to stitch the wound properly to prevent infection and speed recovery.

DEALING WITH BROKEN BONES

On the frontier, a broken bone is no small matter and must be dealt with quickly and with care to avoid long-lasting consequences. In such situations, swift and calm action can make the difference between life and death, and knowing how to treat these injuries is a vital skill for every pioneer.

SPLINTING FRACTURES

When a bone is broken, the first task is immobilizing the injured limb to prevent further harm. You must craft a splint from readily available materials—wooden sticks, branches, or even a rolled-up blanket can suffice. Secure the splint firmly to the limb using strips of cloth, ensuring that the bone is held steady while it begins the long process of healing.

SETTING BONES

In more severe breaks, the bone may need to be returned to its proper place before splinting. This difficult and painful task requires skill and a steady hand. The bone must be carefully manipulated back into alignment. If done improperly, it can lead to deformity or lasting injury, so it is best to seek the help of someone with more experience if possible. However, you may need to handle such matters with only your resolve and knowledge in these remote parts.

HEALING AND REHABILITATION

Once the bone is splinted, the limb must remain immobilized for several weeks to give the bone time to knit back together. During this time, rest is of utmost importance. When the bone is sufficiently healed, gentle exercises should be introduced to restore strength and mobility, but care must be taken not to rush this process, lest the injury worsen.

TREATING BURNS

From Minor to Severe

In these rugged lands, burns are a frequent hazard, especially with open fires essential for cooking, heating, and blacksmithing. Here's how you should tend to burns, from the mild to the more severe.

First Degree Burns

COOLING THE BURN

For minor burns, such as those caused by brief contact with hot surfaces or steam, your first task is to cool the burn to ease the pain and prevent further damage. Use cool water or, if available, a soothing herbal infusion like chamomile or lavender. Take care not to apply ice, as the extreme cold could cause harm to the skin.

APPLYING SOOTHING OINTMENTS

Once the burn has been cooled, apply a gentle ointment to help it heal. If you have access to Aloe Vera, it is highly prized for its healing properties. If not, you may make a salve from beeswax, olive oil, and herbs such as calendula or comfrey. This will help keep the skin moist and shielded as it heals.

Second Degree Burns

TREATING BLISTERS

Second-degree burns, which cause blisters, require extra care. Never puncture the blisters, as this can invite infection. Instead, keep the area clean, and apply a mild herbal poultice or salve to ease the pain and speed healing. Cover the burn loosely with a clean bandage to protect it from dirt and further irritation.

PREVENTING INFECTION

With deeper burns, the threat of infection is high. It is vital to keep the area clean. Settlers often used mild antiseptics or natural remedies such as honey or goldenseal, known for their antibacterial properties, to keep infection at bay. If you notice increased redness, swelling, or pus, attend closely to the burn and apply additional remedies as needed.

Third Degree Burns

EMERGENCY CARE

The gravest burns, which char the skin and penetrate the deeper tissues, are life-threatening and require swift action. First, protect the burn by covering it with a clean cloth, not removing any clothing stuck to the skin. The main aim is to prevent shock and keep the burn covered while seeking further help.

MANAGING SHOCK

Burn victims are at high risk of shock, which can be fatal if not appropriately managed. Settlers would keep the victim warm and calm, ensuring they are lying down and elevating their legs if possible. Fluids are given to prevent dehydration, and efforts are made to keep the victim as comfortable as possible while waiting for help or preparing for a long recovery.

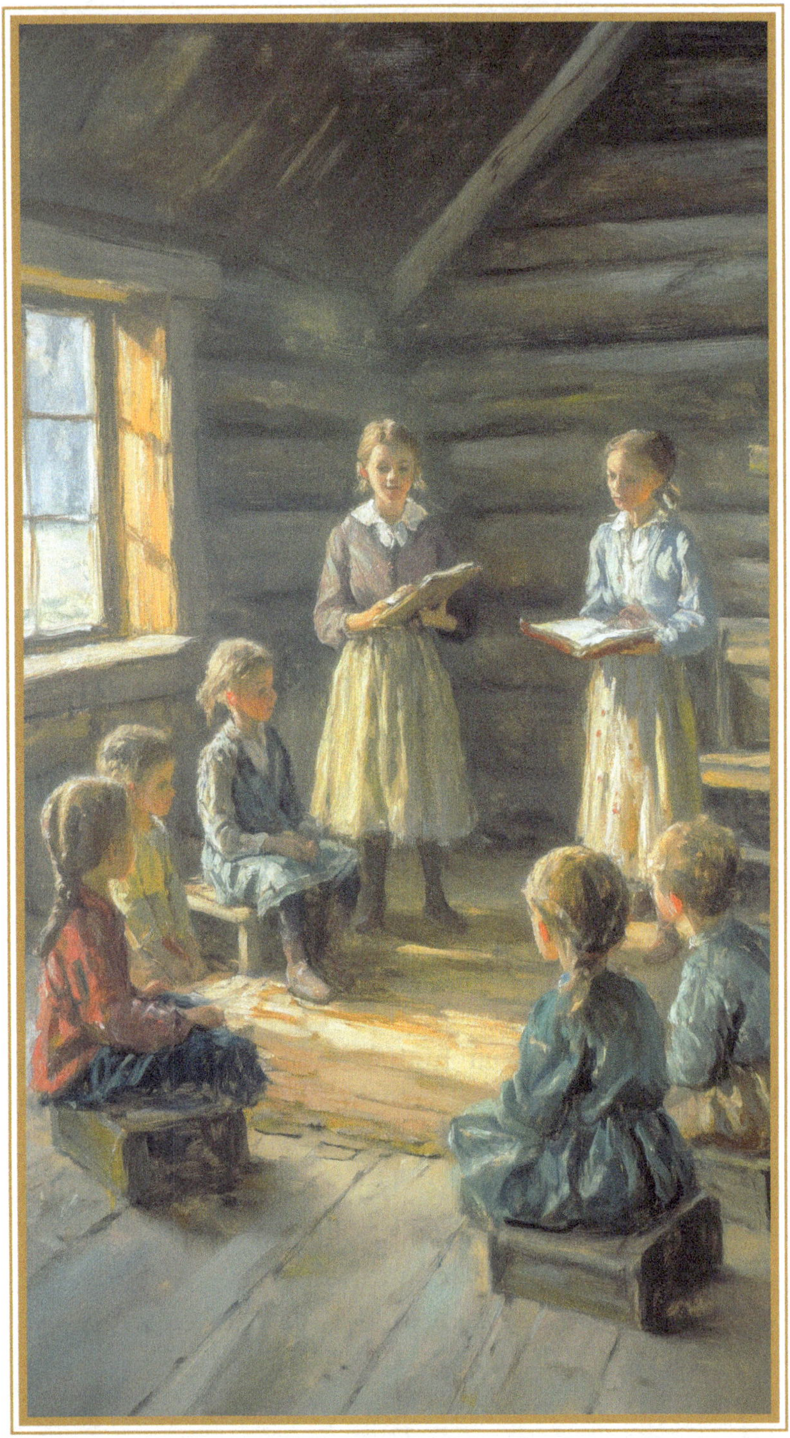

BUILDING A THRIVING COMMUNITY

Community success relies heavily on mutual aid, where families support each other in times of need and collaborate on common goals. From the very beginning, settlers must work together to establish essential institutions such as schools, churches, and local governance structures, which serve as the foundation of a stable society.

To continue growing into a thriving community members must collaborate with external entities, such as land offices, federal and state governments, and even private businesses.

The federal government plays a role in setting up key infrastructure, such as post offices and roads. Postal routes are established through coordination with the government to ensure regular communication, which is crucial for trade, connecting with distant family members, and receiving news.

Roads, bridges, and ferries may also be developed with the assistance of federal or state funds, though much of the labor is typically provided by the local community through cooperatives and mutual aid societies.

For larger projects like the building of churches, schools, or other public institutions, communities sometimes partner with outside organizations or religious institutions that provide support, funding, or leadership to guide the development of these essential services. These partnerships allow the community to create an organized, well-governed environment that can grow and prosper over time.

Those who collaborate with external entities often rise to positions of leadership within the community and may also accumulate wealth. By working closely with land offices, government representatives, and private businesses, these individuals gain access to valuable resources and opportunities. Whether it's securing key land grants, negotiating trade routes, or establishing vital infrastructure like post offices and roads, their involvement places them at the center of the community's development.

In many cases, those who navigate these relationships successfully become not only influential leaders but also prosperous landowners or traders. Their ability to manage external partnerships and bring in resources helps the community grow and often leads to personal financial gain through land acquisition, trade, or leadership roles in local governance. As the community expands, these individuals frequently assume prominent positions in decision-making, helping to guide the future of the settlement and securing a lasting legacy for themselves and their families.

Establishing Educational Institutions

As you settle your family in Orleans County, know that education will play a critical role in shaping your children's future. Many of your neighbors, like you, come from New England, where education is highly valued. These settlers, particularly those of Puritan descent, believe that teaching children to read and write is not just about learning, but also about their spiritual and civic duty. Ensuring your children are literate means they can fully participate in society, both in daily life and in their religious and moral growth.

Just as schools were quickly established in New England settlements, you'll find that your new community will work to build schools early on. This tradition goes back to laws like the 'Old Deluder Satan Law' of 1647, which emphasized the need for education to combat ignorance. As a pioneer, understanding that this commitment to education is part of your new life will help guide your family's success. The knowledge your children gain will enable them to thrive, not just spiritually, but also in the practical aspects of this new frontier, just as it has done for generations before.

BUILDING THE FIRST SCHOOLHOUSE

COMMUNITY EFFORT

As you begin to settle your family in Orleans County, the establishment of a schoolhouse will be one of the community's first priorities. Rest assured, the construction of this important building is a collaborative effort—your neighbors, like you, will contribute labor, materials, and funds to ensure it is built. The schoolhouse is typically a simple, one-room log or frame building, strategically located near the center of your community so that all families may easily access it.

DESIGN AND FEATURES

The schoolhouse itself may be modest, but it will serve as a vital cornerstone for your family's future. With benches or desks fashioned from roughhewn wood, a blackboard, and a wood-burning stove to provide warmth during the cold months, it will be a place of learning and community. Shared textbooks and natural light from the windows will assist the teacher in instructing the children, including yours, in reading, writing, and other essential skills.

SCHOOLING PRACTICES

ONE ROOM SCHOOLHOUSES

In these one-room schoolhouses, children of all ages, from your youngest to your oldest, will be taught together. A single teacher, often a young woman from the community, will guide them through lessons in reading, writing, arithmetic, and more. The school year is usually divided into two terms—one in the winter, when your older boys will be able to attend after the harvest, and another in the summer for the younger children. Though farm duties may sometimes call them away, your children will be encouraged to attend as often as possible.

The curriculum will likely focus on the basics such as reading (often from the Bible), writing, arithmetic, and moral instruction. Older students might learn more advanced subjects, depending on the teacher's expertise and the availability of resources.

THE ROLE OF THE SCHOOL IN THE COMMUNITY

The schoolhouse will serve not just as a place for learning but as the social heart of the community. Community meetings, social gatherings, and even church services may take place there. More importantly, it will prepare your children for life in this new land. Whether they grow up to manage their own farms, participate in local governance, or pursue further education, the schoolhouse will give them the foundation they need to thrive.

Establishing Religious Institutions

CHURCHES AS CENTERS OF FAITH AND COMMUNITY

As you establish your new life in Orleans County, you will find that a church is one of the first structures your community will look to build, often second only to homes. Much more than a place of worship, the church will serve as a center for spiritual guidance, moral instruction, and a gathering point for your neighbors. For you and your family, it will provide a sense of belonging and direction in these uncharted lands.

BUILDING AND MAINTAINING CHURCHES

Much like the schoolhouse, the church will be constructed through the collective efforts of your neighbors. You, along with others, will contribute materials, labor, and funds to see it built. It is likely to be a simple structure, functional rather than ornate, as the focus is on providing a space for worship and gathering. Sometimes, especially in smaller communities, the same building may serve as both a church and a schoolhouse until the population grows enough to warrant separate buildings.

DENOMINATIONS

At the beginning of a frontier settlement, there may not be the luxury of separate churches for each denomination. In those early days, everyone—regardless of their faith—worships together, sharing a common space for prayer and fellowship. As your community grows, you may see more denominations emerge, but in the meantime, unity and cooperation are essential.

The denomination of your church will often reflect the origins and beliefs of your fellow settlers. Methodist, Presbyterian, and Baptist traditions are common among pioneers, though others may be present. Regardless of denomination, your church plays a vital role in binding the community together through shared beliefs and values. It serves not only as a place of worship but also as a hub for social support, moral guidance, and a space where the whole community gathers, reinforcing bonds and strengthening the collective spirit..

RELIGIOUS PRACTICES

Sunday services will be a key event in your week, drawing together families from across the settlement for worship, prayer, and fellowship. For you, this gathering is more than a time of spiritual reflection—it is a chance to socialize, exchange news, and support one another. In more remote areas, your community may rely on a circuit rider, a traveling minister who serves several settlements. This minister will ensure your family's spiritual needs are met, even if a permanent clergyman is not yet available.

THE CHURCH AS A COMMUNITY ANCHOR

Beyond spiritual guidance, the church will offer moral instruction, serving as the place where disputes are mediated and community values are reinforced. During times of hardship, you can expect the congregation to come together to provide food, labor, or financial assistance to families in need.

The church will also be the backdrop for the most important milestones in your family's life—weddings, baptisms, and funerals. These events, shared with the entire congregation, will further cement the bonds of community and ensure your family's place in the growing settlement.

Establishing Local Governance

ESTABLISHING ORDER AND COOPERATION

As your settlement grows, you will soon find the need to establish formal governance to maintain order and cooperation among your fellow pioneers. Local governments must be formed to manage land, settle disputes, and oversee critical communal tasks such as road building and ensuring public safety. This organization ensures that your community runs smoothly and can prosper in the wilderness.

FORMATION OF TOWNSHIP AND COUNTY GOVERNMENTS

Once your community reaches a certain population size, a township may be established to handle local matters such as land records, taxation, and infrastructure. This township will be the cornerstone of your local governance, ensuring that essential services are managed effectively. County governments, overseeing larger areas, handle broader responsibilities, including law enforcement, courts, and public records, while coordinating efforts between different townships. They also represent the community's interests at the state level.

ELECTED OFFICIALS

You and your fellow settlers will elect township supervisors, clerks, and justices of the peace to enforce laws, collect taxes, and manage public funds. These positions are vital to ensuring the community's daily functioning. Elections typically take place at town meetings, where all eligible settlers can participate and have a voice in how their community is run.

LEGAL STRUCTURES AND COMMUNITY DECISION-MAKING

Town meetings will serve as the heart of decision-making in your community. These gatherings give every settler a chance to vote on important issues, such as road construction, school funding, and land use, making them a direct reflection of the democratic spirit. Disputes over land boundaries or community conduct will be mediated by justices of the peace, who blend common law with local customs to maintain peace and order.

PUBLIC WORKS

Your local government will also organize public works such as road and bridge construction, often relying on "work bees," where you and your neighbors contribute labor instead of taxes to complete essential projects. These efforts ensure the community thrives and remains connected with surrounding settlements.

Cooperatives and Mutual Aid Societies

On the frontier, cooperation among settlers is not just a convenience but a necessity for survival. As you settle into Orleans County, you'll quickly find that your success depends on mutual aid and support from your neighbors. Cooperatives and mutual aid societies will help organize collective tasks and ensure families receive assistance when they need it most.

BARN RAISING AND OTHER COMMUNAL WORK

One of the most significant examples of pioneer cooperation is barn raising. When your family or a neighbor needs to build or repair a barn, the entire community will gather to help. Each person is assigned a role based on their skills, from cutting timber to raising the frame. Barn raisings are not just workdays; they are social events often followed by a shared meal, reinforcing the bonds between families.

ROAD BUILDING

Maintaining the roads that connect your community to others is another task that requires cooperation. While local government may organize crews, you and your neighbors will likely contribute labor to ensure the roads remain passable. Each household is often expected to dedicate a few days of work annually to keep these vital routes open.

HARVESTING AND THRESHING BEES

During the harvest season, time is of the essence, and many hands make light work. You and your neighbors will come together for harvesting or threshing bees, where everyone pitches in to bring in crops before bad weather strikes. These gatherings are essential not only for securing food but for strengthening the community's ties, ensuring no one is left without help.

MUTUAL AID SOCIETIES

In times of illness, disaster, or hardship, you can rely on mutual aid societies. These groups operate on the principle of shared risk and mutual benefit. By paying dues into a common fund, you'll have access to support when facing medical expenses, funeral costs, or the need to rebuild after a fire. These societies offer financial help and a sense of security, knowing your neighbors stand ready to support you.

Through cooperatives and mutual aid, your community will thrive, ensuring that every family can weather the hardships of frontier life while fostering a spirit of unity and shared responsibility.

The Role of Women in Community Organization

In your new life on the frontier, you'll find that the women of the community are at the heart of its organization and survival. Far beyond managing their own households, they take on roles that shape the very foundation of your settlement, helping to ensure its long-term success.

LEADERSHIP IN EDUCATION AND RELIGION

When it comes to educating your children, women are often the first to step up as teachers. In these early days of settlement, before formal schooling systems are fully established, it's usually the women who teach in one-room schoolhouses. They don't just provide instruction in reading, writing, and arithmetic—they also serve as moral guides, helping to instill values that are crucial for raising the next generation of settlers.

Women also play a central role in your church. Whether they are organizing Sunday schools, charity events, or social gatherings, their involvement is essential to maintaining the church's presence in the community. You'll often find women cleaning and decorating the church, preparing food for communal events, and ensuring the church remains a place where the community gathers for faith and fellowship.

SOCIAL NETWORKS AND MUTUAL SUPPORT

Women are the backbone of the networks that help families survive the challenges of pioneer life. They organize quilting bees, cooking bees, and other gatherings where essential tasks are done together. These events provide practical help while giving women a chance to share news, advice, and companionship, strengthening the bonds within the community.

Beyond daily chores, women often lead charitable efforts, ensuring that the sick, widows, orphans, and those facing hardship are supported. These acts of kindness ensure that every family in the settlement is cared for, no matter the circumstances. Their quiet strength and leadership build the fabric of a thriving, resilient community.

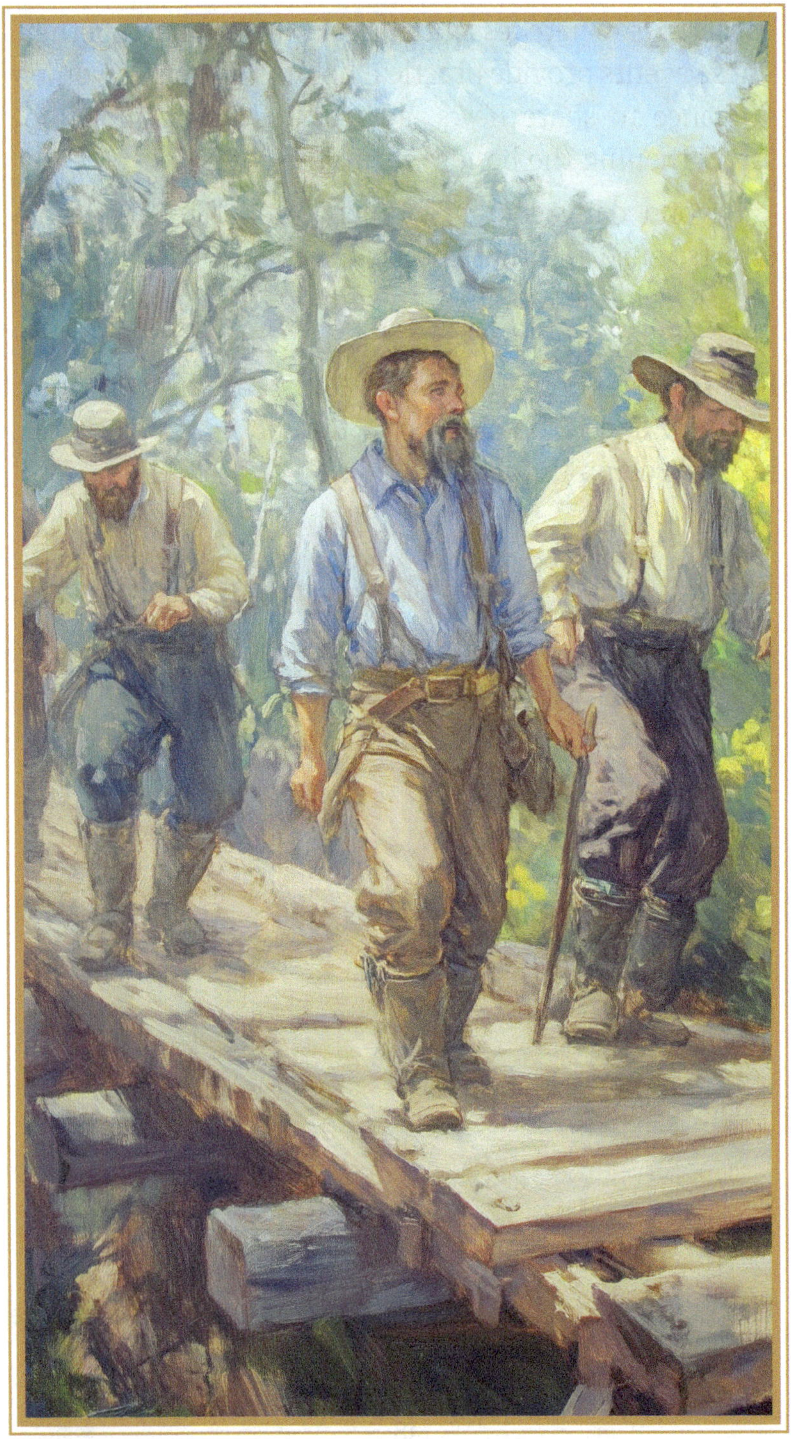

SETTING UP KEY INFRASTRUCTURE

Establishing key infrastructure will be crucial to your community's success. The federal government plays a vital role in this process, especially in setting up post offices and roads. These systems are essential for maintaining trade, staying in touch with family, and keeping up with news from afar.

POSTAL ROUTES AND POST ROADS

With settlers moving westward, the government prioritizes creating post roads—routes designated for carrying mail between towns and settlements. Whether by postal riders or stagecoaches, letters and packages are delivered along these roads, often following main highways and turnpikes. As a settler, you'll depend on these routes to maintain communication with distant family members and business partners.

RURAL POST OFFICES

In small towns and settlements like yours, rural post offices are vital hubs for collecting and distributing mail. Typically, it's a local citizen who initiates the process of establishing a post office. This individual, often the town's storekeeper or another prominent resident, petitions the federal government for the creation of a post office. The process involves sending a formal request to the Post Office Department, outlining the need for reliable mail service in your area.

Once approved, the post office is often set up in a central location, such as a general store, inn, or even the postmaster's home. The local citizen who petitioned for the post office frequently becomes the postmaster, overseeing the mail's arrival and distribution. As the postmaster, they may receive a small salary or compensation in exchange for handling the community's mail.

NAMING THE POST OFFICE

Naming the post office is another important step, as it often reflects the identity of the settlement. The name could be based on a nearby geographic feature, the name of the founding family, or an important local figure. Once the name is approved by the Post Office Department, it becomes the official designation for your town, further cementing its presence on regional maps and postal routes.

Over time, these post offices quickly become central gathering spots where neighbors come to receive letters, exchange news, and conduct business. The arrival of the mail can be a significant event, with settlers often waiting eagerly for news from distant family members, government notices, or trade opportunities.

COMMUNICATION CHALLENGES

Mail service on the frontier can be slow and unpredictable. A letter may take weeks or months to arrive, depending on the season or distance. In the meantime, you might rely on traders or travelers to carry important messages.

TELEGRAPH LINES

With the introduction of the telegraph in the mid-19th century, some frontier settlements began to connect to telegraph lines. This infrastructure allows for faster communication with distant areas, particularly important for business, government correspondence, and emergencies.

WATER INFRASTRUCTURE

WELLS

Access to clean, reliable water is critical for any settlement. The digging of wells is often one of the first major infrastructure projects undertaken. In many cases, individual families dig their own wells, but community wells may also be established.

CISTERNS

Collecting and storing rainwater is also common, especially in regions where groundwater is scarce. Underground and above-ground cisterns can be built to supply water during dry seasons.

IRRIGATION

For settlers farming the land, irrigation systems such as channels or ditches are necessary to divert water to fields during dry spells. Managing water resources effectively can make the difference between a successful harvest and failure.

MILLS AND WATER POWER

MILLS

Once your community grows, the construction of mills—especially gristmills for grinding grain and sawmills for processing timber—will become essential. Many early mills are water-powered and located along rivers or streams.

WATER POWER

Harnessing water for power is an important advancement in frontier communities. Water wheels can drive machinery that not only powers mills but also assists in more industrial endeavors like processing cloth or forging metals.

STORAGE INFRASTRUCTURE

GRANARIES

Once crops are harvested, communities often need to store grain in granaries to protect against spoilage and pests. A well-constructed granary ensures the community has enough food reserves to survive lean times.

WAREHOUSES

As trade increases, a settlement may need larger storage facilities for goods like hides, timber, and agricultural products, which will be traded or transported elsewhere.

COMMUNAL BUILDINGS AND PUBLIC SPACES

TOWN HALLS

As the population grows, your community will need a town hall or similar structure for meetings, elections, and other public functions. These buildings often serve multiple purposes, including spaces for courts, libraries, and community events. Markets and Trading Posts: A central marketplace, often a simple open space at first, will eventually evolve into a designated structure or trading post where goods are bought, sold, or bartered. Trading posts also facilitate exchanges with nearby Native American communities or other settlements.

TRANSPORTATION INFRASTRUCTURE

As your settlement grows, the construction of roads, bridges, and ferries will depend heavily on the participation of your community. While the federal or state government may provide some funding, much of the labor and effort will come from families like yours, working together to create these essential routes.

Through cooperatives and mutual aid societies, you will contribute your share of time and resources to ensure that transportation remains possible for all.

By participating in these essential infrastructure projects, you'll help ensure that your community remains connected, trade routes stay open, and your settlement continues to thrive. These efforts are more than physical—they strengthen the bonds between neighbors and provide the foundation for long-term success in your new life on the frontier.

FERRIES

When rivers are too wide or deep to build bridges, ferries become an essential means of transport. Operating ferries across waterways allows you and your neighbors to cross with wagons, livestock, and supplies.

These ferries, often manned by a local ferryman, are typically located at natural crossing points, where the river's current is slower and the banks are more accessible. Positioned along major roads and trails, these ferries will allow your community to connect with vital trade routes.

BUILDING AND MAINTAINING SAFE CROSSINGS

The building of roads, bridges, and ferries requires a collective effort, with each family contributing labor through "work bees" or mutual aid.

You will likely help construct simple flatboats or paddle ferries to ensure safe river passage, especially during seasonal flooding or high water. Just as important are the community-led efforts to maintain these crossings, reinforcing banks, repairing boats, and ensuring safety for travelers.

NAVIGATING SEASONAL CHALLENGES

Winter presents its own set of challenges. When rivers freeze solid, settlers will create ice roads that allow for travel and transportation across the frozen waterways. In other seasons, fords—shallow areas of a river where wagons and animals can pass through—will be used.

However, these natural crossings can be treacherous, especially during spring floods or after heavy rains, so it is wise to continue scouting these areas to ensure they are safe to use.

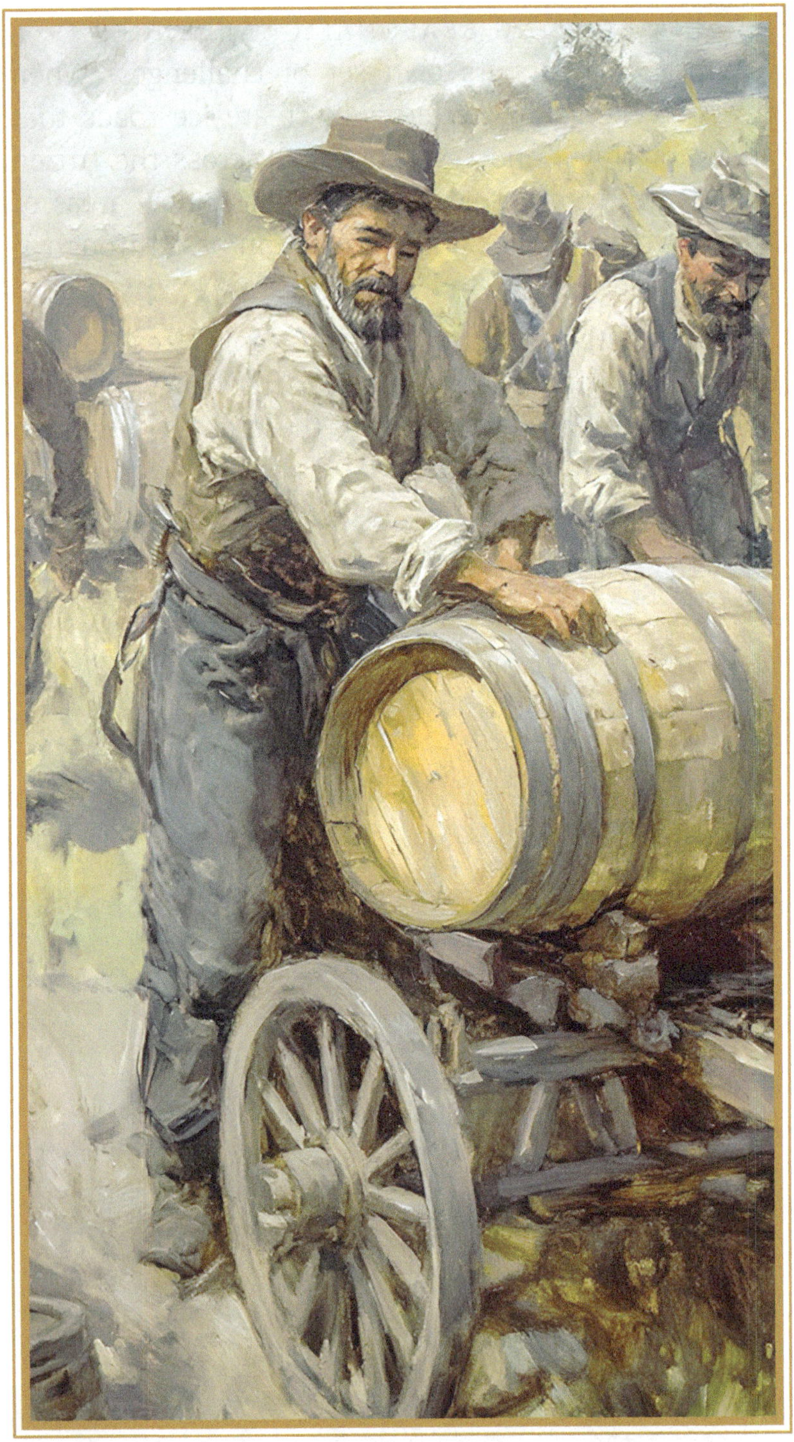

NAVIGATING THE LOCAL ECONOMY

In the pioneer era, the economy is a blend of currency-based transactions, bartering, and credit systems. Settlers often find themselves in situations where cash is scarce, making bartering an essential part of daily life. Understanding how to navigate this hybrid economy, including the use of money, credit, and trade goods, is crucial for conducting business and ensuring the survival and prosperity of your family.

Credit and Trade Goods

In the absence of cash, many transactions are made on credit, with an understanding that payment will be made at a later time, often in the form of goods or services. This system requires trust between neighbors and merchants and helps sustain business when cash flow is limited. Participating in one or more key trades—such as blacksmithing, woodworking, or farming—can provide your family with tradable goods or valuable skills that will help you thrive in this economy.

KEY SERVICES VITAL TO EVERY COMMUNITY

In every thriving pioneer community, certain key industries, trades, and professions take root early on, laying the foundation for survival and future growth. These vital industries are essential to the community's well-being. By becoming involved in one or more of these trades, your family can secure its own prosperity while contributing to the strength and success of the settlement.

BLACKSMITHING

Blacksmiths are crucial for making and repairing tools, horseshoes, nails, and metal parts for wagons and farming equipment.

CARPENTRY AND WOODWORKING

Carpenters build homes, barns, and essential furniture, as well as infrastructure like bridges and fences.

FARMING AND AGRICULTURE

Farmers grow the food needed to sustain the population and often trade surplus crops with other settlers.

MILLING

Grain mills, usually powered by water, are necessary for turning wheat, corn, and other grains into flour and meal.

TANNING AND LEATHERWORKING

Tanners prepare animal hides to create leather goods like shoes, harnesses, and clothing.

GENERAL STOREKEEPING

The general store provides settlers with goods that can't be produced locally, such as tools, fabric, and supplies, and often acts as a hub for trade and news.

TAILORING AND WEAVING

Tailors and weavers provide clothing and textiles, often working with wool, flax, or cotton.

DOCTOR OR APOTHECARY

While rare in early settlements, basic medical care is often provided by someone with knowledge of herbs or simple remedies.

BAKING AND BREWING

Bakers and brewers produce essential foodstuffs like bread and ale, which are staples in many pioneer communities.

LOGGING AND TIMBER

Timber is needed for building homes, barns, and tools, making logging a vital early industry.

PARTICIPATING IN THE LOCAL ECONOMY

Your family can secure its own prosperity while contributing to the strength of the settlement. But first, you must first identify how you can contribute to the essential industries and services needed for survival and growth and then work to establish yourself.

ASSESS YOUR SKILLS AND RESOURCES

Identify the trades, skills, or resources you can bring to the community. If you have skills in blacksmithing, farming, carpentry, or any other essential trade, you'll find that your services are in demand. Even if you don't possess specific trades, you can contribute through labor, bartering goods, or learning new skills from your neighbors.

BUILD RELATIONSHIPS AND NETWORKS

Introduce yourself to established community members, especially those who run key businesses or farms. Most pioneer communities are tight-knit, and relationships are built on trust and cooperation. Participation in community projects like barn raisings or road building is a great way to establish yourself.

BARTER OR TRADE GOODS AND SERVICES

Cash is often scarce, so barter is the most common form of exchange. You may start by trading labor, foodstuffs, or goods you produce, such as homemade tools or clothing. Being open to negotiation and trade will help you build connections and integrate quickly

PARTICIPATE IN MUTUAL AID SOCIETIES AND COOPERATIVES

Joining local cooperatives or mutual aid societies, where the community pools labor and resources, can help you establish a foothold. Whether through helping others with harvests, repairs, or building projects, you'll earn reciprocal support from your neighbors

OPEN A SHOP OR OFFER SPECIALIZED SERVICES

If you have a specialized trade, such as blacksmithing or weaving, you might consider setting up shop. Offering a service or good that the community lacks will quickly establish your role in the local economy. Many communities are eager to support newcomers who provide needed skills or goods.

ACQUIRE LAND FOR FARMING OR LIVESTOCK

Many settlers start by acquiring a piece of land to farm or raise livestock. Selling or trading surplus crops, animal products, or timber can bring you into the local trading network, allowing you to barter for goods and services you can't produce yourself.

WORK WITH LOCAL LEADERS AND GOVERNANCE

Engage with local leaders, join town meetings, and contribute to discussions on issues like trade routes, taxation, or public works. By doing so, you gain visibility and trust within the community, which can open up economic opportunities.

Currency in Pioneer Life

In your new life as a settler, you'll find that the economy is a blend of cash transactions, credit, and bartering. Understanding how to navigate these forms of exchange is essential for managing your finances, conducting business, and ensuring that your family has access to the goods and services you'll need.

While currency is used when available, bartering becomes a reliable means of exchange. Items like produce, livestock, handmade tools, and homegrown crops often serve as valuable trade commodities. Knowing the value of your goods in comparison to others is vital to ensure fair trade. Additionally, some larger settlements or markets may offer goods that can be purchased using hard currency, when available, especially for items not produced locally, such as tools, salt, or fabric.

THE USE OF HARD CURRENCY

Though cash may be scarce, it still plays an important role in the pioneer economy. You'll often use coins, primarily silver and copper, for smaller transactions or when dealing with merchants who prefer hard currency. These coins hold their value based on weight and metal content, making even a few coins valuable for essential purchases. It's wise to save your money for when bartering is not an option or when you're making significant transactions.

PAPER MONEY AND BANKNOTES

In some areas, you might come across paper money or banknotes, often issued by local banks or merchants. However, these vary in value and acceptability. You'll need to be cautious when using or accepting banknotes, as their worth can fluctuate depending on the institution backing them. In times of uncertainty, some settlers prefer to stick with coins or barter to avoid the risks associated with paper money.

CREDIT AND LOANS

Credit is another important part of pioneer life. Trusted settlers often receive credit from local merchants, allowing them to purchase goods now and repay later, typically after a good harvest. Managing credit wisely is crucial; falling into debt can harm your reputation and cut off access to the supplies you need for your homestead.

THE BARTER SYSTEM

Bartering is often the most practical way to exchange goods, especially when cash is hard to come by. You may trade a bushel of corn for a new pair of boots or exchange fresh produce for a repaired tool. Knowing the value of your goods and negotiating fair trades will be key to making sure you get what your family needs.

COMMON TRADE GOODS

Certain items are highly valuable and frequently used in barter. Salt, sugar, coffee, and tobacco are always in demand and can be stored for long periods, making them excellent trade goods. Tools, cloth, and livestock are also valuable commodities. Trading healthy chickens or pigs can provide you with other necessities that may be difficult to produce on your homestead.

NEGOTIATING FAIR TRADES

When bartering, it's important to assess the value of the items being exchanged and negotiate a deal that benefits both parties. Fair dealing builds trust, which is essential for successful trade relationships. You'll find that strong negotiation skills will serve you well in this new economy, ensuring your family thrives.

Markets and Trading Posts

As a settler, you'll rely on local markets and trading posts to access goods and services that may be unavailable on your homestead. These vital hubs of economic activity are where you can buy, sell, and trade the surplus crops, livestock, and handmade items your family produces. By learning when and where these markets operate, you'll stay connected to the broader economy and ensure your family has what they need to thrive.

LOCAL MARKETS

Markets are the heart of pioneer communities, offering opportunities to trade surplus goods, earn cash, and purchase items you cannot produce yourself. Market days are often held weekly or monthly in nearby towns, drawing settlers from miles around. These bustling events give you the chance to sell your goods, such as fresh produce, livestock, or handmade items, and to buy tools, hardware, and other goods brought in by merchants.

In addition to securing vital goods, markets are also where you can build relationships with other settlers. The connections you make here could lead to future trade deals, partnerships, or mutual support within your community.

TRADING POSTS

Trading posts are another essential part of pioneer life, especially for those living in more remote areas. Located along key routes like rivers or crossroads, trading posts provide access to goods such as flour, salt, tools, and luxury items like coffee and tea. You'll often find services like blacksmithing or wagon repair here as well.

For settlers like yourself, trading posts serve as lifelines to the outside world, offering the goods and services necessary for survival. They're also a critical point of contact with Native American tribes, where fur and other local resources can be exchanged for manufactured items.

BALANCING CURRENCY AND BARTERING

In your new life, you'll need to navigate a mix of currency and barter to meet your family's needs. While cash is used for significant purchases like land or livestock, bartering is often more common for everyday transactions. Preserving surplus goods will help you maintain a stockpile for trade, ensuring you're always prepared for opportunities at markets or trading posts.

BUILDING A REPUTATION

Your success in the pioneer economy depends heavily on trust and fair dealing. Those with a reputation for honesty and quality goods find it easier to make trades and form lasting relationships. Engaging with your community, whether at market days, town meetings, or social gatherings, allows you to network, build your reputation, and gain valuable insights into the local economy.

UNDERSTANDING SUPPLY AND DEMAND

By timing your trades carefully, and responding to fluctuations in the economy, you'll secure your place in the local market and help your family prosper in this new life. You need to be attuned to the dynamics of supply and demand locally and in the broader economy. For example, certain goods like fresh produce or livestock might fetch higher prices during the winter when they are scarce. Conversely, items like firewood or preserved food might be more valuable in late fall as winter approaches. By understanding these patterns, settlers can time sales and trades to maximize returns.

RESPONDING TO ECONOMIC FLUCTUATIONS

Economic fluctuations, such as crop failures, market gluts, or trade route changes, can significantly impact the pioneer economy. Settlers who are adaptable and resourceful are better able to navigate these challenges. This might involve diversifying production, finding new markets, or adjusting barter strategies to reflect changing conditions. Flexibility and a willingness to experiment are crucial to thriving in an uncertain economic environment.

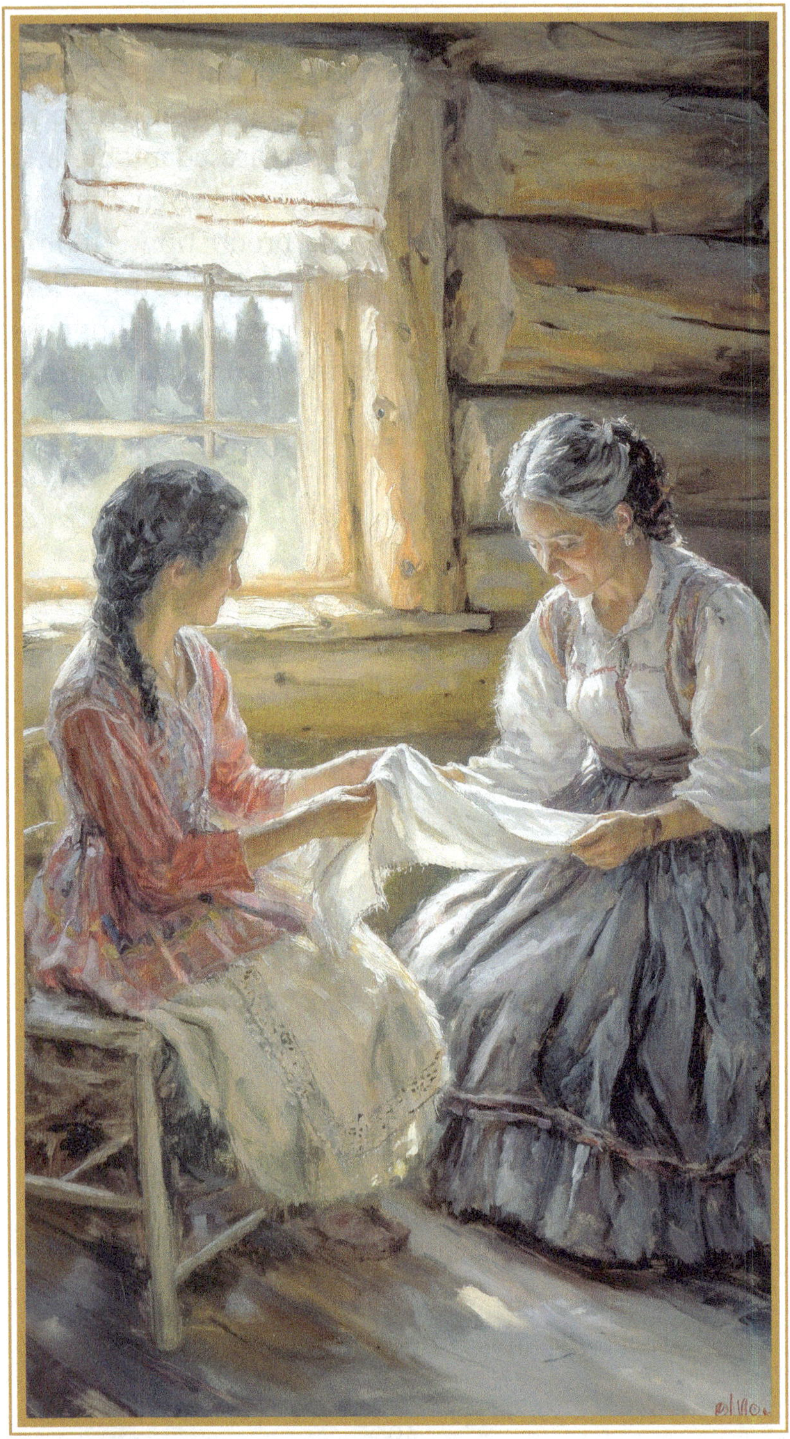

INTERACTIONS WITH NATIVE AMERICANS

As a new settler in Orleans County, it is important to understand that interactions with the Native American tribes who inhabit these lands will play a significant role in your daily life. These interactions—whether in trade, communication, or navigating cultural differences—will shape your success on the frontier.

Maintaining peace with the Native Americans is essential, not only for your survival but for the mutual benefit of all who inhabit this wilderness. To achieve this, you must approach each encounter with respect, understanding, and an open mind.

Navigating Trade, Communication, and Respect

The arrival of settlers has brought significant cultural change to Native American societies, including the introduction of new goods, diseases, and social structures. While trade provides access to valuable resources, it also disrupts traditional ways of life and sometimes leads to dependency on European goods.

The interactions between settlers and Native Americans are complex and multifaceted, resulting in cooperation and conflict. The outcomes of these interactions have lasting impacts on both communities.

Settlers who interact with Native Americans are often exposed to cultural practices that are unfamiliar to them. Respecting these practices, even when they differ significantly from European traditions, is essential for building trust and avoiding cultural offenses. This includes understanding rituals, ceremonies, and social customs that govern everything from trade to diplomacy.

BUILDING TIES

ALLIANCES

Sometimes, settlers and Native Americans form alliances for mutual defense against common enemies, whether they are other tribes or external threats. These alliances are often solidified through trade and intermarriage, creating bonds lasting for generations.

TRADE

Trade with Native Americans is one of the most vital relationships you will form. Both settlers and Native Americans bring valuable goods to the table.

Goods Exchanged

FURS AND PELTS

One of the most significant trade goods exchanged by Native Americans is animal pelts, particularly beaver, deer, and bear furs. These pelts are highly sought after by European and American traders for the fur trade. In return, settlers provide goods not readily available to Native Americans.

METAL TOOLS AND WEAPONS

Native Americans value metal tools such as knives, axes, and cooking pots, which are more durable and practical than traditional stone or bone tools. Firearms, gunpowder, and ammunition are also highly prized, although the trade of weapons is often a source of tension and concern for both parties.

CLOTH AND CLOTHING

European cloth and clothing, including wool blankets, are popular trade items. These goods are valued for warmth, durability, and the variety of colors and patterns they offer, which are often different from what can be produced locally by Native Americans.

FOOD AND AGRICULTURAL PRODUCTS

As a settler, you will often find opportunities to trade surplus crops like corn, beans, and wheat with the Native Americans. In return, they offer traditional foods such as wild rice, maple sugar, and game meat, which are valuable additions to your diet.

More importantly, the Native Americans possess extensive knowledge of the land and its bounty. They will often share techniques for cultivating native crops like corn, beans, and squash, as well as invaluable skills in hunting and trapping local wildlife.

This exchange of agricultural wisdom and survival techniques is crucial to thriving in this new and untamed land, ensuring your family's success in the wilderness.

Trade Practices and Bartering

BARTER SYSTEM

The barter system is the most common method of exchange, so be prepared to negotiate the value of your goods. The value of goods is determined through negotiation, with both parties needing to agree on a fair trade. This system requires a deep understanding of the relative value of goods in both cultures.

TRADE NETWORKS

Many Native American tribes are part of extensive trade networks that predate European contact. These networks allow for the exchange of goods across vast distances. Settlers who trade with Native Americans often find themselves part of these more extensive networks, which can bring goods from distant regions into communities.

SEASONAL TRADE

Trade is often seasonal, with specific times of the year more conducive to certain types of exchange. For example, furs are typically traded in the fall and winter when pelts are thickest, while agricultural products are traded after the harvest.

Communication

Bridging Language and Cultural Barriers

Effective communication between settlers and Native Americans is essential for successful trade and peaceful coexistence. However, this communication is often challenging due to language barriers and cultural differences.

CLEAR BOUNDARIES AND SIGNALS

One effective way to avoid conflicts is to ensure that both parties clearly mark and understand boundaries. This can include physical markers, such as fences or blazed trees, and verbal agreements reinforced through regular communication.

INTERPRETERS AND TRANSLATORS

Language barriers are a significant challenge in frontier interactions. Using skilled interpreters fluent in English (or another European language) and the relevant Native American languages is critical for ensuring that messages are accurately conveyed. These interpreters are often of mixed heritage or have lived among both cultures, allowing them to navigate linguistic and cultural nuances that might otherwise lead to misunderstandings.

PIDGIN LANGUAGES AND TRADE JARGON

Over time, simplified forms of communication known as pidgin languages or trade jargon have developed. These are mixtures of words and phrases from multiple languages, designed to facilitate essential communication and trade. While not fully developed, these simple languages allow for functional communication in specific contexts.

SIGN LANGUAGE

In some cases, particularly where language barriers are significant, Native Americans and settlers use sign language to communicate. This method is prevalent on the plains and in regions with diverse linguistic groups. Sign language provides a way to convey essential concepts and intentions, though it is limited in its complexity.

CULTURAL SENSITIVITY

In many Native American cultures, gift-giving is essential to establishing and maintaining relationships. Settlers who understand and participate in these practices can build goodwill and trust. However, the exchange of gifts is not merely transactional; it is embedded in a system of reciprocity that requires ongoing mutual respect and support. Ignoring or disrespecting these practices can lead to misunderstandings or conflicts.

DIPLOMACY AND NEGOTIATION

When negotiating with Native American leaders, settlers must be clear, patient, and respectful. Diplomatic negotiations often take time, as decisions are made collectively by tribal councils rather than by a single leader. Rushing these processes or dismissing Native American concerns can lead to mistrust and conflict.

Native American tribes often have complex social hierarchies and decision-making processes. Settlers must respect these structures, recognizing the authority of chiefs, sachems, and other leaders. Tribal leaders hold significant authority within communities, and approval is necessary for major agreements or alliances.

These negotiations must be approached respectfully, recognizing the leaders' roles and the importance of consensus in Native American decision-making. Disregarding or bypassing these leaders can be seen as a direct insult to the tribe and lead to hostility.

Respect for Territories and Sovereignty

Settlers need to be aware of land ownership concepts, and the boundaries recognized by Native American tribes. To help prevent actions that can be perceived as disrespectful or aggressive, settlers should also understand and respect Native American cultural practices, such as sacred rituals or hunting seasons. Those who take the time to learn about these practices are less likely to unintentionally provoke conflicts.

TRADITIONAL LAND USE

Native American tribes have long-established territories used for hunting, fishing, farming, and gathering. These territories are often marked by natural landmarks such as rivers, mountains, or forests. Settlers need to recognize and respect these boundaries to avoid encroaching on land vital to the tribe's way of life.

RESPECTING HUNTING AND FISHING RIGHTS

Even as settlers claim land for farming and building, it is essential to recognize the ongoing rights of Native Americans to hunt, fish, and gather within traditional territories. Ignoring these rights or disrupting these activities can lead to severe conflicts, as these resources are essential for the survival of Native American communities.

LAND OWNERSHIP VS. LAND STEWARDSHIP

Native American concepts of land ownership differed from European notions of private property. Many tribes viewed land as a communal resource to be used and cared for by all community members, rather than as a commodity to be bought and sold. Settlers need to understand this difference to avoid misunderstandings and to approach negotiations with the appropriate mindset.

SACRED SITES

Many Native American tribes have specific sites within territories that are considered sacred. These can include burial grounds, ceremonial sites, or places of spiritual significance. It is crucial to respect these sites and to avoid disturbing them, as heresy can lead to severe conflicts.

CONFLICT RESOLUTION

As pioneer settlements expand, conflicts over land become increasingly more common. Settlers' desire for farmland often leads to encroachment on Native American territories, resulting in disputes that sometimes escalate into violence.

When conflicts arise, effective communication is essential for resolving them without violence. Settlers who understand Native American customs and legal practices are better equipped to navigate disputes over land, resources, or trade agreements.

Mediation by respected community members, both pioneer and Native American, is often used to find mutually acceptable solutions.

INVOLVEMENT OF LOCAL AUTHORITIES

In more complex or severe disputes, local government authorities, such as justices of the peace or county officials, might be called upon to mediate. These officials are responsible for upholding the law and respecting treaties. However, involvement can be a double-edged sword; while they provide a formal mechanism for dispute resolution, actions are sometimes seen as biased in favor of settlers.

APPEALS TO HIGHER AUTHORITIES

Disputes are sometimes escalated to state or federal authorities, particularly when treaties are involved. This can include appeals to state governors or even the federal government. However, such escalations often take time, leading to prolonged uncertainty and tension.

FORCED RELOCATION

The pressure of expanding European settlement has led to the forced relocation of many Native American tribes from ancestral lands. This is often done through treaties that are made under duress or through outright force, leading to significant hardship and loss of life among Native American communities.

TREATIES AND AGREEMENTS

Throughout the 18th and 19th centuries, various treaties and agreements have been made between Native American tribes, European settlers, and the U.S. government. These treaties often define specific boundaries and rights to land use. Settlers are expected to be aware of these treaties and adhere to the agreed-upon terms, though in practice, these agreements are frequently violated, leading to conflicts.

ADHERENCE TO TREATY TERMS

Strict adherence to the terms of treaties is essential for maintaining peaceful relations. Violating treaty boundaries, whether through unauthorized settlement, resource extraction, or other activities, can be perceived as an act of aggression by Native American tribes. This can escalate into conflicts that endanger both settlers and Native communities.

Successful Resolution

THE TREATY OF CANANDAIGUA (1794)

This treaty, negotiated between the United States and the Haudenosaunee (Iroquois Confederacy), is an example of successful conflict resolution that has helped maintain peace in Orleans County. The treaty recognizes the sovereignty of the Haudenosaunee and has established clear boundaries, which have been respected by both sides for many years. Settlers who settle in the region are expected to adhere to the treaty's terms.

LOCAL PEACE PACTS

In some cases, individual pioneer communities and Native American tribes negotiate local peace pacts that allow for shared use of resources, such as hunting grounds or water sources. These agreements are often based on mutual respect and the recognition of each other's needs.

Failures and Lessons Learned

THE SULLIVAN CLINTON CAMPAIGN (1779)

The Sullivan Clinton campaign, a military expedition during the American Revolution aimed at neutralizing the Iroquois Confederacy, destroyed numerous Native American villages and crops. The long-term impact of this campaign is a deep-seated mistrust and hatred between settlers and Native Americans, highlighting the devastating consequences of failing to resolve conflicts peacefully.

THE TREATY OF FORT STANWIX (1768)

While intended to establish clear boundaries between settlers and Native American lands, the Treaty of Fort Stanwix was later criticized for being coercive and not fully representative of all Native American interests. The resulting land disputes contributed to ongoing tensions and conflicts, underscoring the importance of fair and inclusive negotiations.

The Role of Women in Conflict Resolution

Women often play a unique and significant role in preventing and resolving conflicts between settlers and Native Americans.

BUILDING BRIDGES

Women often manage household interactions with Native Americans through trade, hospitality, or daily encounters. Their role in maintaining positive relations at the domestic level is crucial for preventing minor misunderstandings from escalating into larger conflicts.

INTERMARRIAGE

Intermarriage between settlers and Native Americans, while not expected, does occur and can serve as a powerful means of building alliances and reducing tensions. These marriages often bring families and communities closer, creating bonds that help prevent conflicts.

WOMEN AS MEDIATORS

In some Native American cultures, women significantly influence decision-making processes, particularly in matters related to family and community welfare. Settlers who recognize and respect these women's authority can engage them as mediators in disputes, tapping into influence to resolve conflicts peacefully.

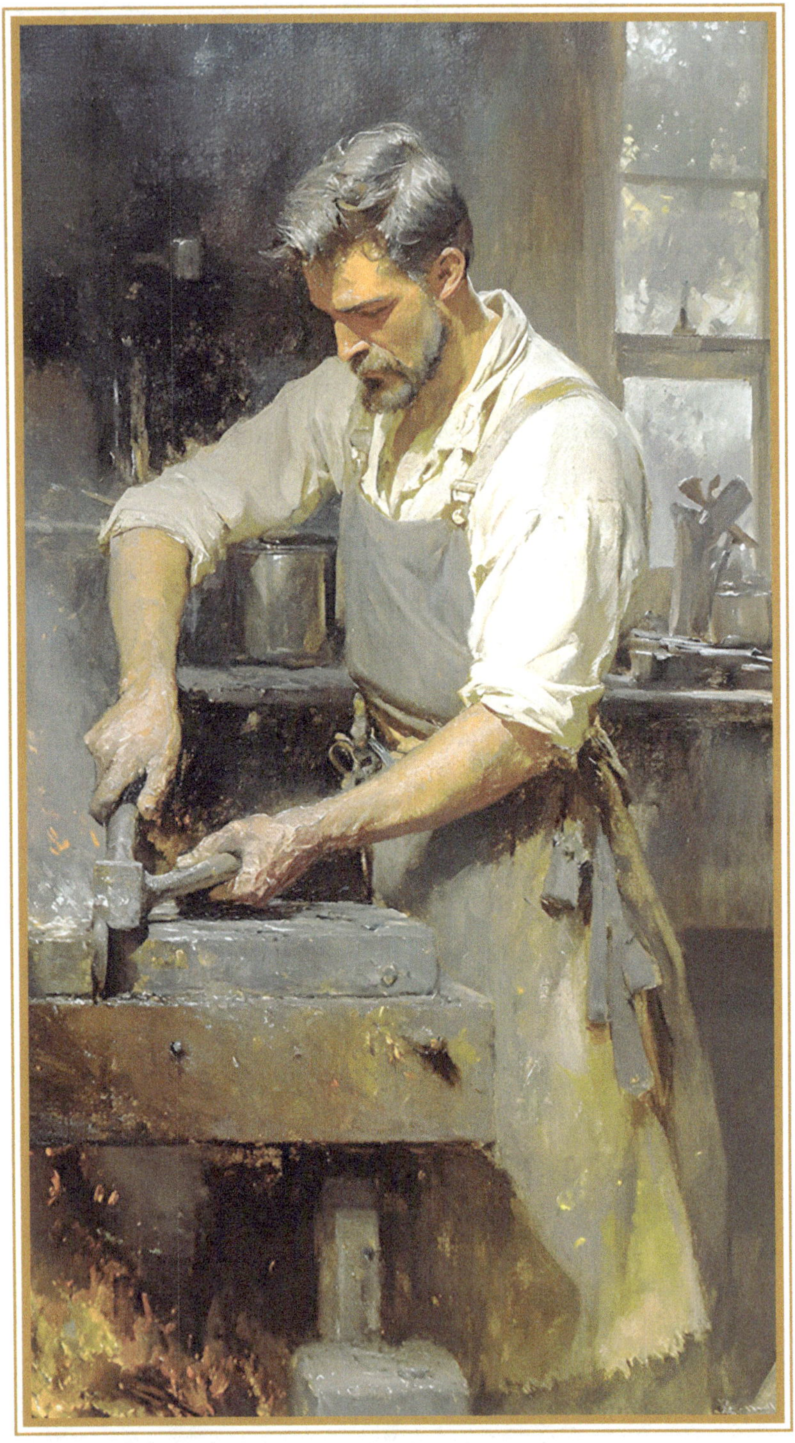

ESSENTIAL CRAFTING FOR HOME AND TRADE

Crafting essential goods for daily life will likely demand a significant portion of your family's time, but it can also become a valuable source of income.

Whether it be blacksmithing, leatherworking, or weaving, mastering such crafts ensures your self-sufficiency and opens up opportunities for bartering and selling goods. In a pioneer community, everyone thrives when at least one individual is proficient in each of these vital skills, fostering cooperation and mutual benefit throughout the settlement.

Preparation of Daily Necessities

Maple Sugaring

Maple sugaring is collecting and boiling sap from sugar maple trees (Acer saccharum) to produce maple syrup and sugar. This task is typically carried out in early spring when daytime temperatures rise above freezing and nighttime temperatures fall below freezing, causing the sap to flow.

The process begins by tapping the maple trees, which involves drilling small holes into the trunks and inserting spiles (small wooden or metal spouts) to guide the sap into buckets or containers.

Once collected, the sap, mostly water, must be boiled down to concentrate the sugars. This is done in large pans or kettles over an open fire or in a sugaring house. It takes approximately 40 gallons of sap to produce just one gallon of syrup.

As the sap boils, water evaporates, and the sap thickens into syrup. The syrup is then filtered to remove impurities and may be boiled further to create maple sugar, a more concentrated and long-lasting form of the sweetener.

Maple syrup and sugar are valuable for cooking, baking, and preserving food, making this process a vital spring activity.

Soap Making

Soap-making is a straightforward essential skill that provides a means to keep clean with limited resources. The process combines animal fat (such as tallow or lard) with lye, a powerful alkaline substance derived from wood ash.

ANIMAL FAT (TALLOW OR LARD)

Fat is rendered from animals like cows or pigs, boiled down to remove impurities, and cooled to create a smooth, solid base. This fat is the main ingredient in soap, providing cleansing properties and lather.

LYE (WOOD ASH SOLUTION)

Lye leaches water through hardwood ashes to extract the alkaline salts. The resulting liquid is then concentrated through repeated boiling, becoming strong enough to saponify the fat when mixed.

MIXING LYE AND FAT

The rendered fat is slowly heated over a fire, and the prepared lye solution is carefully added. The mixture is stirred constantly to ensure even blending. This process, called saponification, turns the fat and lye into soap as they react chemically.

COOKING AND SETTING

Once the mixture thickens into a smooth, pudding-like consistency, it is poured into molds (often wooden boxes or trays). The soap is left to cool and harden for several days. During this time, it solidifies into usable bars.

CUTTING AND CURING

After hardening, the soap is cut into individual bars and set aside to cure for a few weeks. This curing process ensures the soap becomes firm and long-lasting, reducing residual harshness from the lye.

USES OF HOMEMADE SOAP

The intense cleansing properties make homemade soap ideal for laundry and dishwashing, effectively cutting through grease and grime.

Churning Butter

Butter is made by allowing the milk to sit, giving the cream time to rise to the top. This cream is then skimmed off and placed in a butter churn, a large container with a plunger that is moved up and down.

As the cream is churned, the fat particles clump together, eventually forming butter. The remaining liquid, buttermilk, is drained and often used for baking or cooking. The butter is then rinsed, salted, and packed into storage containers for use.

Making Cheese

Cheese production involves curdling milk by adding rennet, a substance derived from the stomach of young animals (or a plant-based alternative). The milk separates into curds (solid) and whey (liquid). The curds are then scooped into molds and pressed to remove excess moisture. After pressing, the cheese ages for several weeks or months to develop its flavor and texture.

Some pioneers use simple, fresh cheeses that don't require aging for quicker consumption.

Bread Baking

SOURDOUGH OR YEAST BREAD

Bread is a staple in the pioneer diet, often baked several times a week. A sourdough starter or yeast was used to leaven the bread. The sourdough starter is made by mixing flour and water and allowing it to ferment naturally, providing the yeast needed to make the bread rise.

YEAST BREAD

Making yeast bread involves adding a yeast culture to flour, water, and salt. The dough is kneaded, raised, and then baked in an oven.

Pioneers often built outdoor bread ovens made from stone or clay, where the loaves are baked until golden brown and crusty.

Making Vinegar

Vinegar ferments fruit scraps, most commonly apple peels or cores. The fruit is submerged in water, and natural yeasts ferment the sugars over time into alcohol. A second fermentation process, led by acetic acid bacteria, turns the alcohol into vinegar.

The resulting product is used in food preservation (pickling), cooking, and cleaning. Pioneers often set aside jars of fermenting fruit in a warm place and stirred the mixture daily to encourage fermentation.

Soap Ash Collection

Wood ash from the stove or fireplace is valuable in soap-making. The ash, typically from hardwood trees, is collected and soaked in water to create lye (potassium hydroxide). The lye is then combined with animal fats or oils to create soap. This routine task is tied to maintaining the household hearth and is essential for making a critical cleaning supply.

Repairing Metal Tools

This is a precious skill if you have access to a forge. Several fundamental principles and techniques must be followed to successfully heat, bend, and mend metal for restoring broken tools. Apprenticing is the best way to learn, but here are a few essential details to give you a basic understanding of the process.

PROPER HEATING

The metal must be heated to the correct temperature, typically around 1,400 to 1,600°F (bright red to orange heat) for most iron and steel. If the metal is too cool, it will be brittle and difficult to work with; it can become too soft or burn if it is too hot.

A bellows-fed forge or a modern equivalent is needed to reach these temperatures. Charcoal or coal is often used as fuel in the forge. Maintain a consistent heat by adjusting the air supply with bellows or a hand-cranked blower.

BENDING AND SHAPING

Once heated to the right temperature, the metal becomes malleable and can be shaped using a hammer on an anvil. Use lighter hammer blows to shape thin or delicate parts and heavier blows for thicker, more vital areas.

Anvils have different surfaces and edges, allowing you to shape metal as needed. The flat surface is for general hammering, while the horn (curved end) is used for bending metal into rounded shapes.

PROPER COOLING (QUENCHING AND TEMPERING)

After shaping the metal, you may need to quench it by dipping it into water or oil to cool quickly. This process hardens the metal, making it durable but also brittle.

After quenching, the tool should be reheated at a lower temperature (around 400°F to 600°F) to temper the metal. This step reduces brittleness and increases toughness, ensuring the tool won't easily break.

WELDING AND JOINING (IF NECESSARY)

If the tool is broken in two or needs a new piece of metal added, forge welding is used to combine two pieces. Both ends are heated to a high temperature and then hammered together until they fuse.

FILING AND FINISHING

Once the tool is shaped and hardened, filing or grinding the edges to sharpen them (especially for cutting tools like axes or plows) and smooth out any rough areas is essential. This ensures the tool functions properly and is comfortable to handle.

INSPECTION

After mending, inspect the tool for cracks or weak spots, especially along welded areas. If necessary, repeat heating and tempering to ensure durability. By following these steps, broken tools can be successfully repaired, allowing them to be used for extended periods without needing replacement.

Clothing and Textile Production

WOOL PRODUCTION

Shearing sheep, cleaning and carding the wool, and spinning it into yarn.

SHEARING SHEEP

Shearing typically occurs in the spring, just after winter, when the sheep no longer need their thick coat for warmth. It's crucial to shear before the hot summer months, as a thick wool coat can cause the sheep to overheat.

A pair of sturdy shears or a specialized sheep-shearing tool is used. The process requires care to avoid cutting the sheep's skin and skill to remove the fleece in one large piece.

After shearing, the fleece is laid out flat. The wool is inspected for quality, with the cleanest parts of the fleece saved for spinning and the dirtier, shorter wool used for other purposes like felting or insulation.

CLEANING WOOL (SCOURING)

The raw fleece contains natural oils (lanolin) and dirt. It must be washed in warm water with a mild soap or detergent. Avoid hot water, as this can cause the wool fibers to feel unusable for spinning.

After washing, the wool is thoroughly rinsed to remove soap and dirt, ensuring the fibers are not agitated too much, which can cause matting.

The washed fleece is spread to dry in a well-ventilated, shaded area. It is important that the wool is dried completely to prevent mold or mildew from forming.

CARDING WOOL

Carding aligns the wool fibers and removes any remaining debris or tangles. This process prepares the wool for spinning by creating a fluffy, organized roll called a rolag.

Carding uses two flat paddles with metal teeth, hand carders, or a drum carder for larger batches.

The wool is gently placed between the carders, and the paddles are brushed against each other to straighten the fibers. Once the fibers are aligned, they are rolled off into a rolag, which is easy to spin.

SPINNING WOOL INTO YARN

Wool can be spun using either a spinning wheel, which allows for faster production, or a drop spindle, which is portable and simple.

The fibers from the rolag are pulled and twisted into a single strand of yarn. The spinning wheel or spindle twists the fibers into yarn by pulling the fibers into the wheel's bobbin or spindle, creating a continuous strand of yarn.

The thickness of the yarn depends on how much fiber is drafted (pulled) at once. A finer draft creates a thinner yarn, while more fiber produces a thicker yarn. The spinner controls the consistency of the yarn as it works.

PLYING AND SETTING YARN

Once spun, the single strand (called a single) can be plied by twisting two or more singles together, creating a more robust, balanced yarn.

To set the twist and prevent unraveling, the finished yarn is soaked in warm water and then hung to dry with a small weight attached to help it straighten and stabilize.

COLLECT LANOLIN

The natural oils in wool, known as lanolin, are often collected during cleaning and used for making soaps or skin care products, making wool production even more resourceful.

DYEING YARN

Once the yarn is spun, it can be dyed using natural plant dyes or other substances to create different colors before being woven or knitted into clothing.

TANNING HIDES

Tanning hides is a crucial process for pioneers, as it transforms animal skins into durable leather used for crafting boots, belts, outerwear, and other essential items. The process is labor-intensive but yields a long-lasting material invaluable for daily life. Below are the critical steps in tanning hides, providing settlers with the knowledge they need to produce quality leather.

SKINNING THE ANIMAL

Once the animal is butchered, the hide must be carefully removed to prevent damage. A sharp knife separates the skin from the flesh, keeping the hide intact.

Any excess fat or flesh is trimmed away from the skin. This step must be done thoroughly to ensure a clean hide ready for tanning.

SOAKING AND CLEANING HIDE

The hide is soaked in water to soften it and remove any remaining blood, dirt, or fat. This step helps prepare the hide for hair removal and further treatment.

After soaking, the hide is scraped with a dull knife or a specialized scraping tool to remove the hair. This step must be done carefully to avoid puncturing the hide. Sometimes, settlers may choose to keep the hair for fur-lined garments, but most leather-making requires removing the hair.

Once the hair is removed, the hide is thoroughly cleaned, ensuring all flesh and fat are scraped away.

TANNING HIDE

Traditional tanning methods involve natural agents, such as oak bark, hemlock, or sumac, which contain tannins that preserve the hide and make it more flexible and durable. The bark is collected, chopped, and boiled to create a tannin-rich solution.

The cleaned hide is submerged in the tannin solution for several weeks. During this time, the tannins penetrate the hide, slowly transforming it into leather. The longer the hide soaks, the more durable and waterproof the resulting leather becomes.

To ensure even tanning, the hide is periodically turned and stirred within the solution, making sure every part of the hide is evenly treated.

BRAIN TANNING

Some pioneers also use "brain tanning," a method that involves soaking the hide in a mixture made from the animal's brain and water. This technique produces exceptionally soft and flexible leather, often used for clothing and moccasins.

STRETCHING AND DRYING LEATHER

After the hide has soaked in the tannin solution for the necessary period, it is removed, wrung out, and stretched to its full size. Stretching prevents the leather from shrinking and hardening as it dries.

The stretched hide is hung in a shaded, well-ventilated area to dry slowly. Quick drying in direct sunlight or heat can cause the leather to become brittle. The hide is monitored to ensure it dries evenly without warping or cracking.

SOFTENING THE LEATHER

Once dry, the leather may feel stiff. Settlers soften it by working the hide over the edge of a wooden post or by kneading it with their hands. This process, known as "breaking," helps loosen the fibers and make the leather more supple.

To further soften and protect the leather, settlers apply natural oils or animal fats, such as bear grease or tallow. The oil is worked into the leather to keep it flexible and water-resistant.

FINISHING THE LEATHER

The leather is trimmed and cut into the desired shapes and sizes for specific uses, such as boots, belts, pouches, or outerwear. Leatherworkers often use a knife or cutting tool to ensure precise cuts.

For a smoother finish, the leather can be polished with a smooth stone or piece of wood, giving it a finer appearance.

SMOKEWORKING

After tanning, some hides are smoked over a fire to make the leather more water-resistant. The smoke infuses the hide with natural preservatives, increasing its longevity.

PREPARING FLAX FOR LINEN

In addition to wool and leather, you will likely rely on cotton and linen to make lighter fabrics, particularly for everyday clothing and household items like sheets and towels. Cotton growing is more common in the southern regions, so cotton cloth will likely be stored in stores.

On the other hand, linen is made from flax plants and is commonly cultivated in northern areas like Orleans County. Growing, harvesting, and preparing these fibers for cloth-making is time-consuming, but having these skills will increase your family's self-sufficiency and could become a good source of income.

GROWING FLAX

Flax is well-suited to the cooler, temperate climate of northern regions like Orleans County, making it a popular crop for linen production among pioneer families.

Flax is sown in early spring, increasing to reach 2-4 feet. It requires well-prepared soil and adequate moisture throughout the growing season.

HARVESTING FLAX

Flax is harvested when the stems turn yellow, and the seeds begin to mature, usually in late summer. Rather than cutting the plant, settlers pull the flax stalks from the ground to preserve the entire length of the fibers.

The pulled flax is left to dry in the sun for several days, ensuring the fibers are adequately prepared for the following processing stage.

RETTING AND BREAKING FLAX

Once dried, the flax is subjected to "retting," a process in which the stems are soaked in water to break down the pectin that holds the fibers together. This can be done in streams, ponds, or special retting vats.

After retting, the dried flax stalks are broken using a flax brake tool. This process loosens the woody outer parts of the stalk, allowing the inner fibers to be separated.

SCUTCHING AND HECKLING

The broken flax stalks are then scutched—beaten with a wooden scutching knife to remove the remaining woody parts of the stem. This leaves the long, fine fibers exposed.

The final step in preparing flax fibers is heckling, in which the fibers are drawn through a series of combs to clean and align them further. The result is long, smooth fibers ready for spinning.

SPINNING AND WEAVING LINEN

The prepared flax fibers are spun into linen thread using a spinning wheel. Linen thread tends to be stronger and more durable than cotton, making it ideal for sturdy garments and household textiles.

Like cotton, linen is woven into cloth on a loom. It can be made into fine linen for undergarments or heavier cloth for work shirts, aprons, and bedding.

BLEACHING AND FINISHING

Linen cloth is often bleached in the sun to create a lighter color. Once woven, the fabric is washed, smoothed, and prepared for sewing into finished garments or other items.

SPINNING WOOL

Use a spinning wheel or drop spindle to turn raw fibers into thread or yarn.

Spinning wool into yarn is essential for pioneer families, allowing them to transform raw wool into usable thread for knitting, weaving, and clothing production. Whether using a spinning wheel or a drop spindle, the basic process involves twisting the wool fibers together to create a continuous strand of yarn. Below are key details of the process to help you understand how to spin wool efficiently.

Before you begin spinning, the wool must be adequately prepared.

CARDING

After washing and drying the wool, the fibers are carded. This involves brushing the wool with two carding paddles and aligning the fibers to make them smooth and more spin-friendly. The result is a fluffy roll of wool, called a rolag, ready for spinning.

DRAFTING

The fibers are then "drafted," meaning you gently pull the wool into a thinner, even section that will feed into the spinning process. This step ensures a smooth, consistent thread.

USING A DROP SPINDLE

A drop spindle is a simple, hand-held tool for spinning yarn. Begin by securing a small amount of drafted wool onto the spindle's hook or notch. This initial twist will start the spinning process.

Hold the drafted wool in one hand and spin the spindle with the other, using a flicking motion to keep the spindle turning. As the spindle rotates, it twists the wool fibers, turning them into yarn.

DRAFTING AND TWISTING

Continue drafting the wool with your fingers while letting the spindle hang and spin. The twist moves up into the wool, creating yarn. As the yarn lengthens, wind it onto the spindle shaft, then repeat the process until you've spun the desired amount of yarn.

PLYING (OPTIONAL)

For a stronger yarn, you can ply two or more strands together. To do this, twist two strands of spun yarn in the opposite direction of their original twist.

Using a Spinning Wheel

A spinning wheel offers a faster, more efficient way to spin yarn and is often preferred by those with larger quantities of wool to process.

SETTING UP THE WHEEL

The spinning wheel consists of several parts, including the drive wheel, the treadle, and the bobbin. The wool is fed through the orifice, a hole in the wheel, and onto the bobbin as you spin.

ATTACHING THE WOOL

Like a drop spindle, start by attaching the drafted wool to the leader (a piece of yarn already attached to the bobbin) and turn the wheel.

TREADLING AND DRAFTING

The spinner uses their foot to operate the treadle, which turns the wheel. As the wheel spins, you draft the wool by pulling it gently with your hands while the wheel twists it into yarn. The treadling motion controls the wheel's speed, which controls the amount of twist added to the wool.

WINDING THE YARN

Once the wool is twisted into yarn, it is automatically wound onto the bobbin. You continue feeding the wool into the wheel while treadling, creating a steady flow of yarn.

PLYING (OPTIONAL)

Like a drop spindle, you can ply yarn by spinning two or more strands together to increase its strength and thickness.

TENSION CONTROL

Managing the tension on the spinning wheel is crucial for producing even yarn. If the tension is too loose, the yarn will not wind onto the bobbin correctly; if it is too tight, it can break the yarn.

CONSISTENCY

The key to good spinning is maintaining a consistent drafting and twisting process to ensure the yarn is even thicker. Based on the drafting method, beginners may find it useful to practice creating different thicknesses of yarn, from fine thread to bulky yarn.

FINISHING THE YARN

After spinning, the yarn is often washed and stretched, or "blocked," to set the twist and smooth out any inconsistencies.

FINAL TIPS

Wool spinning, whether by spindle or wheel, takes time to master. Be patient as you practice keeping the yarn smooth and even.

The drop spindle and spinning wheel are portable and can be taken to different locations for spinning on the go, making it an adaptable tool for pioneer life.

Mastering spinning wool provides settlers with a crucial means of creating clothing, blankets, and other essential textiles. This self-reliance on homemade yarn fosters independence and sustainability in the wilderness.

WEAVING CLOTH

Weaving cloth is a fundamental skill for pioneer families. Mastering this skill will allow you to turn their hand-spun yarn into fabric for garments, blankets, and other household necessities.

The process involves interlacing two sets of yarn—the warp and the weft—on a loom to create a strong, durable cloth. Below are the essential steps and details for understanding the weaving process on a loom.

Preparing the Loom

WARPING THE LOOM

The first step in weaving is setting up the warp threads, which run vertically on the loom. These threads must be strong and even, as they form the backbone of your fabric.

MEASURE THE WARP

You'll measure the warp threads to the desired length of your fabric. These threads are then wound onto the warp beam of the loom, ensuring each thread is evenly spaced and under tension.

THREADING THE HEDDLES

Each warp thread is threaded through small loops called heddles attached to the harnesses. The heddles help control the movement of the warp threads during weaving.

TENSIONING THE WARP

After threading, the warp threads are stretched tight and evenly across the loom, ensuring a smooth surface for weaving.

PREPARING THE WEFT

The weft threads, which run horizontally, are wound onto a shuttle, a tool that allows the weaver to pass the weft threads back and forth across the warp. Depending on the woven fabric, the weft yarn can be spun from wool, cotton, or linen.

The Weaving Process

SHEDDING

This is lifting specific warp threads to create a gap, or "shed," through which the shuttle can pass. The heddles, controlled by the harnesses, raise and lower the warp threads in a specific pattern. By alternating which threads are lifted, different weaving patterns can be achieved.

SIMPLE WEAVES

The most basic pattern is a plain weave, where one weft thread passes over and under alternating warp threads. This pattern is ideal for strong, even cloth.

COMPLEX PATTERNS

More experienced weavers might experiment with twill or herringbone patterns, achieved by manipulating the harnesses to create diagonal or more intricate designs.

PASSING THE SHUTTLE

With the shed created, the weaver passes the shuttle through the warp threads, laying down the weft thread. After each pass, the harnesses are adjusted to create a new shed, and the shuttle is passed back in the opposite direction. This back-and-forth motion interlaces the weft and warp, forming the fabric.

BEATING THE WEFT

After passing the shuttle, the weaver uses the loom's beater (or reed) to push the weft thread down tightly against the previous rows of weaving. This ensures the fabric is tight and even, preventing gaps or loose threads.

The tighter the beating, the denser and more robust the fabric. For lighter fabrics, a gentler beat is used.

ADVANCING THE WARP

As the cloth is woven, the completed fabric is wound onto the cloth beam, and more warp threads are advanced from the warp beam. This allows the weaver to continue working on longer pieces of fabric without interruption.

Finishing Cloth

REMOVING THE FABRIC FROM THE LOOM

Once the desired length of fabric has been woven, the cloth is carefully cut from the loom. The loose warp threads at each end are tied or hemmed to prevent unraveling.

FULLING THE FABRIC

Depending on the type of yarn used, the cloth may be "fulled" to make it firmer and softer. Fulling involves washing the fabric in hot, soapy water and then agitating it to make the fibers mat together slightly, creating a denser fabric. Wool fabrics are often filled to increase durability.

PRESSING AND CUTTING

Once woven and washed, the cloth is pressed flat and ready to cut and sew into garments, blankets, or other valuable items. Weaving produces a continuous piece of fabric, which can be cut and shaped into shirts, trousers, dresses, or other household goods.

Loom Types

BACKSTRAP LOOM

A simple loom where the warp threads are stretched between a stationary object and a strap worn around the weaver's back. This loom is portable and ideal for small projects like belts or sashes.

FLOOR LOOM

A larger, more permanent loom is often used for producing comprehensive, long pieces of fabric. Floor looms can accommodate a variety of weaves and produce sturdy fabric for clothing, blankets, or upholstery.

TABLE LOOM

A smaller, more compact loom that sits on a table. It is suited for narrower pieces of fabric and is easier to move than a floor loom.

Practical Considerations

EFFICIENCY

Weaving on a loom, though labor-intensive, is a highly efficient way to produce fabric, allowing families to make much of their clothing and household linens.

DURABILITY

The strength of handwoven cloth makes it ideal for the rough conditions of pioneer life. Wool fabrics, in particular, are warm, durable, and water-resistant, making them perfect for outerwear and blankets.

VERSATILITY

The loom allows pioneers to create a wide range of textiles, from lightweight cotton for summer shirts to heavy woolen fabrics for winter coats.

Mastering the loom provides self-sufficiency in clothing production, an essential skill in the pioneer lifestyle.

KNITTING AND CROCHETING

The arts of knitting and crocheting are indispensable skills for creating functional garments and decorative items. With minimal tools—knitting needles or a crochet hook—families can produce everything from socks and hats to intricate lacework using available yarn or thread.

By mastering these knitting and crochet techniques, your family can produce essential garments and accessories that provide warmth and comfort while allowing for creativity in design. These handcrafts also serve as a means of relaxation and expression, making them both practical and enriching skills for frontier life.

Basic Knitting Stitches

THE KNIT STITCH

The knit stitch is the foundational stitch in knitting. Using two knitting needles, the yarn is looped through a series of stitches to create a smooth, flat fabric. This simple stitch is ideal for creating sturdy and warm garments like scarves, hats, or blankets. Knitting can be done in rows for flat pieces or in the round for seamless items like socks.

THE PURL STITCH

The purl stitch complements the knit stitch, often combined to create textured patterns in the fabric. By alternating between knit and purl stitches, settlers can make ribbed patterns for fitted cuffs or hems, or create elaborate designs like cable knits for sweaters and socks. Mastering both knit and purl stitches opens up a wide range of possibilities for functional and decorative garments.

KNITTING IN THE ROUND

Using a circular or double-pointed set of needles, knitting in the round allows settlers to create seamless tubes of fabric, which is particularly useful for making socks, hats, or mittens. This method eliminates the need for seams, resulting in a cleaner, more comfortable garment.

Crochet Techniques

BASIC CROCHET STITCHES

Crochet, performed with a single hook, is a more versatile craft for creating smaller, delicate items such as lace, doilies, or decorative edges for garments. The basic stitch in crochet is the chain stitch, from which all other stitches are built. After making a chain, use single or double crochet stitches to create fabric. These stitches form rows of interconnected loops, resulting in a strong yet flexible material.

CROCHETING GARMENTS

While knitting is typically favored for oversized garments, crochet suits smaller pieces or accessories well. Crochet hooks often craft small items like baby bonnets, shawls, or fingerless gloves. The open weave of crochet fabric allows for breathability, making it useful for lighter garments or decorative clothing items.

CREATING LACEWORK

For more decorative purposes, crochet techniques are employed to create intricate lace patterns, doilies, or embellishments for collars and cuffs. Using finer thread and smaller hooks, settlers can craft delicate, decorative items that add a touch of refinement to otherwise practical clothing.

SEWING AND GARMENT CONSTRUCTION

Sewing and constructing garments is vital for settlers, as ready-made clothing is often scarce. By mastering basic sewing techniques, pattern making, and fitting, your family will craft clothing that is practical, durable, and well-suited to the demands of frontier life.

Basic Sewing Techniques

RUNNING STITCH

The running stitch is the most straightforward and most basic hand-sewing technique. It involves passing the needle in and out of the fabric in a straight line, creating tiny, even stitches. This stitch is ideal for sewing seams and combining two pieces of fabric. While quick to sew, itlacks the durability of stronger stitches, so it is typically used for lighter garments or temporary seams.

BACKSTITCH

A backstitch is a more robust and more durable sewing technique, where the needle goes backward to reinforce the seam with each stitch. This creates a tight, continuous line of stitching, perfect for seams that endure wear and tear, such as along trousers or sleeves. Backstitching provides a strong, reliable seam, ensuring garments will hold up during daily activities.

HEMMING

Hemming is used to finish the edges of garments, such as cuffs, skirts, and pant legs. Fold the fabric edge twice to hide the raw edge, then use small, even stitches to secure the fold. This prevents fraying and creates a clean edge that extends the garment's life.

Pattern Making

UNDERSTANDING BASIC PATTERNS

To construct shirts, pants, dresses, and outerwear, settlers rely on simple, hand-drawn patterns. These patterns are typically drawn on paper or cloth and used as fabric-cutting templates. Learn to draft basic shapes for each garment piece—bodices, sleeves, pants legs—and piece them together to ensure a functional and comfortable fit. A well-made pattern ensures efficiency in the sewing process and consistency across multiple garments.

SIZING AND ADAPTATION

Patterns can be adapted to different body shapes and sizes by altering the dimensions. For example, adding extra fabric for a loose fit or reducing fabric for a closer fit. Settlers often pass patterns down through generations, modifying them as necessary to suit individual family members.

CREATING OUTER GARMENTS

When making outerwear, such as jackets or coats, draft more complex patterns that account for multiple layers of fabric or insulation. Factor in larger seam allowances to accommodate thicker materials like wool or leather, ensuring the garments provide warmth and protection from the elements.

Fitting and Tailoring

ADJUSTING GARMENTS

Proper fitting is critical to making comfortable and functional clothing. Adjust garments to fit different body types, allowing for movement and growth. Common alterations include shortening sleeves, tapering waistlines, or adding gussets to pants for extra room.

TAILORING FOR CHILDREN

As children age, make garments with room for growth, perhaps adding tucks or pleats that can be let out over time. Adjustable waistbands or laces ensure the garment remains practical as the child grows.

IMPROVISING AND MODIFYING CLOTHING

If a garment does not fit perfectly after sewing, make modifications. Add fabric to lengthen skirts or pants, insert panels for extra width, or use seams to make garments more fitted. These skills allow you to make the most of materials, ensuring nothing is wasted.

LEATHERWORKING

Leatherworking is an essential skill for creating durable garments and accessories from animal hides. Whether making sturdy moccasins for long treks through the wilderness or crafting belts and hats, knowing how to work with leather ensures that your family is equipped with long-lasting and practical clothing built to withstand the rigors of frontier life.

Making Leather Garments

CRAFTING MOCCASINS

Moccasins are soft leather shoes that provide comfort and durability, which are ideal for navigating forested areas and rugged terrain. To make moccasins, select a sturdy, well-tanned hide, typically from deer or elk. Cut the leather into a pattern, and stitch the sole and upper portion together using sinew or strong thread. Moccasins can be lined with fur for warmth or unlined for lighter use. The soft, flexible soles make them well-suited for quiet movement through the woods, a key feature for hunters and trappers.

BELTS AND HATS

Belts are crafted from leather strips, cut to the desired width and length. Use a leather punch to create holes for buckles and adjust sizing. Hats, especially wide-brimmed ones, are made by shaping softer hides, like deerskin, and stitching the pieces together. Shape the leather using steam and then dry to hold its form.

Hats are an essential part of daily wear for anyone laboring outdoors, offering protection from the sun, rain, and other elements.

DURABLE OUTERWEAR

Leather jackets or vests are crafted for protection against the weather and rugged conditions. Using a hide large enough to cover the torso, cut the material according to a simple pattern. Sew the pieces together with sturdy stitching, and reinforce the seams to ensure durability. These garments protect against wind, rain, and cold, making them valuable for extended work days outside.

Tooling and Stitching Leather

PUNCHING HOLES

Before stitching leather pieces together, holes are punched to make the sewing process easier and to create uniform stitches. Leather punches, made from metal, are used to create these holes along the edges of the garment or accessory. Hole spacing is critical for evenly distributing the stitches, making the final product durable and aesthetically pleasing.

STURDY STITCHING

Once the holes are punched, stitching begins. Saddle stitching is a common technique known for its strength and longevity. Using a thick thread, made from sinew or waxed linen, pass the needle through the pre-punched holes, to create a secure and even seam. This stitch is used to ensure that garments, moccasins, and belts will hold up under heavy use and not unravel over time.

TOOLING LEATHER

For more decorative leather items, settlers sometimes tool the leather, engraving patterns or designs into the surface. Tooling is done with metal stamps or knives, pressing designs into the leather to create intricate textures or symbols. Though decorative, tooled leather is also a mark of craftsmanship and is often reserved for belts, hats, or ceremonial items.

DYEING FABRICS

Natural Dyes

Dyeing fabric using natural materials is a practical and creative skill that allows pioneers to add color and individuality to their homemade garments. By utilizing plants, berries, bark, and roots found in nature, settlers can create a variety of color variations for their wool or cloth. The dyeing process requires knowledge of the dye sources and the methods to ensure even, lasting colors that will endure through washing and wear.

PLANT-BASED DYES

Many plants offer vibrant dyes, with different parts of the plant producing unique hues. Common plants for natural dyes include:

Madder root: Yields reds and pinks

Onion skins: Provide golden yellows

Walnut husks: Produce rich browns

Indigo: A source of deep blues

Dandelions: Offer shades of yellow

Berries like elderberries and blackberries produce purples, blues, and even reds, while sumac berries can create more subtle tones. Be mindful that some berry-based dyes, while beautiful, may fade more quickly and require extra preparation.

Bark from trees like oak or birch, along with nut husks such as walnut or chestnut, can yield earthy tones like browns, tans, and grays. These are particularly valued for their durability.

Dyeing Methods

MORDANTS FOR FIXING THE DYE

Before dyeing fabric, it is crucial to treat the material with a mordant—a substance that helps fix the dye and ensures it bonds to the fibers.

Alum is often used for bright colors and is easy to obtain. Iron is used to darken or "sadden" colors, creating deeper tones. Copper is used to create green hues or enhance blues.

To prepare the fabric, dissolve the chosen mordant in water and soak the cloth or yarn in the solution for a set time (often several hours or overnight), then rinse thoroughly before dyeing.

PREPARING THE DYE BATH

Once the plant material (berries, bark or roots) is gathered, it must be prepared. Most natural dyes are made by boiling the plant material in water for an extended period—typically 30 minutes to an hour—to release the pigments.

Boil the dye material in a large pot of water, then simmer gently, allowing the colors to seep into the water.

Strain out the plant matter, leaving behind a rich, colored liquid known as the dye bath.

Dyeing the Fabric

Once the dye bath is ready, place the mordant-treated fabric into the pot. Stir gently to ensure even dye distribution and prevent the fabric from bunching up. Dyeing wool is best carried out at moderate temperatures to avoid shrinking or loss of natural elasticity.

Allow the fabric to simmer in the dye bath for up to an hour, depending on how deep you want the color.

After simmering, let the fabric soak in the dye bath overnight to intensify the color, stirring occasionally to ensure even coverage.

After dyeing, remove the fabric and rinse it in cold water until it clears. This step removes excess dye and helps set the color. Be careful not to wring the fabric too harshly, as it can cause uneven fading.

Hang the dyed fabric in a shaded, well-ventilated area to dry. Direct sunlight may cause the colors to fade prematurely.

Tips for Even and Lasting Color

PRE-WASH THE FABRIC

Always wash the fabric or wool beforehand to remove oils or dirt, which can affect how well the dye adheres.

AVOID OVERCROWDING THE DYE BATH

Dyeing small batches at a time ensures the fabric absorbs the dye evenly.

TEST A SAMPLE

Before dyeing a whole piece, test the dye on a small fabric swatch to check the color.

By mastering these natural dyeing techniques, settlers can produce beautiful, custom-colored fabrics that add variety and personalization to their wardrobes, while maintaining practical durability.

MENDING AND PATCHING

Pioneer families know the importance of keeping their clothing in good repair. With limited access to new fabrics and the time-consuming nature of making clothes by hand, mastering the skills of mending and patching is essential for prolonging the life of garments.

Repairing Clothes

DARNING SOCKS

Socks and stockings wear out quickly, especially in the heels and toes. Darning involves stitching over the hole in a way that reweaves the fabric. Using a needle and sturdy thread or yarn, settlers weave crisscrossed stitches over the hole, reinforcing the thin areas and extending the sock's life. A darning egg or smooth stone is often placed inside the sock to hold its shape during the repair.

PATCHING WORN FABRIC

Worn spots on shirts, trousers, or outerwear can be patched using scrap fabric. Patching is done by cutting a piece of fabric slightly larger than the hole or worn area and then stitching it in place with a solid running stitch or backstitch. Edges of the patch are often folded under to prevent fraying. Patching is essential for high-wear areas like knees, elbows, and pockets.

REINFORCING SEAMS

Over time, seams may weaken or come undone, especially in heavily used clothing like work shirts or pants. Reinforcing seams by sewing a second line of stitches along the original seam helps to strengthen the garment. For extra reinforcement, settlers might add a strip of fabric to the inside of the seam before restitching.

Recycling Old Clothes

REPURPOSING WORN GARMENTS

When garments become too worn, settlers don't let them go to waste. Old shirts, skirts, or trousers are often cut up for new purposes. For instance, worn-out shirts can be turned into patch material for other clothes, while sturdier fabrics, like old wool coats, can be made into quilt squares or blankets.

MAKING NEW ITEMS FROM OLD CLOTHES

Pioneers are thrifty and resourceful, and old clothes are frequently transformed into something new. Worn-out dresses or pants might be taken apart, and the fabric used to make smaller garments for children, aprons, or even linings for jackets. This practice ensures that even the oldest, most worn garments are used to their fullest potential.

By learning to mend, patch, and recycle clothing, settlers ensure that their limited resources last as long as possible, making the most of every stitch.

SEASONAL PROJECTS

Pioneer families must adapt their clothing to the changing seasons, ensuring warmth in winter's bitter cold and comfort in summer's heat. Mastering the creation of garments suited to both extremes is essential for survival and comfort on the frontier.

Winter Garments

Insulating Against the Cold

WOOL COATS AND OUTERWEAR

For the harsh winters, warm outer layers are crucial. Wool, known for its insulating properties, is spun into thick yarn and used to create heavy coats, cloaks, and capes. These garments, often lined with additional layers of woven fabric, provide excellent protection from the cold. Leather from tanned hides is also used for crafting durable and wind-resistant outerwear like fur-lined cloaks or heavy overcoats.

MITTENS AND SCARVES

Hands and necks need special protection during winter. Wool mittens, knitted using double layers of yarn, trap warmth and allow fingers to stay functional even in freezing temperatures. Scarves and shawls are knitted or crocheted with dense wool and wrapped securely around the neck to prevent cold air from seeping through clothing layers. These accessories are both practical and easy to make at home.

WOOLEN BLANKETS AND BEDDING

In addition to clothing, wool is used to craft warm blankets and bedding for winter nights. Large woven wool blankets can be layered on beds, or used as wraps during travel in winter sleighs or sledges. Wool's ability to insulate and retain heat even when damp makes it reliable for keeping families warm through the night.

Light Summer Clothing
Staying Cool in the Heat

COTTON AND LINEN GARMENTS

Pioneers rely on breathable materials like cotton and linen for the warmer months. These fibers are woven into lightweight fabric, ideal for shirts, dresses, and trousers. Cotton and linen absorb moisture, allowing sweat to evaporate and keeping the body cool. Summer garments are typically looser-fitting to promote airflow and reduce the heat's discomfort.

SIMPLE, FUNCTIONAL DESIGN

Summer clothing is often made with simplicity in mind, using fewer layers than winter garments. Lightweight shirts, skirts, and trousers are crafted with minimal decoration, focusing on comfort and ease of movement. Short-sleeved shirts, wide-brimmed hats, and cotton bonnets are standard to protect from the sun without trapping excess heat.

SUN PROTECTION

While warmth is the primary concern in winter, shielding the skin from the sun's harsh rays is vital in summer. Long cotton skirts, wide-brimmed hats, and linen shirts with high collars are worn to prevent sunburn. These lightweight garments allow coverage without overheating, essential for outdoor work during long summer days.

MAKING AND MENDING SHOES

Sturdy shoes or boots are essential for daily labor and travel. Pioneer families craft footwear from leather, using basic cobbling techniques to create durable shoes, boots, and moccasins.

Crafting Leather Shoes and Boots

Leather from tanned animal hides is cut and shaped into uppers, soles, and heels. These pieces are then sewn together using strong, waxed thread. The soles are often reinforced with additional leather or wooden inserts for durability, especially in rugged terrain. Moccasins, a simpler form of footwear, are made by cutting a single piece of leather and stitching it to fit snugly around the foot, often with added soles for protection.

BASIC COBBLING REPAIRS

Footwear endures wear and tear, and learning the art of cobbling is vital for keeping shoes functional. Worn soles can be replaced, torn leather patched, and broken seams stitched back together. Using awls to punch holes and cobbler's wax to secure the stitching ensures long-lasting repairs. Wooden or leather inserts are sometimes placed inside shoes to extend their lifespan.

MAINTAINING FOOTWEAR

Regular care helps preserve footwear. Leather shoes and boots are often treated with animal fat or oil to keep them soft and waterproof, while moccasins benefit from regular re-stitching and sole replacement. Knowing how to care for and repair shoes means settlers can extend the life of their footwear without needing to replace them frequently.

UNDERGARMENTS AND LINENS

In addition to outerwear, settlers must produce practical household items and undergarments to maintain hygiene and comfort.

Undergarments

Essential undergarments and nightshirts are often made from lightweight cotton or linen fabric.

These are simple, functional garments designed for comfort and cleanliness. Basic undergarment patterns allow for easy sewing and adjustments, with minimal embellishments. Soft linen or cotton is preferred for underclothing to prevent irritation and keep the body cool in warmer weather.

Household Linens

Families also need to produce linens for the home, including towels, curtains, and bed sheets. These items are made from sturdy cotton or linen, woven or sewn by hand to fit the household's needs. Curtains provide privacy and insulation, while bed sheets and blankets ensure warmth and comfort during rest. Towels, made from absorbent fabrics, are essential for personal hygiene and household chores.

PRACTICAL SEWING FOR LINENS

Like clothing, linens must be durable enough to withstand frequent use and washing. Strong seams, reinforced edges, and hemming techniques prevent fraying. Pioneers often recycle old or worn-out fabric into rags or patchwork quilts, ensuring no material goes to waste.

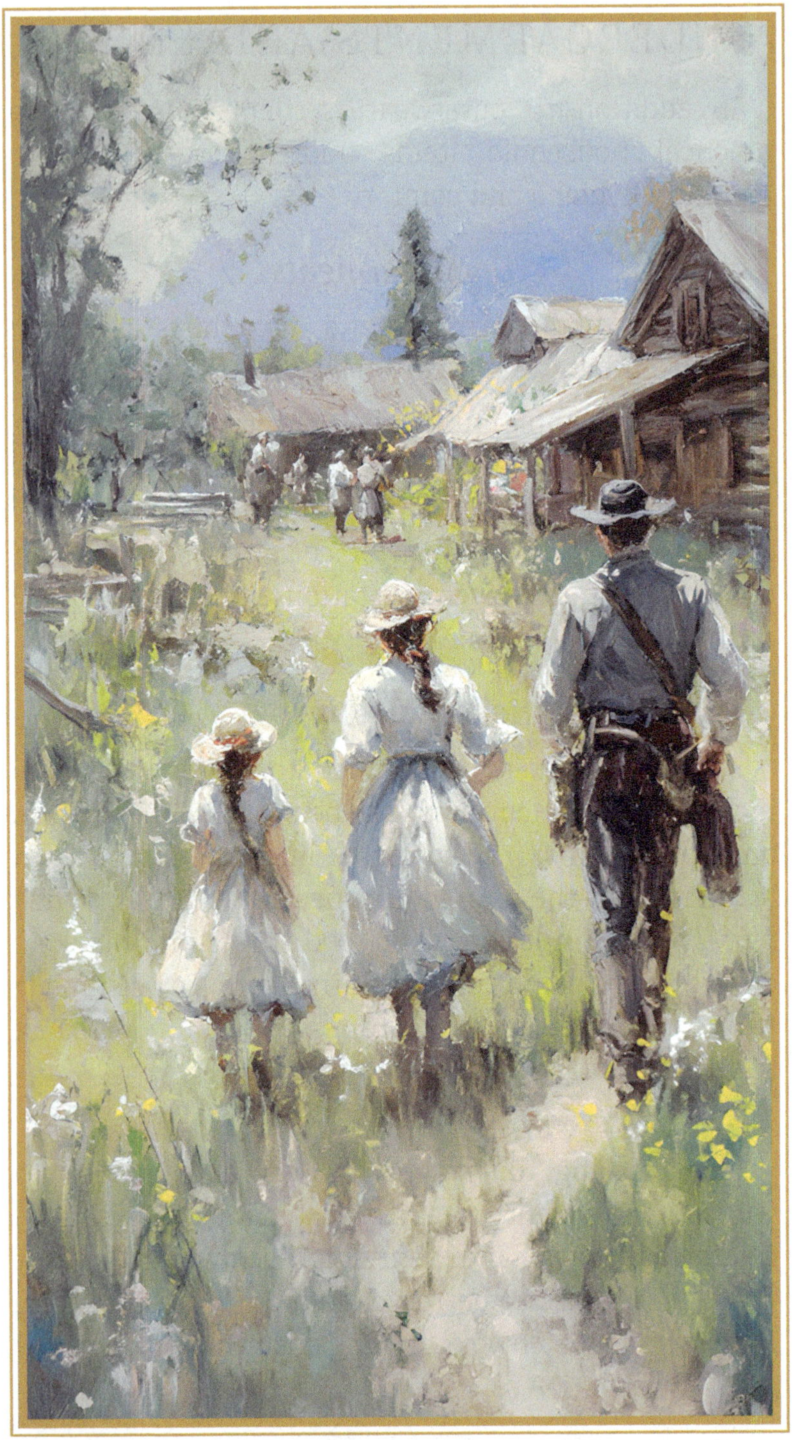

FAMILY RELATIONSHIPS

As you prepare to embark upon your journey into the wilderness, it is vital to consider the structure of your household, for the success of your homestead relies upon the diligence of each family member. In the wilderness, family is not merely a social bond but the very foundation of your livelihood. A husband's leadership, a wife's support in managing the home, and the labor of children and elders all contribute to the welfare of the family and its survival on the frontier.

GENDER ROLES

The duties of men and women on the frontier are clear. The husband, as head of the household, is tasked with defending and providing for the family, clearing land, planting crops, and hunting for game. The wife oversees the domestic sphere, caring for the children, preserving food, maintaining the home, and ensuring all have what they need to weather the challenges of wilderness life. Both roles are essential to the success of the homestead, and each must honor the other's contribution.

EDITOR'S NOTE: The understanding and expectations of gender roles have evolved considerably since the early 19th century. Today, family roles are far more flexible, with both men and women taking on a variety of responsibilities in and outside the home. Many households now emphasize equal participation in work, childcare, and decision-making, reflecting a broader cultural shift toward gender equality. The contributions of all individuals, regardless of gender, are valued in shaping both family dynamics and community structures.

CHILDREN'S CONTRIBUTIONS

Even the youngest family members will have important tasks, such as gathering firewood, collecting eggs, or helping in the garden. Children's labor, though light at first, will grow as they do. Instilling a sense of responsibility early will help them take pride in their contributions.

EXTENDED FAMILY AND COMMUNITY SUPPORT

ELDERS AS KEEPERS OF WISDOM

If your family includes elders, consider yourself truly fortunate. Grandparents hold the key to generations of wisdom, from farming techniques to herbal remedies and survival skills. Their counsel will guide you as you forge your new life in the wilderness. In their wisdom lies the strength to persevere through the trials of pioneer life.

INTERGENERATIONAL SUPPORT

Having extended family nearby provides great advantage. Relatives work together to build homes, tend crops, and care for the young and vulnerable. The ties of kinship form a sturdy foundation of mutual support, ensuring that your family can weather the harshest of trials.

MARRIAGE AND PARTNERSHIP

Partnerships in Labor

Marriage on the frontier is more than a romantic bond; it is a partnership of labor and survival. You and your spouse must stand shoulder to shoulder, sharing the burdens and the bounties of wilderness life. A good marriage will be your refuge during the harshest winters and a source of joy during times of plenty.

LOVE AND PRACTICALITY

While love holds great importance, the practical considerations of marriage cannot be ignored. A spouse who is strong and capable can determine whether you thrive or fall into hardship. Choose wisely, for your success on the frontier depends on it.

FAMILY GROWTH AND CHALLENGES

BIRTH AND RAISING CHILDREN

Bringing new life into the world fills your home with hope, but it also brings great challenge. Childbirth is fraught with danger, and raising children in the wilderness requires not only patience and strength but also the support of your community to help them grow and prosper.

DEATH AND LOSS

Loss is an ever-present reality on the frontier, be it from illness, accident, or misfortune. When death visits your family, resilience is your greatest ally. The bonds of family will provide the strength to endure sorrow and move forward, together.

CELEBRATIONS AND TRADITIONS

FAMILY GATHERINGS

Though daily life is hard, there will still be moments for celebration—weddings, the birth of children, harvest feasts, and holidays. These gatherings strengthen the ties within your family and offer a reprieve from the labors of the land. They are reminders of joy amidst the trials of life.

PASSING DOWN TRADITIONS

Whether through tales told by the hearth, recipes passed from generation to generation, or customs brought from the old country, traditions offer comfort and continuity. It is your duty to teach these to your children, so that they may carry your family's legacy into the future.

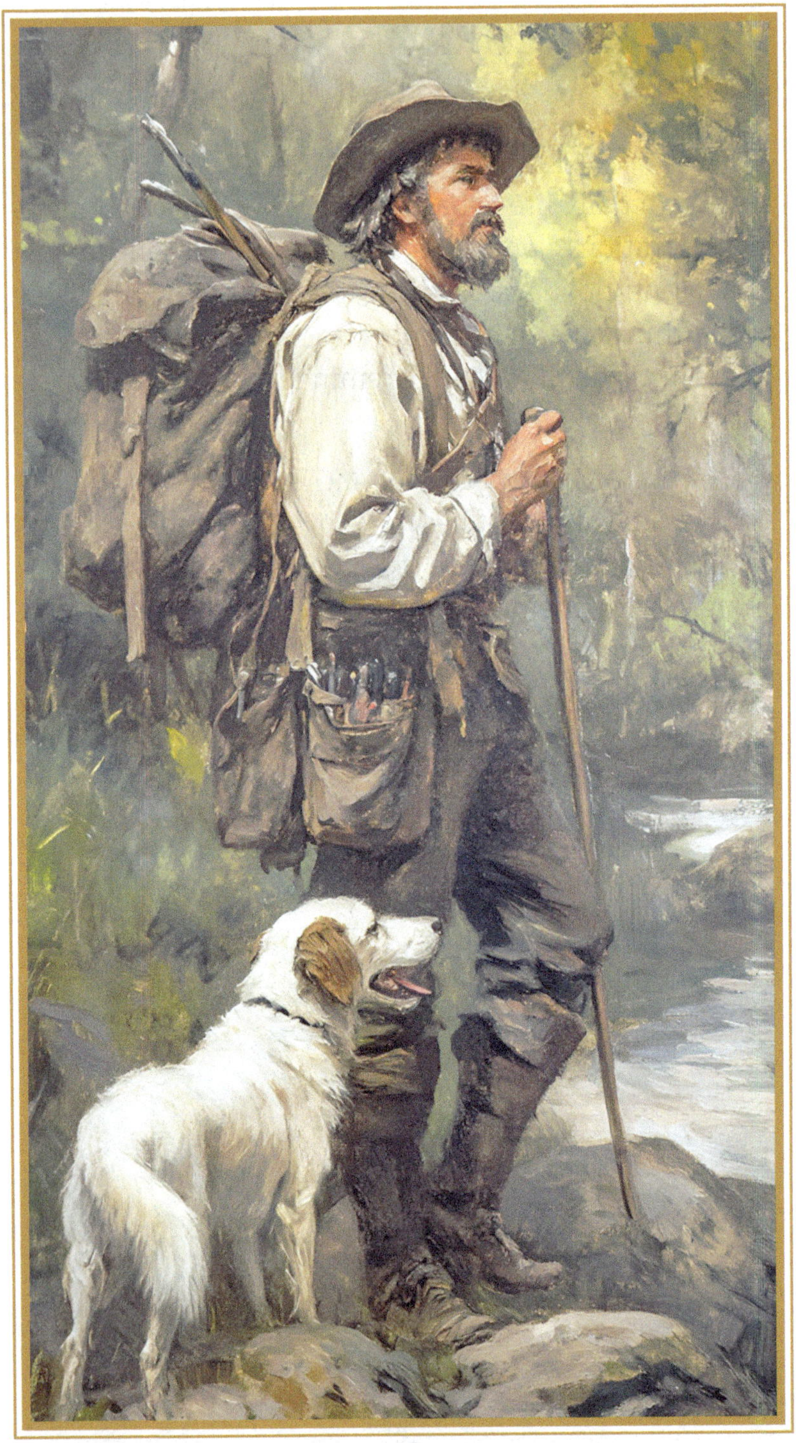

CONCLUSION

Embrace the Journey Ahead

As you prepare to take your first steps into the wilderness of Orleans County, remember that you are not only embarking on a journey to claim and cultivate land but also becoming a vital part of a growing community.

Just as your forebears relied on the knowledge of the land, the strength of community, and the wisdom passed down through generations, so too will you. Each skill you acquire, from crafting essential goods to building lasting trade relationships, brings you closer to a self-sufficient life and strengthens the community around you. The success of your venture depends not only on your hard work but also on the mutual aid and cooperation of your neighbors.

Your journey does not end with securing land; it is only the beginning. With each season, you will face new trials—storms, blizzards, droughts—but you will also grow stronger and more resilient. Through these experiences, you will contribute to the fabric of your community, ensuring that future generations will inherit a thriving, well-ordered society.

As you settle into this new life, draw upon the collective knowledge contained in these pages. Trust in the guidance of your fellow pioneers, the land's resources, and the strength of your own resolve. Every fence you build, every crop you plant, and every trade you make is a step toward not only your success but also the prosperity of Orleans County.

With faith, perseverance, and the support of your community, you will not only survive but thrive. Welcome to your new life on the frontier.

END

Want to know more about the Pioneers of Orleans County?

Visit pioneerhistory.us for additional content
and notices of updates as they occur.

And if you have not already done so,
check out the two companion volumes
"*Pioneer History of Orleans County, New York*" and
"*Pioneer Cookbook: Wilderness Recipes of Orleans County.*"
These two books provide a wealth of information
to help you better understand the life and times of
the Orleans County Pioneers.

Language translations are available.
Visit folk.studio for more information.

INDEX

A

Above-Ground Cisterns, 389
Accidents, 17, 41, 337, 351
Acorns, 105-106, 167, 204, 310-311
Adverse Possession, 54
Agricultural Tools, 114
Agriculture, 24, 28, 45, 145, 270, 280
Ague, 317, 343-344
Albany, 23
Albion, 23
Alluvial Soils, 34
Amphibians, 255, 262-263, 265-266, 268, 271, 281, 295
Animal Hides, 62-63, 74, 78, 123-124, 397, 448, 457
Animal Tracks, 4
Animal Trails, 13
Arithmetic, 66, 376-377, 384
Ash, 63, 89, 147, 149, 153, 165, 169, 338, 340, 422-423, 425
Ash Collection, 425
Axes, 2, 63, 122, 135, 137-138, 152, 409, 427

B

Bandages, 2
Bark, 5, 7, 53, 63, 122, 159-163, 165-169, 172, 189-190, 286, 293, 298, 300-301, 311, 335, 341, 345, 357, 360, 431, 450-451
Barn Construction, 126
Barn Raising, 37, 65, 76, 382, 398
Barns and Stables, 110-111
Barred Owl, 255
Bartering, 65, 395, 398, 400-402, 404, 410, 421
Basic Medical Supplies, 2
Basket Weaving, 147
Basswood, 163
Beans and Squash, 96
Bear, 13, 16, 25, 112, 159, 228, 249, 260, 262, 273, 304-311, 409, 432
Bear Behavior, 310
Beaver, 21, 142, 228, 283, 298, 409
Bedding, 2, 110, 193, 252, 258, 327, 435, 456
Beech, 73, 159, 200, 310-311
Beech Nuts, 73, 159, 200
Beechnuts, 310-311
Bees, 76, 163, 381-382, 384, 392
Beneficial Plants, 157, 173, 210
Birch, 153, 166, 334-335, 451
Birds of Prey, 330
Bison, 302
Black Walnut, 201
Blacksmithing, 63, 127, 150, 370, 395, 398-399, 403, 421
Blankets, 2, 62, 107, 174, 339, 409, 438, 441-443, 454, 456, 459
Blaze, 7-8, 338-339
Blazed Trees, 53, 411
Blazing Trails, 4, 7
Blizzards, 76-77, 80, 467
Blueberry, 72, 180
Bluebird, 253
Boiling Water, 361
Boundary Disputes, 56

Boundary Markers, 133
Breeding Practices, 107
Brick Houses, 129
Bridges, 373, 391-392, 396
Broken Bones, 365, 369
Buck, 226, 228, 299
Bucket Irrigation, 45
Buffalo, 23
Building Materials, 143
Bullfrog, 271
Burns, 126, 146, 151, 333, 339, 343, 363, 367, 370-371

C

Cairns, 8
Campsites, 3
Canals, 352
Carpenters, 396
Carpentry, 64, 127, 147, 398
Cash Transactions, 400
Cattle, 96, 104-105, 109, 113, 211, 217, 228, 304, 307
Celebrations, 465
Chaff, 102
Chanterelles, 207
Chestnuts, 203
Childbirth Complications, 350
Chimneys, 74, 124, 151, 337
Chinking, 122, 124
Chipmunk, 285
Cholera, 42, 111, 325, 345
Churches, 37, 65, 149, 373-374, 378
Cisterns, 41-45, 47-49, 83, 389
Clay Soils, 33, 98, 115
Clearing, 8, 13, 22, 48, 55, 59, 71, 118, 134-135, 137-138, 145, 154, 199, 262, 270, 281, 462

Clearing Land, 145, 262, 281, 462
Clothing, 2, 59, 62-63, 75, 107, 226, 228, 258, 284, 287-288, 291, 299-300, 302, 306, 317, 352, 371, 397-398, 409, 428, 430, 432-433, 435, 438, 442-443, 445, 447-448, 453-456, 459
Clothing Production, 435, 443
Cold Season, 273
Collaboration with Native Americans, 356
Common Raven, 259
Common Trees, 158
Communal Buildings, 391
Communal Events, 384
Community Arbitration, 56
Community Gatherings, 76
Community Support, 64, 463
Companion Planting, 60
Compass Navigation, 10
Composting, 43, 89
Composting Pits, 43
Conflict Resolution, 415, 417-418
Controlled Burns, 339
Cooking Utensils, 2
Corn, 32-33, 60, 72, 86, 94-96, 98-101, 103, 109, 323-324, 396, 401, 409-410
Cougar, 283, 303
Courthouse, 56
Cover Crops, 88, 90
Cranberries, 191
Credit Systems, 395
Crocheting, 443
Crop Diversity, 98
Crop Management, 93
Crop Rotation, 46, 60, 86, 91, 97, 323

Cross Marks, 7
Cultivation, 26, 118
Cultural Practices, 67, 408, 413

D

Daily Necessities, 421
Deeds, 54-56
Deep Wells, 41
Deer, 13, 21, 133, 141, 161, 204, 226, 228, 231, 283, 299, 301, 303-304, 311, 319, 409, 448
Deer Hunting, 226
Dense Forests, 1, 4, 7, 10-12, 25
Digging, 45, 132-133, 135, 138, 339, 389
Dispute Resolution, 416
Dog, 112, 307, 309
Drag, 115
Drainage Systems, 35
Dried Meats, 1
Dry Goods, 153, 326, 337
Drying Herbs, 360
Dyeing Fabrics, 450
Dysentery, 42, 325, 346

E

Early Mills, 20, 390
Early Settlers, 17, 25, 114
Echinacea, 357
Economic Stability, 57, 113, 304
Edible Mushrooms, 157, 205
Edible Plants, 60
Education, 65-66, 375, 377
Educational Institutions, 375
Elderberry, 177, 359, 451
Elk, 13, 300, 304, 448
Elm, 71, 164

Emergency Preparedness, 339
Endurance, 2, 25, 105, 269
Environmental Impact, 154
Erie Canal, 18, 23, 29, 155
Essential Supplies, 1
Exposure, 5, 121, 126, 347, 352
Extended Family, 463

F

Family Members, 2, 373, 387-388, 446, 462
Fencing, 131, 135, 139, 309
Fertile Soil, 15, 31, 34, 57
Fevers, 176, 182, 190, 357, 361
Fire Building, 333
Fire Safety, 125, 337
Fire Tools, 340
Fireplaces, 337
Firewood, 62, 74-75, 78, 121, 127, 131, 137, 139, 146, 150-151, 154-155, 334-335, 338, 404, 462
First Aid, 343, 351-352, 367
First Schoolhouse, 376
Fish, 14, 20, 22-24, 221-225, 229, 231, 414
Fish Creek, 22-23
Fish Preservation, 225
Fish Species, 24, 231
Fishing, 2, 20, 23-24, 27-28, 40, 60, 221-224, 414
Fishing Seasons, 223
Fishing Techniques, 222
Fishing Villages, 20
Flint and Steel, 335-336, 341
Flood Plains, 35-36, 79
Flooding, 34-36, 45, 48-49, 76, 78-79, 99, 121, 392

Folk Medicine, 355
Food Preservation, 60, 425
Food Production, 60
Foraged Nuts, 200
Foraging, 60, 65, 71-72, 75, 109, 157, 173, 194, 202, 208, 257, 262, 288, 305, 310-311, 355, 360, 365
Fords, 16-17, 393
Forest Clearing, 137, 199
Fox, 112, 142, 228, 283, 294, 297
Freshwater, 22, 239, 241-242, 244
Frog, 21, 271, 273-275, 277-279
Frozen Rivers, 16
Fur Trade, 298, 409
Fur Trapping, 228

G

Game Animals, 283
Game Birds, 227
Gender Roles, 462
Genesee, 18, 36, 233
Genesee County, 18
Genesee River, 233
Genesee Road, 36
Goldenseal, 181, 358, 368, 371
Goose, 252
Grain and Apples, 23
Grain Mills, 396
Granaries, 103, 314, 331, 390
Gristmill, 390
Groundwater, 39-41, 389

H

Hammers, 2, 152
Hardships, I, 383
Hardtack, 1

Hardwood Trees, 425
Hare, 227, 286
Harrows, 99, 115-116
Harvesting Techniques, 101
Hawk, 256, 307, 330
Health, 2, 42, 46-47, 61, 72, 82, 87, 96-97, 103-104, 112, 139, 154, 157, 178, 211, 271, 282, 310, 313-314, 317, 343, 347, 353, 359, 362, 367
Hemlock, 147, 150, 162, 176, 210, 214, 431
Herbal Remedies, 318, 329, 345, 355-356, 360, 363-365, 463
Herbal Salves, 317, 363
Herbs, 2, 60, 72, 208, 287, 327, 360-365, 368, 370, 397
Herds, 300, 302
Hickory, 73, 146, 150, 152, 202, 333-334
Hickory Nuts, 73, 202
Holley, 28-29
Holley Canal Falls, 29
Holley Gorge, 28
Home Insulation, 124
Home Remedies, 111, 355, 365
Horse, 86, 96, 104, 115, 138, 217, 367
Hospitality, 418
House Raising, 61
Hudson River, 23
Hunting, 2, 12, 27-28, 60, 65, 67, 141-143, 221, 226-229, 231, 256, 262, 283, 294, 300, 302, 308, 330, 410, 413-414, 417, 462
Hunting and Trapping, 141, 308, 410
Hunting Techniques, 221
Hunting Wild Game, 226

I

Ice Roads, 16, 393
Indian Trail, 25
Informal Schools, 66
Infrastructure, 65, 345, 373-374, 380, 387, 389-391, 396
Injuries, 2, 343, 351, 357, 365, 367, 369
Insect Pests, 250, 316
Insulation, 61, 69, 74, 78, 110, 121, 123-124, 128-129, 131, 428, 447, 459
Iroquois, 25, 27, 417-418
Irrigation Ditches, 22
Irrigation Systems, 389
Irrigation Techniques, 45

J

Johnson Creek, 21, 36
Journey, II-4, 7-8, 11, 14, 17-20, 23, 25-26, 223, 229, 461, 467

K

Kendall, 21
Key Landmarks, 1, 18
Knitting, 435, 443-444
Knowledge Sharing, 65

L

Lake Erie, 23
Lake Ontario, 18, 20-21, 26-27
Lakes, 14-16, 19, 23, 40, 44, 155, 221-223, 235-240, 242, 244, 247, 252, 265, 267, 271, 277, 280, 301
Lambsquarters, 196
Land Boundaries, 381
Land Clearing, 138, 270
Land Disputes, 54, 418
Land Grants, 51, 374
Land Management, 56, 137, 139
Land Office, 53, 56, 373-374
Land Ownership, 53, 55, 57, 413-414
Land Records, 380
Language Barriers, 411-412
Leather Tanning, 63
Leatherworking, 421, 448
Legacy, 57, 374, 465
Linen Production, 433
Livestock, 2-3, 17, 26, 37, 39-40, 57, 61, 72-74, 76, 78-81, 83, 86-87, 95-96, 98, 103-105, 107-113, 126-128, 131-134, 141, 153, 155, 157, 194, 210, 212-217, 219, 228, 231, 247, 259, 261, 268, 290, 293-295, 303-308, 318, 329, 392, 399-400, 402-404
Livestock Management, 61, 104, 107
Loamy Soils, 31-32, 34, 94-95, 97
Local Economy, 23, 231, 395, 398-399, 404
Local Governance, 373-374, 377, 380
Local Government, 51, 55, 380-382, 415
Log Cabins, 61, 121, 148
Looms, 62, 442
Lumber, 155, 171

M

Magnetic North, 6
Magnetic Variations, 11
Malaria, 317, 343-344
Mallard Duck, 258
Mammals, 24, 169, 226-227, 248, 255-256, 260, 262, 271, 283, 291, 303, 306
Managing Shock, 371

Managing Supplies, 2
Maple, 71, 146-147, 150, 153, 159-161, 334, 410, 421-422
Maple Sugaring, 71, 421
Maple Syrup, 71, 146, 421-422
Maps, 4, 7-8, 10, 388
Marriage, 419, 464
Marsh Creek, 22
Medical Supplies, 2
Medicinal Plants, 356, 361
Medina, 23-24, 29
Medina Sandstone Formation, 29
Melting Snow for Water, 48
Mending and Patching, 453
Merchants, 395, 400-401, 403
Metalworking, 63
Mills, 20, 28, 39, 65, 144, 390, 396
Moose, 13, 301
Morels, 71, 206
Mortar, 128, 134
Moss, 4-5, 61, 122, 124, 341
Moss Growth, 4-5
Mountain Gaps, 14
Mountain Lion, 303
Mountains, 9, 12, 14-15, 414
Muck Soils, 28, 31, 33-35
Mucklands, 28, 97
Mulching, 32, 46, 83
Murray, 21
Mutual Aid Societies, 373, 382-383, 391, 399
Mutual Respect, 412, 417

N

Nails, 2, 63, 132, 149, 396
Native American Trails, 14

Native Americans, 19, 28, 67, 96, 181, 188, 190-192, 203-204, 210, 231, 233, 239, 244, 260, 262, 267, 269-271, 274-277, 279-282, 284, 287, 292-293, 295, 300-303, 306, 311, 346, 348-349, 352, 355-356, 365, 407-412, 414, 418-419
Natural Disasters, 76-77
Natural Landmarks, 5, 12, 15, 414
Natural Repellents, 321, 324
Natural Water Sources, 39, 41
Navigate, I, 1, 10, 12, 18, 25, 374, 395, 400, 404-405, 411, 415
Navigation, 4, 6, 10-12, 15, 18-19, 26
Newt, 280
Niagara Escarpment, 18, 26
North Star (Polaris), 6
Northern Flicker, 257

O

Oak, 20-24, 27-28, 35-36, 78, 122, 146-147, 149-150, 153, 167, 204, 207, 333-334, 431, 451
Oak Orchard, 20-24, 27-28, 35-36, 78
Oak Orchard River, 20-24, 27-28, 35-36, 78
Oak Orchard Swamp, 27
Older Children, 2
Organic Matter, 32-33, 86-88, 96, 114, 116
Outbuildings, 35, 37, 78, 80, 126-127, 148, 150, 162
Overburden, 2
Ox, 25, 105, 115, 138

P

Passes, 14, 23, 102, 227, 440
Pemmican, 191

Peppermint, 358
Pest Control, 276, 280, 313, 330
Pickling, 205, 209, 225, 425
Pioneer Healthcare, 363
Pioneer Spirit, 179
Plan Carefully, 1
Plantain, 358-359, 362, 368
Planting Techniques, 99
Plows, 63, 99, 114-115, 427
Pneumonia, 348, 350, 353
Point Breeze, 20, 27
Poison Ivy, 186
Poisonous Plants, 60, 157, 210
Ponds, 40, 47-48, 174, 238-239, 242, 258, 265, 267-271, 273, 275-277, 279-280, 290, 298, 301, 434
Post Office, 373-374, 387-388
Post Roads, 387
Postal Routes, 373, 387-388
Potatoes, 32, 86, 94, 97, 99, 102
Poultices, 111, 177, 193, 356, 362
Predator Control, 228
Predators, 9, 13, 61, 72, 110, 112, 228, 269, 279, 283, 286, 289, 303-304, 307-309, 313, 324, 330
Preparing for Your Journey, 1
Preventing House Fires, 337
Property Boundaries, 54, 132, 134
Property Taxes, 55
Prosperity, 23, 67, 76, 82, 93-94, 113, 139, 143, 395-396, 398, 468
Protecting Crops, 131
Proximity to Roads, 36
Public Spaces, 391
Purslane, 72, 195

Q
Quilting Bees, 76, 384
Quinine, 345

R
Rabbit, 227, 283, 287
Raccoon, 112, 142, 228, 283, 288
Rafters, 122, 148
Rainwater Harvesting, 41
Ranges, 14
Raspberry, 72, 197
Rattlesnake, 260-261
Reading, 4, 8-9, 11, 66, 376-377, 384
Red Oaks, 204
Religious Institutions, 374, 378
Remedies, 2, 111, 180-181, 188, 318, 327, 329, 345, 355-356, 360, 363-365, 371, 397, 463
Reptiles, 246, 248, 256, 260
Resourcefulness, 59, 64, 259, 289
Respect for Territories, 413
Ridge Road, 18, 25-26, 36
Ridges, 12, 34, 277
Riverbanks, 17, 36, 185, 199
Rivers, I, 4, 8-9, 12, 14-16, 19, 34-36, 39, 44, 48, 78, 144, 155, 164, 221-223, 229, 233-236, 238-242, 244, 247, 252, 258, 262, 265, 268, 270, 290, 295, 317-318, 343-344, 390, 392-393, 403, 414
Road Conditions, 1, 3
Roads, 4, 12, 16, 18, 24-25, 36, 55, 373-374, 382, 387, 391-393
Robin, 254
Rodents, 103, 248, 256, 263-264, 313-314, 316, 330-331
Role of Women, 384, 418

477

Root Beer, 190
Root Cellars, 72, 75, 80, 102, 109, 127
Rotational Grazing, 61

S

Safe Harvesting Practices, 205
Safety During Travel, 3
Salamander, 281-282
Salmon, 233
Salted Pork, 1
Salves, 317, 356, 359, 363
Sandy Creek, 21-22, 28, 35, 78
Sandy Soils, 32, 266
Sanitation Practices, 43, 47, 351
Sawmill, 154-155, 390
Saws, 2, 64, 122, 135, 137
Schoolhouses, 376, 384
Schooling Practices, 376
Scythes, 101, 116
Seasonal Changes, 15, 59-60
Seasonal Construction, 130
Seasonal Hunting Cycles, 228
Sections, 136-137, 350
Seeds, 2, 73, 99-101, 106, 115-116, 118, 161, 165-166, 169, 174, 197, 284-285, 311, 315, 434
Self-Sufficiency, 59, 63-64, 66, 433, 443
Settlement Patterns, 54, 343
Sewing, 75, 368, 435, 445-447, 449, 454, 459
Sewing Techniques, 445
Shadow Sticks, 5
Shallow Wells, 40
Sheep, 62-63, 104, 107-109, 304, 307, 428

Shelter Building, 61, 121
Sickle, 101, 117
Sleds, 16
Small Game Hunting, 227
Small Mammals, 24, 169, 227, 248, 255-256, 260, 262, 271, 291, 306
Smallpox, 345
Snakes, 260-261, 263-266
Snowfall, 69-70, 74, 77
Soap Making, 63, 107, 422
Social Gatherings, 113, 377, 384, 404
Sod Houses, 61, 129
Soil Amendments, 34, 89
Soil Fertility, 85, 88-90, 94, 97-98, 105
Soil Management, 85, 90
Soil Types, 31, 95, 97, 172
Soups and Stews, 195, 268
Sovereignty, 413, 417
Splinting, 369
Split Logs, 123
Spring Peeper, 273
Spring Thaw, 35, 48, 78
Springs, 39
Squatters' Rights, 54
Squirrel, 161, 204, 283-284, 311, 314
Stars, 4, 6, 12
Starvation, 78, 320
Stone Construction, 128
Stone Quarry, 36
Storage Infrastructure, 390
Strawberry, 72, 178
Streams, 14, 18, 39, 47, 144, 155, 174, 201, 221-223, 231, 233-234, 237, 262, 269-270, 273, 277, 279, 295, 318, 390, 434

Stumps, 134-135, 137-138
Sturgeon, 232
Summer Droughts, 49
Summer Growing Season, 72
Sun, 4-5, 12, 129, 225, 229, 434-435, 448, 456-457
Sun Position, 5
Sunday Schools, 384
Surface Irrigation, 45
Surveying, 52, 54, 56
Surveyors, 52
Survival Skills, 66, 463

T

Tanning Hides, 430
Teachers, 384
Teas and Infusions, 361
Temperature Fluctuations, 42
Textile Production, 63, 428
Threshing, 101-102, 382
Thunderstorms, 76, 79
Timber, 36, 57, 121, 123, 126, 128-130, 132, 135, 137-139, 143-145, 148-150, 152, 154-155, 168, 201, 304, 322, 382, 390, 397, 399
Timber As a Cash Crop, 154
Timber Harvesting, 139
Timber Resources, 144
Tinctures, 357-359, 361-362
Title Deeds, 54
Toads, 266, 276
Tools and Implements, 152
Tornadoes, 76, 80-81
Town Meeting, 56, 381, 399, 404
Townships, 380
Toxic Plants, 210

Trade Goods, 20, 228, 395, 402, 409
Trade with Native Americans, 409-410
Trading Posts, 3, 14, 391, 402-404
Traditions, 113, 143, 251, 355, 379, 408, 465
Trails, 4, 7, 9, 12-14, 25, 36, 228, 392
Transit Line, 26
Transit Line Road, 26
Transportation, 1, 19, 23, 34, 36, 96, 391, 393
Transportation Infrastructure, 391
Treaty, 415-418
Tree Growth Patterns, 4, 12
Trees, 4-5, 7-9, 21, 26, 53, 61, 71, 79-81, 99, 122, 130, 134-135, 137-139, 142, 144-145, 148, 154, 157-158, 164, 201, 204, 207, 246-247, 250, 257, 278, 284, 286, 293, 297-298, 301, 310-311, 322, 411, 421-422, 425, 451
Tuberculosis, 346
Turtle, 267-270

U

Underground Cisterns, 41
Uplands, 34

V

Valleys, 4, 12-15, 34, 93
Venison, 229
Village of Medina, 24

W

Water Conservation, 45-46, 49
Water Filtration, 44
Water Infrastructure, 389
Water Power, 390

Resources, 36, 39, 389
Waterborne Diseases, 42
Waterfalls, 19, 28
Waterfowl Hunting, 229
Waterport, 24, 28
Weather, I, 1-3, 6, 10, 47, 59-61, 69-70, 76-77, 98, 101, 110, 124, 131, 136, 149-150, 260, 273, 333, 338, 347-348, 352, 383, 449, 459, 462-463
Weather Patterns, 60, 69-70
Weather Variability, 77
Weaving Cloth, 75, 438
Wells, 40-41, 43, 47-49, 69, 83, 389
Western New York, 48, 76-77, 80, 83, 172, 245, 260, 277, 301-302
Wetlands, 20, 22, 28, 33, 35, 174, 185, 191, 229, 258, 263, 265, 267, 273, 275-280, 290, 317, 329, 343-344
Wheat, 32, 72, 86, 94-95, 98, 100, 103, 396, 409
Wild Animal, 131, 334
Wild Grapes, 199
Wild Leeks, 71, 194
Wild Plants, 157-158, 173, 206, 355, 360, 365
Willow Bark, 357
Wind Patterns, 4-5
Winter Survival, 74
Wolf, 25, 112, 141, 228, 283, 304, 307-309
Wood for Construction, 158
Woodlots, 90, 137, 139, 154
Woodworking, 64, 148, 395

Wool Production, 428, 430
Wool Spinning, 438
Wound Care, 353, 368
Writing, 66, 376-377, 384

Y

Yarrow, 176, 362, 368

Made in the USA
Monee, IL
25 March 2025